Three Years with Company K

AUSTIN C. STEARNS. This photograph is believed to have been taken around 1864.

Three Years
with Company K

Sergt. Austin C. Stearns
COMPANY K
13TH MASS. INFANTRY
(DECEASED)

Edited by Arthur A. Kent

RUTHERFORD ● MADISON ● TEANECK
FAIRLEIGH DICKINSON UNIVERSITY PRESS

LONDON: ASSOCIATED UNIVERSITY PRESSES

E
601
S815
1976

Associated University Presses, Inc.
Cranbury, New Jersey 08512

Associated University Presses
108 New Bond Street
London W1Y OQX, England

Library of Congress Cataloging in Publication Data

Stearns, Austin C.   1835-1924.
    Three years with Company K.

    Bibliography: p.
    Includes index.
    1. United States—History—Civil War, 1861-1865—Personal narratives.
2. Massachusetts Infantry. 13th Regt., 1861-1864. Company K. 3. United
States—History—Civil War, 1861-1865—Regimental histories—Massachusetts
Infantry—13th. Company K. 4. Stearns, Austin C., 1835-1924. I. Title.
E601.S815   973.7'81   74-4989
ISBN 0-8386-1480-9

Contents

Preface

This narrative was written by my great-grandfather, Austin C. Stearns, who passed it down, along with some of his Army equipment, through the family.

I have kept his wording, also his spelling with a few exceptions: for example, Stuart for Stewart, where he obviously refers to Lt. Gen. James E. B. Stuart, CSA, and Meade for Mead, where he refers to Maj. Gen. George G. Meade, USA, and certain others.

The diary contains over two hundred sketches, of which forty-three are here reproduced.

So this is his story, as he wrote it more than 85 years ago. May you enjoy his adventures in the "Grand Old Army" as much as he did.

Three Years with Company K

1

If I Had Known Then

Recruiting—Formation of regiment in Boston Harbor—Going to the Front—Incidents on the way—Arrival at Hagerstown, Md.

*T*he Spring of '61 found the South arrayed against the North. A Confederacy was formed with Jefferson Davis for it's President. Richmond, Va. was it's capital.

Fort Sumter had fallen and the little army of the United States was treacherously surrendered, leaving President Lincoln no other alternative than to call on the loyal people to maintain the supremacy of the laws and the integrity of the Union.

A proclamation was issued calling for seventy five thousand men, and the loyal, regardless of party, quickly responded. A living stream then commenced to flow from the North, which abated not, but increased in volume for four long years, till secession was conquered and peace was declared in our land.

My native town failing to raise a company and hearing that Westboro[1] wanted a few more men to make her com-

1. Westboro, Massachusetts.

pany full, six of us Bear Hill boys came over and offered ourselves. We were voted in and commenced to drill immediately. The company was already formed, with the following named officers: for Captain, William P. Blackmer (Methodist Minister), 1st Lieut., Charles P. Winslow (Expressman), 2nd Lieut., Ethan Bullard (Carpenter), 3rd Lieut., John Sanderson (Carpenter), 4th Lieut., Abner Greenwood. The Company was known as the "Westboro Company," but men from Shewsbury, Southboro, Hopkinton, and Upton were in its ranks.

After visiting each town by invitation and partaking of collation, we were ordered on the 29th of June to Fort Independence in Boston Harbor, then and there to form a regiment, to be known as the 13th Mass. Our Regiment was composed of companies from the following named cities and towns. Boston, four companies, calling themselves "the 4th Batt." and lettered A, B, C, and D, Roxbury E, Marlboro F, Stoneham G, Natick H, Marlboro I, and Westboro K. Samuel H. Leonard was commissioned Col., N. Walter Batchelder Lieut. Col., and J. Parker Gould Major.

We passed a very pleasant time learning to be soldiers, drilling down on the Point, doing Guard Duty inside and out of the Fort, [having] dress parade inside the Fort at sunset, and occasionally a ride on the "Nellie Baker."

The last was not compulsory, but was taken for pleasure, as every one who had been on guard was excused from all duty for the forenoon and had the privilege of riding down the Harbor to Fort Warren, to visit the 12th Mass.

I remember of going down one day, with four or five others; when we arrived at the Fort it was raining hard. We concluded not to land but kept on to Nahant. How mad the Captain was, when we were coming back, because we would not pay our fare. It was cheeky, I know, but others did it the same; why couldn't we?

The *Nellie Baker*

On the 16th of July, about 10 A.M., Company K was marched up into the Fort, and there took the oath that

Going to take the Oath

made us Uncle Sam's soldiers. I noticed, as we marched in, a boyish looking fellow with a tall hat on, who followed us, and also Charles B. Fox, a Sergeant of Company B, but did not think they were to be our Lieutenants, but such was the case.

Our old Lieutenants were allowed to go where they pleased. Greenwood went in K as a Sergeant, Sanderson as a Sergeant in C, while Winslow and Bullard went home.

William B. Bacon was the name of the boyish looking fellow; he was mustered in as our 1st Lieutenant. I have nothing to say about the old Lieutenants, only this: I think they were used as mean as men could be, and I justify them in the course they took. I do not know who was responsible for this. Fox was a good man and officer, and always treated the men as men. Bacon, as far as he knew, did the same, but he was a young man, just from school, without any knowledge or experience of the great principles one should have who is called upon to command. In fact he was a boy; boyish principles and boyish impulses governed all his acts. To put such a boy in command over men who were better qualified, as far as age, experience, and knowledge of human nature, was one of the fatal mistakes of the Executives of Mass. in the early days of the war, and I have no hesitation in saying that full one fourth of the men who marched into the Fort that morning were better qualified to be commissioned than he.

Of Captain Blackmer, I have but a word to say. He entered at the big end of the horn, with a loud flourish, declaring he would "wade in blood to his ears," and then in three months came out at the little end, from a hole too small to be seen with the naked eye.

Bull Run[2] battle was fought and lost. Troops were hurried forward as fast as they could be [armed, with] English muskets—[for] an English gun was selected for us; selected? there was no choice, it was all the Government had—and with them we were ordered on the 29th to start for the Front. With pleasant memories of our life there, we again, and for the last time, embarked on the Nellie Baker and were soon landed at Long Wharf; as but half of the Regiment could be taken up at a time, we made ourselves as comfortable as we could under the sheds, while the

2. Battle of First Bull Run (First Manassas), July 21, 1861.

steamer went for the rest. When all were landed, we were formed—in the rain—and marched through some of the principal streets and partook of a collation in Faneuil Hall,[3] where we were bidden in the name of the State a "God speed for the conflict."

Leaving Boston at 5:30 P.M. over the Norwich route, we stopped at Worcester and paraded the principal streets, after which we partook of a collation which awaited us in Mechanics Hall. As only a part of the Regiment could enter at a time, the right wing entered first, and from the tables bountifully supplied they made a most substantial meal. After eating all they could, they filled their haversacks and canteens. The waiters, thinking all the Regiment was in the hall, generously brought forward all they had and urged it upon them. When the left wing entered, with blank faces they confessed they had nothing but the broken food on the tables. The coffee was nothing but slops; disgusted with the fare, we went out. The rememberance of it to this day is not pleasant. Whose fault it was, at this day it is not best to say, but it is evident some one neglected their duty.

The train was waiting and we left immediately for New York, where we arrived the next morning and marched up to City Park. After stacking arms, Col. Leonard dismissed the men till a certain hour in the afternoon. One of the City officials expressed surprise and offered a "squad of police" to keep the men within certain limits, telling the Col. he never would get all his men together again. He declined all offers, saying all his men would be on hand at the appointed hour. At the specified time every man was in his place, and the march was resumed down Broadway in "column by platoon," reaching from "curb to curb," the band playing and the men singing "John Brown."

3. Faneuil Hall in Boston was originally built as a market and was used as a patriotic meeting place before and during the American Revolution.

It was a perfect ovation all along the whole way. The sidewalks were crowded, and from every window were waving handkerchieves to cheer us on our way.

We took the Steamer near the Battery, which was to convey us through the Kill-Von-Kull to Amboy.

All the way, till night came on, the same enthusiasm was displayed. At short intervals the Steamer whistle was blowing, and some of the boys had taken possession of the bell; this was rung continually, adding to the general din.

The citizens, hearing us coming, would hasten to the banks and in every way manifest their interest in us. If they were far away, we could see the waving handkerchief of its owner.

At Amboy transportation awaited, and we were soon off for the City of "Brotherly Love," about 2 A.M.

We marched to the "Soldiers Retreat," where refreshments were served. While marching through the streets at that early hour, heads would pop out of the windows, and this question would be asked: "Where you from?" On learning from Mass., it would immediately bring the person out. After being well served we marched through the city, beyond it's western limit, to an open field where we could sleep while transportation was being provided for our further journey.

The officials of the road tendered cattle-cars for our immediate use, but the Col. declined them, choosing to wait a few hours till more convenient cars could be found. At 10 A.M. the train was made up, consisting of about twenty cars. We were soon moving towards Harrisburg. The day was extremely hot, every seat was filled with a soldier who had a gun with it's equipments, knapsack, haversack and canteen, with overcoat and blanket, which made the spare room exceedingly small. At Harrisburg we stopped but a few moments, long enough to pay several stores a visit. The shop keepers at first were afraid of us; they began putting up their blinds and closing their stores. The reason for this was, some soldiers who were passing through the place [had] helped themselves to what they wanted, without as much as "I thank you."

We quieted their fears by promptly paying for everything we wanted. The train was soon underway, and we were off for Chambersburg. At a little place called Mechanicsburg we stopped—found all the inhabitants at the station with baskets of goodies. They were waiting for some soldiers who were natives of this place, and were now in camp, but were soon going to the Front. Hearing that a train full of soldiers were coming, they had rushed to the station thinking, it was their friends. They were no less glad to see us and freely distributed the contents of their baskets.

Let it ever be said to the honor of the good people of Penn., that they never withheld anything from the soldiers that was for their general good. From the earliest to the latest day, they were the same loyal, generous people. A Massachusetts soldier never wanted for anything they could give.

With cheers for the good people of Mechanicsburg, the train rolled away. Being tired, I fell asleep and did not wake till morning. I found the train was not in motion; taking a look out of the window, I found we were in a cut of the Railroad with banks so high we could not see over them. The rain was coming down "so easy" and the weather so warm, [that] the very ground seemed to steam.

About the first of my recollections that morning was, on looking out of a window, I saw a soldier step off the car and go ankle deep in mud, yes genuine Maryland mud, with which we were so familiar afterward.

Soon the order was to get our traps on and get out of the cars, up on to the bank—a thing a great deal easier said than done, but at last it was accomplished.

Slatery could not find his cap anywhere and had to substitute his sleeping cap instead. Afterwards; when we used to laugh at him about it, Jim would say "By gard, if I had known then as much as I do now I would had a hart,"

"If I had known then as much as I do now, I'd had a *hart*."

which was a byword with us for a long time when any one was laboring under a difficulty. We were at Hagerstown, Md. We marched from the depot up to the town. Stacking arms, we were dismissed to make ourselves as comfortable as we could. Some of the boys went into a hotel and had breakfast—a good one, for twenty-five cents. Darkies waited on the table. This was quite a novelty with some of us.

They had a contrivance for keeping off flies which created

Breakfast at Hagarstown, Maryland

considerable amusement, or that portion that gave the machine its motive power, which was a stout, buxom girl, black as the "ace of spades," with a face as round as a full moon, and a mouth which seemed to stretch from ear to ear, filled with exceeding white teeth.

The contrivance was a rope with a spiral spring, fastened at the end to a staple in the ceiling, running along directly over the table, its full length. The end hanging down [was] grasped by the girl. At regular intervals, a piece of cotton cloth was suspended which reached almost down to the food. The girl giving it a gentle pull, then easing up, caused it to swing back and forth, thus keeping the flies at a respectful distance.

Al Sanborn, always full of fun, kept talking to her, which kept her on the broad grin all the time, with such questions as, "How are you Dinah?" "Are you glad we've come?", and then asked some of the boys how they would like "a smack from those lips."

After breakfast was over, I went out on the street. The Regiment was disposed of in various places. The boys were trying, with good success, to sleep. It was clearing up, and the sun broke through the clouds, sending down what promised to be exceeding hot rays—at least to us, who had come from the cool and delicious breezes of Boston Harbor. Seeing an open door and stepping in, I found it to be the County Clerk's office. That official, with several citizens, were seated at a table, while on the settees and floor were sleeping soldiers. Unrolling and spreading my blanket on the floor, I joined them.

2
Meeting the Enemy

Leaving Hagerstown—March down the valley;
bivouac—Ordered to Sharpsburg, Md.—Our
camp life—Ordered to Darnstown—Arrived at
Middletown; ordered to Pleasant Valley—I and K
detached and sent to Harpers Ferry

A*bout* 1 P.M. the order was given to pack our traps and move out of the village about a mile or so, where we pitched our tents. After that we took a bath in one of the Maryland creeks. We stayed two nights here. The second night there was an alarm. The long roll was beaten, we were ordered to fall in at the shortest notice, guns were fired, and we expected an immediate attack from the enemy, who, to say the least, were a hundred miles away. As no enemy appeared, quiet was restored and we were dismissed to sleep again. The Col. wanted to see how quick we could be in line of battle, in case of a real attack.

Just at night of the third day we were ordered to "strike tents," and be ready to march. The teams were ordered to take our knapsacks, and thus, in light marching order, we commenced a ten miles march to Boonsboro; being unused to marching and the weather extremely warm, and in a strange country, and the water scarce, made it the hardest of our many hard ones. We reached Boonsboro in the small hours of the morning. Finding a well of good water, we quenched our thirst. Then we turned into a field, with the order to make ourselves comfortable. The night was dark, so we could not see, but by the smell we judged it was not new mown hay. In the morning we found we were not the only occupants, for there were boys that claimed a prior right, and they were busy in establishing their claims by rolling up huge balls. The fact was, we were in a field that had long been used as a mule pen.

Starting early in the morning, we passed down the west side of the South Mountain Ridge. The morning was foggy; as we passed along the fog would lift, and we could see peaks far above us bathed in the morning sun, which made a picture long to be remembered.

We marched down and bivouacked in a piece of woods close up to Elk Ridge.

We stayed here three or four days, pitching our tents, for the weather was warm and dry. We were then ordered to Sharpsburg. Md.

We crossed Elk Ridge—marched through the valley —over Antietam Creek on the stone bridge, which in after time was made famous by Burnside.[1] The day was extremely warm, and as we were not accustomed to such heat, it told with effect on us boys.

We formed a camp at Sharpsburg, or about a mile from it, in a piece of woods.

The first night we were here, there was an alarm given. I was on guard at the time, and Pat Cleary, who was on the

1. Maj. Gen. Ambrose E. Burnside, USA, who commanded the Left Wing of the Army of the Potomac during the Battle of Antietam (Sharpsburg) in September 1862.

next beat, fired at what he always afterward declared to be a man. I saw and heard nothing. The men turned out and after a few moments were dismissed.

A day or two afterward a hog was found badly wounded in a wheatfield, which bounded our camp on one side.

We were sent out on picket toward the Potomac, with orders to keep a strict watch of the opposite shore. While out at one time with Corporal Stone and Henry Gassett, after spending the day alone, a squad from Company F was sent out to lengthen the line, with orders to keep a strict watch all night as the enemy might be expected at any moment.

Corporal Stone posted his men at places about ten rods apart. As my post was on the line and next to the other Company, he spent most of his time at the other post. Along in the night, well toward the small hours, as I was sitting on a rail, the man at my right fired. I jumped up, expecting we were attacked and ready to run if need be. Stone came up to see what the matter was and went to the man who fired. He said he saw a man coming up from the woods and "let drive at him."

The Corporal went back to his post, and I sat down. Soon the man fired again. To the enquiry as to what he saw, he said "I saw horsemen coming up from the woods." His shots must have frightened them all away, for he saw them no more.

In the morning an old horse was seen down in that direction. As he was unhurt, we were never satisfied whether he was the target or not. No one for a moment would entertain the thought that a man of the 13th was so nervous he couldn't hit a horse.

Company D was sent down to the mouth of Antietam Creek. While there a squad went over into Virginia and captured Alexander R. Boteler—a former member of Congress, but now a Secessionist. He was brought to camp and sent down toward the headquarters of General Banks.[2] Before reaching there he was released by order of the President.

Our food was not of the best kind, or it was a little different from what we had been accustomed to—perhaps that was it. Our hardtack—about the first we had issued to us—was rightly named hard. It came in round cakes about as large as a saucer and about half an inch thick; to break it was impossible; water made but very little impression on it.

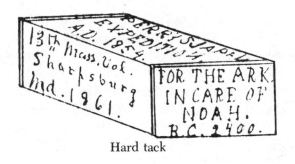

Hard tack

I saw some that had been soaked twenty four hours; when scraped with a knife, just a little could be started from the outside. With downcast looks we surveyed this article of food. To us it ment but one thing if we tried to masticate or swallow it whole. The boys said that Perry carried it with him to Japan for balls for his cannon; as he had no occasion to use them, they were issued by mistake to the infantry for food when they were intended as balls for the artilery. Those who saw the boxes said they were marked B.C. 2400;

2. General Nathaniel P. Banks, USA.

that would bring it back to Noah's time. I cannot vouch for this. The citizens used to visit the camp with their fried cakes and Maryland pies to sell. To appreciate a Maryland pie, one must eat it. One of some kinds would be a great plenty.

On the whole, our stay at Sharpsburg was a pleasant one. About the first of September we were ordered to join General Banks at Darnstown. We started on the march —crossed the South Mountain Ridge of the Blue Ridge into Middleton Valley. Arriving there, we were ordered to Pleasant Valley, where we bivouacked for the night—the usual way on a march.

Companies I and K were detached and sent to Harpers Ferry—C to Monocacy Bridge. Four men were sent from D to a place on top of the mountain called "The Lookout," with orders to shoot anyone who came up by the river path in their front. After I and K were sent to the Ferry, a man was sent to tell them of the change. Edwin Smith of K was the man selected. He started up the path that ran direct to their post. It was almost dark when he started, and quite dark when he reached there. He went along, expecting every minute to be challenged by "Who comes there?" Instead, he received a volley from their guns and fell, severly wounded.

After they fired they found out what they had done. They took Smith down to the Regiment, after which he was sent to the hospital at Baltimore.

He lingered about two years, dying from the effect of the wound. No one ever knew which of the four shots hit him, and nothing was ever done about it. He was the first man of the Regiment hit by a bullet.

I and K spent the night crouching on the tow-path. In the morning quarters were assigned us. I's men [were] in some building between the canal and the river, K between the canal and the mountains, formerly occupied by Cook, of John Brown notoriety.

We were not—strictly speaking—in Harpers Ferry, but on the Maryland side opposite.

Here we stayed nine weeks, while the Regiment was in Darnstown.

3

Heroes and Real Enemies

*P*erhaps a few words about the country would not be
amiss. The Blue Ridge runs in an almost north east and
south west direction, while the Potomac's course is generally south east. It looks as though, in some far remote ages,
the river broke through the mountain barrier and it's waters found an outlet to the sea, for the pieces of rock in the
river bed, and the jagged appearance of those on it's banks
all testify to such an event.

The Ridge takes to it's self names. For instance, the
principal ridge is called the South Mountain Ridge. At the
Ferry—Maryland Heights. At the east of South Mountain
Ridge across Pleasant Valley is the Catoctin Ridge.

The place where the river runs through is called Point of Rocks. To the west is Elk Ridge, and still farther away is Old North Mountain Ridge.

The Shenandoah River comes up from the south west and empties it's waters into the Potomac at the Loudoun Heights. On that point of land between the two rivers is the village of Harpers Ferry. It's principal street runs up to the Shenandoah. Up the Potomac were the great Government workshops, now in ruins. Bolivar Heights was the high ground between the two rivers. On the level point between the two rivers were stores, hotels, depot, and the Arsenal Buildings with the parade ground, and last but not least in interest for us, was the Engine House in which John Brown[1] defied the whole State of Virginia, and was only captured after a determined fight by a company of United States Marines under the command of Col. R. E. Lee,[2] now of the Confederacy.

The Baltimore and Ohio Railroad came down from the west and crossed from the Point to the Maryland side on a bridge now in ruins.

Everything about the Ferry bore marks of war. The fine large houses on the side and top of the Heights—the residences of the officials of the works—had not escaped. A road wound round and up a hill to the village of Bolivar. Loudoun Heights commanded the place, and from the Maryland Heights (which commanded both), the country could be seen for miles up the river. Sandy Hook was a mile down the river on the Maryland side, where the headquarters of Major Gould were, in Command of the detachment.

1. The abolitionist who invaded Virginia, captured Harpers Ferry Arsenal on Oct. 16, 1859, and hoped to cause a slave insurrection. He was tried, convicted, and hanged on Dec. 2, 1859.
2. Later General Robert E. Lee, CSA.

Captain Scriber[3] established his headquarters on a canal boat—so [as] to be ready to retreat at any time, his men said. Blackmer took for his quarters the rooms over the store on this side, which stood up close under the Heights.

The canal was on the Maryland side of the river, and there was a road that ran up about a mile to the Lock and turned up into the Valley between the Ridges. There were two locks in the Canal at the Ferry; up the river about a mile there was one Lock and a mile beyond this were two more. This was the limit of our picket duty this way. Down the river we went as far as the Hook, and at times still farther down. At "Two Locks," which was our outpost, were two houses; one was occupied by the Lock-keeper and the other, which was only an old flat-bottomed canal boat, by a family named Reed. One of our posts was directly in front of her door, where we had a bank of dirt thrown up. I remember of being on picket there one day, [and] while I was sitting on the bank talking with Mrs. Reed, a bullet from a Rebs gun came over and struck the bank close beside me. She said, "They ment you that time." She wanted to take my gun and have a shot at one of the "d——d Rebs." I let her have it and she fired, but not holding it up tight enough against her shoulder, it sprung back, giving her a blow, laming her for several days.

As the nights began to grow long and the weather cold, we fixed up our quarters by building banks and taking our ticks out to a neighboring farmer's haystacks, [where we] filled them, paying for it of course.

We found two old twelve pound ship cannon without any carriages. Corporal Jones and George Emery were detailed to make some. They succeeded and soon had them mounted. We built a breastwork or fort, with port holes for

3. In command of Company I, 13th Mass.

the cannons, by piling up a quantity of timber and logs. The powder was supplied—for balls we wired railroad spikes together. William Jones, an old "Man of Warsman," was placed in charge. We fired several times at Loudoun Heights. A few spikes reached the shore, but the greater part fell into the river. They served for a scare if nothing more.

We frequently crossed the river to the sacred soil of Virginia. I remember of crossing over on the ferry boat one day—five or six of us; we tried to manage the boat ourselves. The current was quite rapid and we lost control of her—away she went—down the river, striking one of the piers of the bridge, turning her completely round. Down we went toward the rocks, but good fortune favored us; the current here turned in shore. We caught hold of some bushes, holding her fast, escaping a good ducking if nothing more. Someone went for the boatman; he came and took us over with out any difficulty.

We amused ourselves by walking about, looking over some of the unoccupied houses, bringing away some things that were amusing if not very useful.

Some young men who were there gave us an invitation to go up to Bolivar with them and get grapes. As we had not our rifles with us, we declined to go out of sight of our men on the other side of the river, and thus, I think, we escaped eating grapes in Richmond.

I was on an expedition under Lieut Fox that went over to the Loudoun side and up in the valley two or three miles. We captured four or five horses, then went for the geese—getting a dozen or so; these we cooked and tried to eat. I might as well have tried to chew leather as the flesh of the goose I had. I have never tried to eat goose since.

Captain Scriber had a good deal of trouble with his men. Some were in the guard-house about all the time. Some were fond of whiskey, and would contrive all ways to get it. He seemed to have a particular grudge against one named Sullivan; he told him he would put him in the guard-house and keep him there almost forever. One day he was drilling them in the manual of loading and firing. He told them he would put every man in the guard-house if they didn't do just as he wanted they should. He told them to load —aim—aim higher; about one half mistook the order for aim—fire, and fired. It was fun to see the Dutchman rave and storm, using language not generally heard on drill. More of the men were put into the guard-house.

No liquor could be obtained at the Ferry, but at Sandy Hook, if one wanted it, and had the money, it could be had without much trouble. William Jones had a natural longing for something stimulating, and he was up to all manner of tricks to get past the guard and reach the Hook. At night he would take off his clothes, tie them on his head, and swim down the canal past the guard, and so reach the Hook. On returning he would do the same. At other times he would creep through the brush with cat like stillness, and accomplish his aim.

Old Shepard of I was often thirsty. He was detailed by Captain Scriber to carry messages. When he felt his thirst coming on, he would take a large yellow envelope and start; on approaching the guard he would walk as though he carried an order for the immediate advance of the Army, and so pass unquestioned.

We had several members who were troubled with an optical illusion—especially in the night when on guard. They could see millions of boats, loaded to their utmost capacity with rebels armed to the teeth crossing the river to massacre us, advance, take Washington, and subdue the North. Just at the critical moment, when the Nation's life hung by a thread, he would fire. The Corporal with a file of men would double quick to his post to find out the cause. He would relate what he saw; but the dull eyes of the Corporal could see nothing but the running water on it's way to the sea. The next week an extract from the heroic soldiers letter would appear in the Westboro paper, through the kindness of friends, giving the details of the Nation's narrow escape through his vigilance.

All the boats, scows, and skiffs, for miles up and down the river, we had destroyed or taken to our side.

Lieut Fox with a score of men—I was one of them—had been down the Virginia side and destroyed everything we could find that would float. Other parties had gone up the river on the same kind of an errand.

There was a most violent secessionist who kept a drug store in the Ferry, who at all times never failed to show his hatred toward us. His insults were unbearable, so one day [when] we were ordered to the Ferry, proceeding to his store, we commenced to clean it out. We made a clean sweep of everything he had, and carried it across the river. Some of it was used for hospital purposes, but the greater part was, I think—by the cigars smoked, and the general appearance of the boys—used here. We saw no more of the druggist. The guard at the outpost under charge of Sergeant Greenwood was not at the clean out, so at night some of the boys started up there to carry a few cigars and a canteen of Harpers Ferry Water. They went in for a good time and got up a dance; not having men enough to complete the set and wanting all to have a good time, Corporal Sanborn went out and called his relief, that were on the posts, in.

Some of the boys, realizing what their danger might be, if not from the enemy, from the officer of the guard if he should find it out—he was expected on his guard rounds —talked with the Sergeant, and he sent them back.

The supply of stimulants failing, order was restored. I was not there but give it as it was told me.

Dan Warren, another victim of misplaced confidence, was on guard at the abutment of the bridge in plain sight of the officer's quarters. He felt tired and sat down, leaning against the piers with his gun between his legs. Being in the sun, he went to sleep; he was seen by Fox, who started for him. Some of the boys threw stones, others whistled to wake him, but he was too sound asleep to wake. Fox reached him and took his gun away before he awoke.

Warren was marched to the guard-house, but as he was a good soldier and there was nothing to be gained by punishing him, he was released and cautioned not to be caught so again.

A day or two after, under Sergeant Cordwell, I was at the out-post, at night when the "Officer of the day" had made his "guard round," and we had escorted him part way back to the Ferry; he dismissed us and we started to return. The Sergeant, who had not quite recovered from the raid, saw a hog, and without a moments thought, up with his gun and fired. Such a squeal as that hog set up I think never was excelled.

The Sergeant was afraid the Lieut. heard the shot and would come back to learn the cause of it—for it was strictly against orders to fire unless there was sufficient cause. All kinds of stories were thought of; we decided to tell him we heard a noise and fired. The Lieut. did not come and we heard nothing from it.

One day Company I went up the river about ten miles to the mouth of Antietam Creek to look after some salt. While they were away the Rebs thought to have some fun with us, and perhaps scare us a little if nothing more.

They mounted a Thirty-two pounder on a platform car and ran it down on the track from up the river, so they could almost sweep our side to the Ferry. The grape came down, causing considerable commotion among us. We packed up and got ready to start. None were hurt. After firing a few times they left us masters of the field.

I have no doubt but what they had a good laugh over the scare they gave us. We in turn laughed heartily over the conduct of some of our officers. Their bravery was unquestioned.

At another time five men rowed up the river some five or six miles, going round through the country. In coming back, they took the tow-path, as it was much nearer. When they were within a few rods of our out-post at the "Two Locks," they were fired upon by a party of Rebs, from across the river. One named Spencer from Company I fell dead. The others, dismounting, took to the canal. The alarm was sent down to the Ferry, and from there to Col Geary of the 28th P.V.,[4] commanding the upper Potomac. He came up with two or three companies and a section of a battery, and we made things lively there for awhile, shelling the woods and houses, and men when seen. Scarcely a day passed now but what there was more or less skirmishing.

Harvey Ross, my brother John, and myself was detailed one day to go down to Sandy Hook and there join some citizens employed by Major Gould to go up into the country and help get some cattle left there by Genl Banks.

We went to the Hook and found the men had gone. Having nothing else to do we stayed down there till noon. No men—no cattle came, so we thought we would go up to the Ferry and report for orders. Major Gould and Captain Blackmer were dining with Captain Scriber in the canal boat that day. After getting our dinner, we did not know

4. Pennsylvania Volunteers.

what to do. The orderly told us to report to the Captain. We went to the door of the boat and reported our condition and asked for orders. Captain Blackmer looked up with all the dignity of a Major General, and asked where we had been all the forenoon. Before we had time to reply, Major Gould said, "Go right back, boys, and wait till the men and cattle come." We went back, and when the cattle came we helped them get to a safe place, then went to the Ferry well satisfied with our days work.

Citizens used to cross the river quite often. We thought then that a communication was kept open between the two sides at this place, and I have no doubt of it now.

An order was issued against all citizens crossing, and it created quite a stir among a certain few who were in the habit of crossing every day. One day, [I] being on guard where the dam was built to turn the water into the canal to carry the government works at Harpers Ferry, which at low water one could cross the river, a lady came up with a pass from the Lieut. of the guard granting her the privilege of crossing there. Of course I allowed her to go; when she was part way across, the Lieut came running up and said "Call her back, threaten to shoot her if she doesn't obey." I called her; at first she pretended not to hear, but when I told her I should speak with my rifle, she turned back. She was not very choice in her language about yankee soldiers. She refused my help in getting down from the dam. The Lieut. had disappeared.

Our quarters were on the banks of the canal, being but a few feet from a lock. The Sergeant of our mess, when on guard one night, tried to come to quarters crossing on the gate. It being dark he lost his footing and went plump into the lock; the water was eight or ten feet deep, [and] he got a good ducking. His voice brought the guard, who soon fished him out.

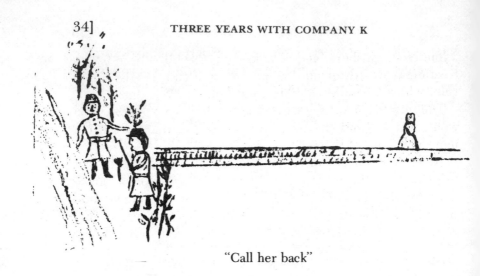

"Call her back"

One of our number on guard one night got tired; leaning his hand on the muzzle of his gun [he] put his foot on the trigger; it slipped off and so did the gun, taking his little finger.

One day a detachment of I and K under Major Gould went over the river to the "Sacred soil" and up the Shenandoah to some Flouring Mills, where there was quite a quantity of wheat stored. After staying an hour or so we went back, K in advance. All was quiet till the boat I was in was half way across the river, when the bullets commenced to whistle over our heads, fired at us from Bolivar Heights. It seemed they had been watching us all the time. As we outnumbered them, they had not dared to open fire till we were partly over the river. Co. I was coming down Shenandoah Street and they were fired upon too. We did not return their fire till we were over, for the boat was crowded. Orders came to recross. We went back, threw out a line of skirmishers, and advanced up the hill, the rebs retreating as we advanced. We picked up a gun, a Mississippi rifle, which Chandler Robbins sent home to Westboro.

The citizens said they carried away three in a wagon. We went over beyond the town and stayed till night. Nothing more was seen of the rebs.

Now commenced stirring times, for it was decided that the wheat in the mills was wanted at Washington to make flour for the Soldiers. We were sent to picket out beyond the mill a mile or more. I remember the first squad that was sent out, for I was one of them; we went out by daylight and the posts were all established; we were on the river road. When it came my turn to go on the post it was dark, and as my post was the farthest from the rest, and the Corporal [was] becoming frightened, he sent me alone to find my man, which I did without much trouble. I can remember now of standing out there alone, so dark you could hardly see your hand when held before you. When I came off, that post was discontinued and two men were placed together.

All the citizens and negros that could be found were employed. A rope was stretched across the river. Co. I was at the mill to sack the wheat, teams drew it to the river, it was then ferried across and loaded into canal boats.

When we were picketing beyond the mill, Capt Blackmer sent a Corporal out with the instructions to send in all of the large men. He instead picked out all those of small stature; I suppose he thought they were large in other respects. How mad Blackmer was when we reported to him. He wanted them to unload the wheat from the ferry boat and carry it up the bank and load it in the canal boats. We had to go to work at it.

Things began to look squally, [and] there was a good deal

of commotion. Stonewall Jackson[5] was reported to be at Winchester, thirty miles away. Co. C was ordered up from Monocacy, three companies from the Third Wisconsin regiment, a section of a R.I. battery, and Col. Geary's[6] regiment was close at hand. Meanwhile the wheat was being taken across as fast as possible. Co. C, the Third Wisconsin, and the battery were taken over the river as Stonewall was coming. The Home Guard came up with their thirty pounder and attacked, but were quickly driven away, with the loss of their old gun which our boys brought down to the Ferry.

Stonewall now appeared upon the scene with a force of about five thousand men. A battery was placed on Loudoun Heights, which was on our flank and also commanded the Ferry. He attacked just at night,[7] drove our men back a short distance, and waited for the morning.

Gov. Sprague[8] came up, a council was held, and it was decided to withdraw all troops to the Maryland side. A busy night it was, for we only had a small scow boat to convey the troops across. In the morning our batteries looked down on Stonewall from Maryland Heights. Cannonading commenced but there was nothing special; after a few shots it died away. Stonewall contented himself by burning the mill, staying a few days, then going back to Winchester. The casualties on our side were three men killed and twelve wounded in the 3d Wisconsin, four wounded in Co. C. Companies I and K were next to the river and so escaped unharmed.

We secured for the Government about sixteen thousand bushels of wheat, which we loaded on canal boats and sent to Washington.

5. Brig. Gen. (later Lieut. Gen.) Thomas J. (Stonewall) Jackson, CSA.
6. Col. John W. Geary, USA, commanding the Union Forces in the area. At about this time he was appointed Brig. Gen. and later Maj. Gen.
7. Engagement at Bolivar Heights on October 16, 1861.
8. William Sprague, Governor of Rhode Island.

During our stay over the river, a valuable horse was secured which Capt Bertram of the 3rd Wisconsin claimed; so
also did Capt Jackson of Co. C. A serious quarrel was most
happily averted by leaving the ownership to Major Gould.
I was on guard at the Major's quarters and overheard the
conversation between the Officers. After hearing the different claims the Major proposed to settle all disputes; they
gave the horse to Gov. Sprague, which both readily agreed
to do.

I have said that the courage of our officers was not to be
questioned, neither do I now intimate any such thing, but
the day after the fight spoken of above, our Capt. sent in
his resignation and left immediately for home, without waiting for it's acceptance or even telling his own brother that
he was going.

We as a company was glad to get rid of him, for he was
one of the smallest specimens of an officer I ever saw and
in the three years I saw some pretty small ones.

Nothing more of an exciting nature happened during our
stay at the Ferry.

The weather was now quite cool, fires were needed.
Stoves were procured from the Ferry, and coal from the
boats as they passed along down the canal. Quite a number
of the boys were sick with the chills and fever. The labor
we performed was immence.

The regiment had been ordered to Williamsport, Maryland and were now there. We were ordered to pack up and
join them. Our baggage was placed in the hold of some
canal boats and, taking a deck passage, we bade adieu to
Harpers Ferry after a stay of nine weeks. As we passed up
through the two locks at the outpost, Corporal O'Grady of I
was so over-come by his feelings or something else that he
fell heels over head into the lock; the water being eight or
ten feet deep and the night cold, his feelings in a measure
revived somewhat quicker than he expected. After being

fished out, he retired to the hold and was seen no more that night.

The labor performed by us at the Ferry was immence. I was on guard nine days in succession at the time of the wheat harvest.

Still, my recolections of our life there are pleasant. In the years that followed, we used to say with Slatery "If we only had known then as much as we do now, what a time we would have had."

4

An Army Travels on Its Stomach

*Journey to Williamsport—Co. C, 4th Batt.
Fever—Billy Jones—Second mess—Building
houses—Thanksgiving—Old Corporal—Guard
duty—A new Captain—Falling water, Dam No.
5—Sergeant Fay—Trip to Hancock—Flippers
and beans—Four Companies from Boston and
the rest from Massachusetts—The first
death—Sick*

At night we tied up at the mouth of Antietam Creek, and
resumed our journey the next morn. When
tired of riding, all we had to do was to jump off and travel
on the tow-path. Co. C, who had the start of us by several
hours, reached Williamsport before dark, where the regiment was drawn up to receive them, and with the band
playing and colors flying they escorted them to camp,
where coffee and soft bread were in waiting. Speeches were
made and Co. C were lauded to the sky. I and K did not
arrive till after dark; only a messenger was there to pilot us
to camp, no band, no speeches, no welcome awaited us,
who had for nine long weeks worked hard and gained for

the regiment an honorable name. Co. G. came over with coffee and in many ways showed their interest in us; tired, and without tents we laid our weary selves down to sleep. Company C were the lions of the hour, not enough could be said in their praise. Chaplain Gaylord preached on the following Sabbath, taking for his text Co. C. He could hardly find words to express the fullness of his love and gratitude for that noble company. "I thank God for Co. C.," he said; not a word did he utter about I and K, who had labored hard and exposed their lives in an equal degree with the favored company. The reason for this was [that] we did not belong to the "Fourth Batt." That fever was raging very hard at this time.

Our camp was about a mile from the village in a pleasant grove just off the Hagerstown Pike. After being here a few weeks we built houses, as we were rather cramped for room in our tent. We lay around within a circle with our feet inside. If anyone from the side fartherest from the door wanted to go out—nine times out of ten, he would step on every man's gut as he went out; then there would be language used neither complimentary or of a high order.

I was awakened one night by someone stepping on me; on opening my eyes I found it was as light as day. I saw Billy Jones standing by the stove with the blaze going out the top of the funnel, which did not reach but about half way up the tent. He came in late, and having a little down, he saw the kindlings, and, being cold, thought to have a fire. I said "What are you doing Billy?", and such a stream of oaths and invectives as he uttered I have seldom heard. He went for his bayonet; what might have happened I don't know, if some of the other boys had not woke up and quieted him down. He had forgotten all about it in the morning.

The second mess thought they did not need a house, so

they dug out the earth to the depth of two feet within the tent and battened up the sides and thought they were comfortable for the winter. As long as the weather remained fair they were all right, but there came a storm of rain and the wind blew, and one night when they were sleeping sound and thought they were all right, the earth around the tent gave way, and down came the tent; the water ran in and filled the hole. Out from the debris crawled the half drowned boys, more like fish-worms than soldiers. They got permission to go to a straw stack a short distance from the camp. I was one of the boys of our mess who opposed building a house, thinking a tent would do as well; after the experience of the 2nd mess I was heartily glad that we were so comfortably housed.

When we voted to build, out of twenty, thirteen voted yes, five no, two would not vote at all, although all agreed to pay their share. I was one of those who voted no, but was chosen to go ahead and buy the lumber, and make all the necessary arrangements. I went to Williamsport and bought the lumber, nails, and windows, and had them all delivered in camp so we could commence work in the afternoon. Being excused from drill, all took hold and pushed the thing along quite fast; having only an axe, saw, and hammer, we did not make very good joints. The next day we finished our house, that is, the outside; it was nearly a week before the inside was done. Those who were the fastest to build were the first to get tired and leave all the work to a very few. We were to pay for the lumber when the paymaster came; I was chosen to collect. All payed promptly but two; those were the fastest to build and offering at that time to pay a double share. The result was, I had to pay three shares, the boys having spent money for other purposes. In the spring when we sold back the lumber, I thought to get my pay, but the one who was left in charge, after selling all he could, got a furlough to go home; he brought up in Canada. I have not seen him since.

Our cooking was done by men detailed for that purpose, in a building or shed made for that purpose and called the cook house.

We built an oven where we could bake meat and beans. On the whole we lived quite comfortably. Lyman Jones, John Flye, Dan Warren, and Alden Lovell were the cooks for a considerable portion of the time.

Lovell wore a pair of over-alls which by long wear had become pretty well saturated with grease. We used to have a good deal of sport over them, and with him, by advising him to try them out and make a soup, as we thought they would make a richer one than we had had for a long time, but we would not listen to our advise and we did not have the pleasure of partaking of an over-all soup.

Thanksgiving was a general holiday. All unnecessary work was suspended. Turkeys were provided and a genuine Plum pudding—these were amongst the luxuries of the day. For amusements we had ball playing, races, a greased pole to climb, and a greased pig. We tried to make it as much of a Massachusetts day as possible.

Among the oddities was an old dog that came to camp, so old that he had not a tooth in his head. He was a white dog with black spots. A regular bull, with nose so short, and turned up so, one had to look twice to see that he had any. When he came to camp he took up his quarters at the guard house. He stayed there all winter as happy and contented as an old dog could be. We gave him the name of "Corporal," for the reason that every time the Sergeant called for the relief guard to "fall in," he was the first to respond. No matter what the weather was, how hard it rained, or snowed, or how cold it might be, he would go around with the guard, come back to the guard house, and take his place by the fire. He had plenty to eat and grew fat. He was a favorite with all. In the spring he was sent to Boston and provided for, for the rest of his days.

Soon after our arrival here the guard duties were performed by companies. When our turn came we went on duty. It was a cold, raw, rainy day. In the night the Sergeant got asleep. We had been on our posts about two hours and a half, [and] we thought it time for the relief, but there were no signs of their coming. One of the boys called for the "Corporal of the Guard," giving a different number from his own; soon every man was calling; the noise woke up the whole camp. Some expected the enemy were upon them. An investigation was made the next day, [but] as no one was hurt, nothing further was done about it.

We were without a Captain; it was time to have one; Lieut Bacon aspired to the place. There were a few of the boys wanted he should be, thinking they would have an easy time. A petition was circulated to get signers for him. Those who brought it to our mess said if we did not have him we should have to have the senior Lieut. of Co. A. Of the two evils, we chose the least, signing for Bacon. After doing so, some of us went out and enquired of the Field, Line, and Staff, and learned that the Col. wanted to promote Lieut Hovey of Co. D. Another petition was circulated for him without consulting the friends of Bacon, [and] the result was [that] we had Hovey for Captain. Our nine weeks stay at Harpers Ferry gave us no time to drill, [so] when we came to the regiment we were one of the poorest drilled companies. The Boston Companies looked upon us with an air of superiority. Hovey, on taking command, said, if we pay strict attention to drill, he would do his best to make us second to none in point of drill, or anything that goes to make a soldier. He said he was satisfied the material was there, and all it needed was to be brought out, and he would do his best to bring it out. His predictions were all filled.

After he took command, one of the first things we did was to go to Falling Waters. The rebs were all up and down the river, and where they thought they could make anything, or scare, they were there.

Falling Waters was about six miles down the river; Co. F was down there where the rebs made their appearance. Capt Whitcomb sent up for reinforcements and Capt Hovey was sent to their help.

We started just at night, in a bright star-light; the ground was frozen just enough to echo our steps as we went tramp, tramp, tramp. At this late day I can almost hear the ring of our steps as we marched over the frozen ground.

We came up with Co. F and it was decided to go down to the river. I was one of the twelve who were selected to act as skirmishers on the advance to the river. We could hear the enemy plainly and see the light of their fires. They were in a sort of a ravine partially hid from our view. We descended the hill that overlooked the river and went down to the canal, where we stayed an hour or two, then we were ordered back up the hill, where we remained till morning. A section of Artilery came down, a few shots were fired, but nothing of any consequence was done. This was only a feint, as their principal point was Dam No. 5 up the river. There was quite an engagement there, and a portion of our regiment took part in it. A few men were wounded in our regiment there.

After staying that night and the next day, we went back to camp. Capt Hovey paid strict attention to drill, and there was soon a marked appearance in our soldierly qualities.

At another time the enemy appeared at Dam No. 5 some six or eight miles up the river. Companies D and K were

ordered to go up there. As at the other time we went in
the night, arriving there in the early dawn. Sergeant Fay,
with twelve men, were left at a little village of three or four
houses and a store, while the rest went on up to the dam.
No rebs were there, and after staying all day, we went back
to camp in the night.

Sergeant Fay got a little balmy, and in the afternoon ordered us out to drill for the amusement of the citizens and
to show off his military skill and knowledge.

Drilling under Sergeant Fay

His mind and tongue would not work together, for when
his mind wanted to say a certain thing his tongue was sure
to give the wrong order; after trying awhile and finding he
could not make things work, he threatened terrible things
and dismissed us. The citizens were all pleased with the
Yankees performance.

Four of our companies went to Hancock, Md., thirty miles up the river, where they stayed two or three weeks and were then ordered back to camp. One Sunday morning, after they had been back a week or two, I was down at the brook washing, when two of Co. A men came down and commenced to talk. One said: "Of course we shall go, it would be a disgrace to us if the Col. should send any other companies." The other expressed a doubt about their going. What it was I did not know then, but on going back into camp I found that Stonewall Jackson had turned up at Hancock and threatened to burn it.

Reinforcements were called for, and Col Leonard, who commanded all the troops then on the Upper Potomac, was requested to send help immediately. Four companies from the 13th were ordered to start at once; they were all different ones, and K was one of them. We started, on as pleasant a Sabbath afternoon as one could wish to see, on a thirty miles tramp. We arrived at a place called Clear Spring about dark, where we halted and rested about an hour. After leaving it began to cloud up, and before reaching Fairview a snowstorm was upon us—a regular storm, one that would do honor to old Massachusetts.

Dan Warren and myself stragled ahead of the rest of the command arriving there sometime before the others. We sat down on some door-steps, [and] I went to sleep, but woke up in season to join the company when it came up. The different companies were assigned to their quarters; ours were in a fine house in the center of the village. As there was no one in the house, all having left on the arrival of "Stonewall," the doors were fastened. We had no key, and not knowing where to call for it, we took a panel out of the door with the butt end of a Musket. The first thing on entering was to search for eaterables. We found a very little [supply of] preserves in the cellar. Nothing of bread kind could be found. One of the boys, in his eagerness to find some goody, found an earthen pot with something in it; fearing that others might come and claim a share, he took it and started out, but thought he would taste and see what it was. He did so, then dropped the pot, not caring for a second taste; it was soft soap. After a thorough search we rolled our selves up in our blankets and slept till morning. The wind changed and it blew bitter cold over the snow-clad mountains of Penn.

I went up back of the house on the hills to see what there was over the river. Stonewall's men had some big fires over in a ravine, I should think, by the way the smoke rolled up. This was all I could see.

We were as hungry as bears, having left camp in a hurry, taking only one days rations with us and eating that on the march up. Some flour was procured, and some of the boys were detailed to cook flippers. I think we had three apiece for the first installment, eating them without butter or sugar.

The call came from the kitchen, "more flippers," and the Sergeant went down to get them while we waited with breathless anxiety to receive them. Report says that he got the large number of three and started back, but thinking that three would go a good ways with one and not very far with twenty, he ate them on the stairs in coming back. A few beans were found and they were stewed and served out to the men.

The Sergeant [knew] that Billy Jones did not eat his beans in camp and thought he would not now, so he asked him for them. Billy looked at him with a face as black and fierce as a tornado and roared out "What do you think I am going to live on, air?" A shout from the boys, and Billy ate his beans.

The ration wagons came up the next day and we had

plenty to eat. While there I saw Gen'l Lander,[1] who was the commander of the forces in West Virginia. He died soon after.

Some of the boys went into a neighboring house where there was an old lady; she wanted to know where they all came from, asked what regiment and State. They told her the 13th from Massachusetts. She laughed and said there were some soldiers there before we came, who said when she asked them, "that four companies were from Boston and the rest from Massachusetts." That was a home thrust for the "Fourth Batts," and it was a long time before they heard the last of it.

After doing guard duty for four days, a brigade of troops arrived and we took up our line of march for Camp Jackson, going back in the daytime. A thaw having commenced, the snow melted freely. We were two days coming back, stopping overnight at Clear Spring, and sleeping in a church, some of the boys taking the pews, but I chose to sleep in the open space at the left of the desk. We arrived at camp just at night of the second day.

Two of our number died while at Camp Jackson—John Burnap, who was sick in the village, and George H. Haradon, who died very suddenly of heart disease. He was not in our mess, yet he was one of my special friends. Both bodies were sent home for burial.

I caught cold and was almost sick one day, and, it being my turn to go on guard, I thought to go to the Surgeons and get excused from duty. I went up with the others in charge of a Sergeant. When it came to my turn to be examined, the Surgeon asked me what the matter was. I told him my complaint. He wrote on his paper, and when through with the list, the Sergeant marched us down to the

1. Brig. Gen. Frederick W. Lander, USA, who died in March 1862 from the results of an old wound.

Hospital tent where the medicine was served out. When my turn came the Steward mixed for me a dose of salts. Now if there is one thing more than another that I detest, it is salts, and when I took the glass and smelt of it I turned and threw it on the ground. The remedy was worse than the disease.

The Surgeon could or would not distinguish between the really sick and those who were playing off. It was my first, and last visit to the Surgeon. I ever after preferred to do my duty if not feeling well, than to trust myself in the hands of a man who could not tell a real sick man from one who was not. I went on guard that day; Lieut Fox, who knew I was not well, and who also knew that I never shirked, came out to me on my post and wanted me to call a supernumerary. I told him "No Sir." I would do my duty, and I done so, although I thought that I had more on my hands than I could carry through before we were relieved. The next day after I came off guard, Fox had me excused from drill, and Corporal Stone made me some composition tea, which I drank and went to bed, the boys lending their blankets. I took a good sweat and felt better, and in a day or two was all right. I have no hard feelings against the Surgeon, although at the time I did not think he did his duty as he ought to have done. And at this late day I am more impressed than ever that he did not. I know that the boys used to play it on him by feigning sickness, and in all ways imaginable, but he should have looked to ones record and enquired of the company officers if he could not of himself decide.

I know that he used to excuse men of the "Fourth Batts." from duty on the most trifling complaint. Perhaps he had the "Fourth Batt. fever" and thought that none others than they were worthy objects of his great learning and skill.

One of the boys in the 2d mess, Jaber Blackmer, lost his

voice and was excused for several weeks from guard duty. But one unlucky night for him, he got to dreaming and talked as plain as any man in the mess. Some of the boys heard him talking and reported him, and from that time forth he had to do his duty the same as the rest of us.

5

Taking Martinsburg

Drill—"Ho Parrott"—The John Brown song—Advance into Virginia—Who took Martinsburg?—On Picket—Advance to Bunker Hill—Baltimore Plug—Winchester—The ladies of Winchester—Shield's Division—Ordered to Centreville—"Aunt Abbie"—No rails to be taken—Ordered back—March continued—Goose Creek—Raid to Middleburg—Cleary's lamb—Death of Cleary

*C*aptain Hovey was as good as his word. He drilled us every day, and took great pains to go into all the details of the drill, and here let me say that there was not a better drill-master, or Officer who took greater pains to instruct his men in the whole regiment, than Captain Hovey. And the men taking as great an interest, the result was that by the first of March Co. K was second to none in point of drill or discipline, and in many ways far surpassed all other companies, as in bayonet and skirmish drill. How well I remember now the drills we used to have in the field, and on the hills that ajoined our camp, drilling the skirmish drill by the sound of the bugle. No other company could do it as well as K company. Thanks to Captain Hovey.

Contrabands[1] came into camp from over the river; each Officer had his choice of a servant. Captain Hovey had a great big strapping Negro who was called Parrott, [and] many were the times during the spring and summer, when we were down on the sacred soil of old Virginia, [that] we heard the stentorian voice of Hovey from our camps and bivouac calling "Ho Parrott!"

There were three came over from Martinsburg named respectively, Wash, Clay, and Thomas Jefferson. I do not know whether they were brothers or not, and as far as that is concerned it makes no difference for they are all off the same piece. They were quite good singers. Many were the evenings they sang to us. A favorite piece with them and also us was the "John Brown Song"; as I have forgotten part of it, I will only give a few verses.

THE JOHN BROWN SONG

There is a place in old Virginia,
    they call it Charlestown
Where they hung an Abolitionist,
    his name it was John Brown
He tried to free the darkies,
    but he found it was no fun
For Gov. Wise, he made him sing,
    the whole hog or none

CHORUS

Old John Brown, don't you see
Twill never do for you to try, to set the darkies free
For if you do the people, will come from all around
They will take you down and hang you up in old Charlestown

---

1. Slaves that had escaped.

He came to Harpers Ferry,
  in the middle of the night
And thought to scare the citizens,
  by showing them some fight
The people, they were all in bed,
  a sleeping very sound
Says John, "I think we're safe enough,
  lets us walk around

CHORUS

Just then a train of cars came by,
  a making such a clatter
When off stepped the Conductor,
  to see what was the matter
Says Mr. Brown to Capt. Phelps,
  "Don't you move or stir"
"For if you do I'll shoot you down,
  as sure as you are here"

CHORUS

With his pistol pointed to his breast,
  he took him to his train
And told him he'd five minutes,
  the Maryland side to gain

CHORUS

The gallant boys from Berkley,
  to protect Virginia's right
They jumped aboard a train of cars,
  and hurried on to fight
Into the Engine House,
  Captain Brown retreated
Says Stevens "Burn the town down,
  or else we'll be defeated"

CHORUS

They procured a long ladder,
  and they busted in the door
And then commenced the bloody work,
  the Harpers Ferry war

Mr. Brown he cut an ugly frill
    and so did Mr. Stevens
And for the bloody deeds they done,
    I rather think we're even

CHORUS

Now to all you Abolitionists,
    I would say just take a friends advice
And don't team up with colored,
    because it is not nice
For if you do the people,
    will come from all around
They'll take you down and hang you up,
    in old Charlestown

CHORUS

As the spring was now advancing, plans were being made and indications were for an early advance of the Grand Army.

Being on the upper Potomac, we did not hear all the rumors and reports that those did who were lower down, but we heard enough to know that there was to be an advance of the whole Army. My recollections of the life spent at Camp Jackson are pleasant. There was no picketing, nothing but guard duty, and drill when the weather was suitable. We were quartered in good substantial houses with plenty to eat, a good warm fire adding to our comforts. What was in store for us none knew, but all were quite confident that there was to be plenty of hard work and fighting. We had gotten brave over the thought that the war was soon to close, at least not before some fighting was done, and we were all eager for the fray.

We received orders to cross the river on the first of March; preparations were made accordingly. Extra clothing was disposed of, our houses sold or burned, as some of the boys preferred to burn rather than sell them for the paltry sum offered, and to leave them standing was out of the question.

We were all day crossing the river, having only one flat-boat to cross on. We were all feeling good that at last the time had come and we were on the "soil of old Virginia." When Company K crossed, we were marched up the hill about half a mile in advance of the regiment, and at night when all were over, we kept the advance toward Martinsburg. Report says that there was considerable feeling shown by some of the companies because K company had the right. Let that be as it may, we held on our way and were the first in Martinsburg. When within two miles, to appease Company A, it was sent around with a guide on another road, to come in and so bag all the rebs that should be caught out at that late hour of the night.

We reached Martinsburg about midnight, and were marched up to the center of the place, where we halted beside the Court House. We stacked arms, with orders not to leave the immediate stacks. Being [that] most of the boys sat down on the sidewalk, I leaned back against the house and was soon asleep, but was quickly awakened by the sound of Muskets being fired. "Fall in K," said Captain Hovey as calmly as on drill. Every man was soon in his place awaiting events. It was soon explained: the advance guard of Co. A just then coming in heard us and, without enquiring, fired. They thought they were the first in the place, and that we were rebels, [but] they soon found out their mistake. For a long time after, when Co. A was having the "Fourth Batt" fever, someone would say "Who took Martinsburg?" Another would reply "Co. A," and this would generally reduce the fever.

During our stay in Martinsburg, we were quartered in

some of the houses near the center. Our mess had the attic, and the board of that floor for hardness surpassed any that I ever saw.

In the immediate vicinity of the depot, I counted upward of fifty locomotives that had been run in there and partly burned. I visited the estate of Charles James Faulkner, who was when the war broke out our Minister at the Court of France.

Our stay at Martinsburg was about a week. K Company went out on picket about a mile on the Winchester Pike; the snow was between two and three inches deep. While here we made our headquarters at a farmhouse. We talked with the lady of the house, who was quite talkative, [and] she had two sons in the Confederate service. One was with Jackson when he made his winter raid to Hancock. Some of the boys in speaking of the cold said "Jackson had two or three men froze to death up there." "Oh no," said the old lady "not froze to death but perished with the cold." We failed to see any great difference between freezing and perishing. My post was out on a dirt road leading from the pike, [and] while I was sitting on the corner of the fence trying to keep warm in the sun, a team came up with two men going towards Martinsburg to sell fried cakes and pies. They did not see me until they got near. I could hear them talking. When one saw me he said "Do you see him?" "Where?" said the other, who was driving. He stopped the horse immediately. I went and spoke to them, told them what my orders were in relation to their going into the village, [then] after talking the matter over for a few minutes, they concluded to go on. I took a fried cake and let them pass.

The command moved toward Winchester while we were out; the next day we followed on, guarding the train. We found them at a little place called Bunker Hill.

We were quartered here in a flour mill with some of the

"First Maryland Volunteers," Col Kenly commanding. The
first night we were here we lay on the floor of the first
story, the Marylanders above. During the night one of the
latter had occasion to go out; he came creeping downstairs
in the dark, mistaking the door, came down stepping on
the feet of some of the boys, [and] they cried out "Get off
my feet." Al Sanborn said "Put him out." The Marylander,
squaring himself off, said with a fearful oath "I'm a Baltimore Plug; if anyone wants, let him pitch in." As no one
was inclined that way at the time, a light was procured and
the plug showed the door.

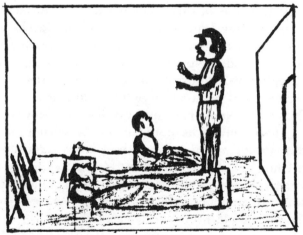

Baltimore plug

Our stay at this place was short. We soon marched toward Winchester, halting at night within a short distance of
it. Here we found the rest of Bank's Division. Early in the
morning we formed a line of battle and moved across the
fields to meet the enemy if they should be there. Jackson,
thinking that "discretion was the better part of valor,"

withdrew in the night further up the valley. When we found the enemy had fled, we reformed the line by column and marched into the city with bands playing and colors flying. I noticed one or two small Union flags. Some of the citizens came out to see us. A few were pleased, some cried, but the greater part maintained a sullen indifference.

Company K, with three other companies from as many regiments, were detailed as Provost Guard. We took up our quarters in quite a respectable house on one of the main streets, the company from the 9th New York being nearly opposite. Over our entrance we hung the Stars and Stripes, and the New Yorkers did the same.

The female portion of the city were violent[ly] secesh. They showed their dislike to the Yanks in every way they could, and to pay them off was a constant study with the boys. One day, having captured a small secession flag and seeing two well dressed ladies coming, we thought to play a little joke on them. On a former occasion they, or some other ladies, had turned out, going round instead of under the Old Flag. Now the captured flag was spread on the walk, so they must walk under it's folds or step on the secesh flag; they came down and saw what was in store for them. One daint[i]ly picked her way past on the curb stone, while the other stepped boldly out into the muddy street, preferring to walk through Virginia mud two inches deep then under the old Flag.

One of the boys in an out house of our quarters found an "Arkansas Tooth Pick," a knife about a foot and a half long, with a curved blade. It was sent home as a relic, I believe.

When off duty I spent my time in looking over the place. I visited the home of Mason, of the famous Mason and Slidell.[2] Also the Medical College. I was detailed one of

2. James M. Mason and John Slidell were Commissioners of the Confederate States enroute to Europe on the British Steamer *Trent* when captured on Nov. 8, 1861, by Capt. Charles Wilkes of the USS *San Jacinto*. This act nearly brought England into war with the United States.

Under the Old Flag

eight to go on guard at Gen'l Banks headquarters, but after one day's duty his regular guard came up and relieved us. While quartered in the city, "Shields'[3] Division" from West Virginia passed through, going up the valley. McClellan[4] forces had moved down to Yorktown, and Banks Division

3. Maj. Gen. James Shields, USA.
4. Maj. Gen. George B. McClellan, USA, commander of the Army during the Peninsular Campaign, April to July 1862.

was ordered to Centreville. Our stay here had been somewhere about a fortnight. Gen'l Hamilton, who had been our
brigade Commander, was ordered to the command of a division with McClellan. Gen'l Abercrombie[5] was given the
command of the Brigade. "Aunt Abbie," we called him. He
was an old officer of the regular army and not used to
commanding volunteers. We marched towards Centreville,
passing through Berryville, and crossing the Shenandoah on
a pontoon bridge at Snickers Gap of the Blue Ridge out to
within a few miles of Aldie. When we started on the march
the commanding Gen'l gave orders that there should be no
foraging. No rails, hay, or straw should be taken. Now it
happened on this night, which was a cold and blustering
one, [that] the field into which we were turned was surrounded by a high dry rail fence, and in one corner was a
large stack of hay.

When we were in line, with guns stacked, the Col. said,
"The Gen'l commanding orders that no rails," pointing to
the fence, "or hay," pointing to the stack, "shall be taken."
"Break ranks, march."

The last order was quickly obeyed with a shout. Some of
the boys attacked the fence, while others went for the
stack, and in less time than it takes me to write this, we
had the rails, and hay enough to keep us warm all
night—much to the surprise of the rest of the brigade coming in, who soon joined in the attack. We never knew, or
thought to enquire, what "Aunt Abbie" said.

In the morning orders were received to be in readiness
to march back at any moment. Stonewall Jackson, seeing
our departure, thought to make easy work of Shields, and
he (Shields), fearing this, sent for us to assist him, or to
have us within supporting distance. We lay there all day,

5. General John J. Abercrombie, USA.

and just at night we started and marched all night back to the top of the Blue Ridge. In the morning when we arrived there, we found the pontoon bridge out of order, and had to wait till it could be repaired. From where we lay we could hear the guns from the distant battlefield.[6] Shields in the meantime was whipping Jackson, and caused him to retreat farther up the valley.

As our presence was no longer needed, after a day's waiting and a good nights rest, we started on again and halted at night in the vicinity of Goose Creek. Early the next morning we were roused up and went on an expedition of three miles to Middleburg, where we expected and hoped to find some Johnie Rebs, but none were there, or at least no body of rebs, but from what we saw, I think if we had been a small force we should have found some opponents. After a season spent in foraging—and the Col. had told some of the boys who were helping themselves to some honey right from the hive "that he thought they were getting more then their share and to come away so the others could have a chance to fight bees"—we returned to our bivouac, where we remained all day and night.

It was strictly against "Aunt Abbie's" orders to forage, but for all that, the boys would steal out, and if they could keep clear of the patrol guard they would bring in something to eat. Pat Cleary and Warren W. Day of our mess were out when they came across a flock of sheep. As the patrol was around, they had to be careful, [but] at length an old ram (old enough, and thought to have come over on the same ship with John Smith) came within range and was quickly dropped by Cleary's rifle. They dragged him into the woods where they soon had his hindquarters dressed; keeping a sharp lookout for the guard, they soon came into

6. Probably the Battles of Winchester, Va., March 23, 1862, and Kernstown, Va., on March 24, 1862.

camp, where they generously distributed the lamb, so called by them, amongst the boys of our mess. I fried some for my dinner and tried to eat it, but failed.

Tough sole-leather was tender as chicken beside it. We laughed at them for their choice of lamb and threw it away. Day sat up all night boiling a portion of it for Cleary and himself to take on the morrow on the march. And the next day, whenever a halt was made, they were trying to reduce a piece or get it into a condition so they could swallow it. We marched all day on the Aldie Pike in the direction of Centreville, and pitched our tents that night within a few miles of it. That night, as we were sleeping as only tired soldiers can, Cleary was taken sick, with a great pain in his side; he took on fearfully, [and] some of the boys, not realizing the extent of his sufferings and remembering the old ram (for they had plagued him all day), said it was the old fellow trying to get out, and they thought it best for him to get up and let him out. Others got up and assisted him to the Surgeons tent where all was done for him that could be. Poor fellow; I never saw him again; he was placed in an ambulance and taken to a hospital tent in Centreville where he lived but two days. His body was sent to Southboro, Mass. and laid in the paupers lot, [w]here it remained for fifteen years, when through the exertion of his friend, W. W. Day, assisted by a few of his comrades from Westboro who contributed towards the expense, his body was removed to the lot of Mr. Forest Day, who gladly granted the priviledge.

Cleary was a good soldier, and was mourned by the whole Company.

6

A Terrible Place

*March resumed—Heights of Centreville—Our stay
there—Bull Run Creek and wood—
Manassas—March continued—Warrenton
Junction—Departure of "Aunt Abbie"—Gen'l
Hartsuff—Incidents of camp life—March to
Falmouth—Gaining his freedom—Incidents—
Good bye Sibleys—Ponchos.*

*T*he morning was cold and cloudy, with every indication
of rain, which commenced soon after we started
and continued all day. Now, ever since we had been in the
army, we had heard of Centreville, and Manassas, and also
Manassas Gap, and we had got them all mixed up and con-
founded together, not thinking that the Gap was in the
Blue Ridge Mountains fifty miles away. And we had also
heard how strongly fortified those places were, in fact we
had heard them called the "Gibralter of America," and we
thought they abounded with batteries that were masked,
and all the other dreadful engines of war that stood with
open mouths ready to swallow up the army that should
dare approach.

[63]

"Manassas." The name had been held up to us as a terrible place; it was used as a by-word when something awful was wanted to be expressed. In fact it was the great Bug-a-boo held up before our eyes, to frighten us, the same as some folks frighten their children.

So this morning we expected to see great things, in an enormous and strongly fortified place, with batteries that were so masked that their presence could not be defined until they poured forth their deadly fire.

How sadly we were disappointed, for after a few hours march we came to what had been called the "Heights of Centreville" and instead of a hill terriable to climb, and honey combed, and interlaced with earth-works and batteries, we found a gentle elevation easily climbed and surrounded by an earth-work that in a later period of the war I have helped build in one night and not work very hard, either. There was scattered around in different places, but more especially to the east of the road to Manassas, a good number of good built log huts where the Johnnies had lived through the winter. Some were in good condition and were clean; others, when the evacuation took place, were left in a condition anything but possessing the latter virtue. Into the former we were told to make ourselves as comfortable as we could till our tents came up, or it ceased raining, for it was raining in torrents.

We stayed here two nights and one day; most of the time was spent in looking over the ground and searching for relics, [but] we found nothing of any value. On the banks of Bull Run Creek is a shrub called "High Laurel," the root of which can be worked into any shape; we dug quite a quantity which we made into pipes, rings, and charms and sent them home to friends as relics, calling them "Bull Run wood." At one time they commanded almost fabulous prices.

On the morning of the second day we left the vicinity of Centreville and, fording Bull Run Creek at Blackburn Ford, went on down towards Manassas Junction.

Everything at the Junction that could not be moved away had been burned. We spent a few hours in searching for relics, finding nothing but a few buttons from some of the Southern states. Collecting buttons from the different states, North as well as South, had been quite a mania for some time with us, and a button from a Secesh was something to be prized. We continued our march alongside the Orange and Alexandria Railroad, fording Kettle Run and crossing Cedar Run on a temporary bridge of the railroad. The Runs were full bank, which made fording extremely unpleasant for us.

We marched on down to Warrenton Junction, where we halted and pitched a regular camp in some woods on ground that at this season of the year was quite damp. It was here that we first saw what was soon to be our tents for the remaining time of our service, Ponchos. Blenkers[1] Division of German troops were camped here having those tents for their shelter. They soon marched away to join Fremont[2] in West Virginia. Here another change in our Brigade Commander took place. Brigadier General George L. Hartsuff relieving Abercrombie of his command,[3] a good change it was for us, for one of his first acts was to move our camp from the low ground up to an open field where we were high and dry.

While at the lower camp in the woods some of the boys of the 1st mess commenced to cut a tree down that stood in the Company street, [and] by the way they commenced to chop I knew it would fall and strike the tent of the 4th

1. General Louis N. Blenker, USA.
2. General John C. Fremont, USA.
3. The 3rd Brigade.

mess. I told them so and tried to have them cut more on the other side, but they knew more about it than I did, and offered to pay for all damage done; so well satisfied was I

Falling a tree in camp

that it would strike the tent that I went and told the boys of their danger. All in the tent but one came out and, agreeing with me where the tree would fall, quickly removed all their traps; the other, beginning to realize that there might be danger, started for the door, pipe in his mouth, and just as he parted the flap of the tent, down came the tree, knocking him over and breaking his pipe that he valued at ten dollars. If he had remained laying down, in all probability he would have been badly hurt if not killed, for the tree fell just where he was laying. The tent was knocked down and torn in a few places, and afterwards served the 1st mess. While out on picket from this place one cold rainy morning, when I got up I found a snake coiled up with me in my blanket, rather an unpleasant bedfellow to have.

About this time we received our first installment of recruits, about one hundred to the regiment, Co. K receiving thirteen. At this time several of the boys received their discharge. The battle of Pittsburg Landing[4] was fought and won, and the boys were much elated. McClellan was on the "Peninsular," and we were all very anxious to join that portion of the army and share in the glory of taking Richmond, for none were so foolish as to think that it could not be taken. "Little Mac," he was called, and his name was on the tongue of every soldier. Great deeds and heroic actions were expected from him, but alas, how soon were we to be bitterly disappointed and the "On to Richmond" changed.

We stayed here till into May, when we were ordered to Falmouth, directly opposite Fredericksburg on the Rappahannock, to join McDowell's[5] Corps preparatory to his joining McClellan before Richmond. The weather was warm and it was a pretty severe march for us, unaccustomed as we were to marching. Where we bivouacked one night, in the morning a darkey boy came driving into the field a small pair of oxen hitched to a cart to pick up whatever we might leave behind; he and the team belonged to the owner of the field in which we stayed.

Some of the boys of K company began to talk with him

4. The Battle of Pittsburg Landing (Shiloh), April 6-7, 1862.
5. Brig. Gen. (later Maj. Gen.) Irwin McDowell, USA.

"Marvel" gets his freedom

and, amongst other things, asked him if he did not want his freedom, and if he did to go with us; he was highly delighted with the thought of being free, but said he could not go and leave behind a half dollar that he had earned and had up at the house. We told him to leave his team and go for the money, but he was terrible afraid his "Old Marsar" would see him coming back, but after thinking it over concluded to make the attempt; he stole up to the house unobserved, got his money, and came running back just as we were marching off the field.

He went with us and stayed with us for a long time, being a good, faithful boy. We gave him the name of Marvel, for some cause which I have forgotten. What became of him at last I do not know.

It was raining when we reached Falmouth, and as we passed through the place some of the troops quartered there (the 14th Brooklyn, New York), seeing our clean uniforms and well kept equipments, thought we were a new regiment just out, and commenced to chaff us by such remarks as "Wait till they have been out as long as we have and you will see a different uniform." "Yes," says another, "after a few weeks camping out you'll see the shine of those brasses." At length one thought to enquire, "How long have you been out, boys?" And the answer coming back "Nine months," they had nothing more to say, for we had been out three months longer than they had.

When Hartsuff reported to McDowell the arrival of his Brigade, "What"! says that officer "Brigade! I saw your train and I thought there was an Army Corps, at least," such was the length of the wagon trains during the first year of the war.

A good story is told of this march. After Hartsuff had reported to McDowell his arrival, that officer enquired "what kind of troops he commanded." "Good," said Gen'l H; "they called me a son of a B———, and men that dare call their Commander to his face by such a name had dare go anywhere." Hartsuff never had an occasion to change his mind of us, for the fighting of our old Brigade won for him the two stars and the command of a Corps. And we could never wish for a better Commander than Hartsuff.

I well remember the occasion that called forth this story, although I did not hear it. It was at a well where the boys were trying to get some water, and they were pushing and crowding each other out of the way so as to get to the water first. Gen'l Hartsuff, seeing the confusion, suggested that if they fell into line they might all be served in a much less time.

We pitched our Sibleys[6] for the last time on the heights of Falmouth, and spent two or three weeks in drilling, both by Battalion and Brigade, preparitory for the "On to Richmond" . . . which we all so longed for. McDowell reviewed his troops and in our impatience we called him Mc

6. A large cone-shaped tent of tepee design, which would house about 15 men.

Do Nothing, when in fact he was as impatient as we were, only held back by his orders. In those first months of the war we did not understand these things.

One day we were ordered to pack up everything but our tents and in our ignorance thought the time had come when we were to join the "Grand Army" under "Little Mac." We packed up quickly and, slinging our knapsacks, were off, and by the direction we took we knew it was Richmond. After going a short distance we turned in a different direction from what was the overland route. Our ardor was somewhat cooled but still some believed we were going to take transports and go by water, an easier way for us; they were always studying an easy way for the soldier. After marching two or three hours we reached the banks of the Potomac, but no transports were in sight, [so] we halted and, sitting down, rested for a half hour, when we commenced our weary march back through the mud and rain seven long miles back to our old camp. The Sibleys had forever departed during our absence; we were ordered to pitch our shelters and make ourselves as comfortable as we could. We did so with a good deal of grumbling and, I fear, many stronger expressions were used as to what seemed a useless exposure of person (for we were all wet through) and a waste of strength to accomplish what might have been done in a short half hour without any exposure whatever, but our experience in after years taught us to expect just such things. Alas, how many times the poor soldier was called upon to undergo exposure and fatigue of a similar nature to gratify the whim of some officer.

We pitched our shelters, which were simply a piece of cloth about six feet square with a row of buttons and button holes on three sides; two men pitched together by buttoning their pieces together and getting two sticks with a crotch at one end and one to go across at the top and then

placing their cloth over and pinning it down tight; if extra
pieces could be procured to button over each end, quite a
comfortable shelter was obtained, but if the ends were left
open, it made simply a shelter for our heads and a good
draught for the wind. On the whole, after we got used to
them, we liked them quite well.

7
Lights Out in K

Ordered to move—Anxiety whether it be up or down—Disaster in the valley—Ordered, and march there—In the vicinity of Strasburg—Incidents there—Recrossing the Shenandoah—Camp near Front Royal—Ordered to Manassas Junction—Incidents—Ordered Warrenton town—How the news of the capture of Richmond was received—Camp at Warrenton—"Lights out in K"—Visit of Gen'l Banks—Again on the march

*M*ay was now drawing to a close, and every day brought its round of stories of our speedy departure for more stirring scenes. Night generally gave the quietness to all, and we remain still in camp. One day orders came to pack up and [start] marching immediately, going directly to the mouth of Aquia Creek.

Here transports were in waiting, and speculation was rife whether it would be up or down the river. We all wished it to be down, and with what anxiety we watched the first Steamer as it left the wharf and ran out of the mouth of the Creek to see if it headed up stream. The boat steamed smoothly down the Creek, and then turned up the broad Potomac. We knew then for a certainty where our destination was to be.

Rumors were in the air that there had been disasters in the Valley. Stonewall had made his appearance there and Banks[1] was driven back with great loss. Washington was again threatened,[2] and all available troops were hurried on to the scene of disaster and conflicts. All was bustle and confusion. Aides were riding here and orderlies there, giving and receiving orders and trying to hurry on the troops. In the afternoon when we reached Alexandria, we were ordered aboard some platform cars and left immediately for Manassas Junction, stopping overnight here but leaving early in [the] morning for a tramp through the Thoroughfare Gap of the Bull Run Mountains towards the valley of Virginia.

We bivouacked at night in some locality near a spring or creek where water was plenty. We were now 3rd Brigade, Hartsuff,[3] 2nd Division, Ord,[4] 1st Corps, McDowell.[5]

At Peidmont on the east side of the Blue Ridge and at the entrance of Manassas Gap, we were ordered to pile up our knapsacks and leave them under guard and go through in light marching order. How well now I remember that march through the mountains, for I was not feeling well and thought at one time that I should have to give up, but the thought that there might be work ahead for us bouyed up my spirits and I hung to and came out all right. It was a cold, raw day and it commenced to rain in the afternoon, which added much to our discomfort. We came out of the

1. Maj. Gen. Nathaniel P. Banks, USA.
2. The results of Gen. Thomas J. (Stonewall) Jackson's operations in the Shenandoah Valley in late May 1862.
3. Brig. Gen. George L. Hartsuff, USA.
4. Maj. Gen. Edward O. C. Ord, USA.
5. Maj. Gen. Irwin McDowell, USA.

Gap and bivouacked in some small pines near Front Royal, the rain coming down in torrents, and our knapsacks, with blankets, twenty miles away on the other side of the mountains, but we made our coffee and passed the night away. In the morning, which was bright and clear, we sat in the sun to dry ourselves and await events; we only moved a short distance where we remained all night. General Officers were as thick as bees around a hive. The next morning we marched down and crossed the north fork of the Shenandoah on a temporary bridge, going along the railroad some four or five miles towards Strasburg; the weather was very warm and showers were of hourly occurance. Our rations also were running very low and we were getting very hungry. Some beef was found and killed, which was eaten before it was hardly dressed. Col Coulter of the 11th P.V.[6] found some flour, which was distributed amongst the Brigade, a pint or so to a man.

I saw a house about a mile away and with a comrade started for it, thinking that we might find something that we could buy or take that we might eat, but how vain were our hopes, for when we got there, there was so many ahead that they had confiscated everything that was eatable.

When I asked the long, lean, and lank girl of about twenty if she hadn't a chicken she could sell, she put on such a smile or grin and answered, "If you Yanks should stay here a week there wouldn't be a chicken left in all Clark County." I turned away, satisfied that if I wanted chickens I must travel in another direction. Dan Warren of our mess was more fortunate than all the rest for he returned with the carcas of a lamb, a genuine lamb this time and no mistake. We procured a mess kettle and commenced to boil it to make a soup, each one contributing of

6. 11th Pennsylvania Volunteers.

"Chickens" of Clark County

his flour to make the thickening. How eagerly we stood around the fire and watched the process of boiling with the thickening being put in: how savory it smelt, and how our mouths watered for the delicious morsel that we thought was in store for us. We had invited Lieut Sanderson of Co. C to share with us in our feast and he had come with his dish, but alas, how vain are all earthly expectations, for when it was pronounced done it was quite dark and those having it in charge, when taking it off and setting it down quickly, set it on a stub and over went the kettle spilling about two thirds; the Lieut. seeing what happened ran quickly to his company, [and] what remained was divided around, a few mouthfuls to a man. During the afternoon I went with two or three comrades out to an old church that was fast going to decay and secured all the boards we could bring in, and fixed us up a comfortable shelter with use of boughs at the ends, laying a floor as well. Most of the boys preferr[ed] to lay down on the ground rather than work to prepare them a place. During the night the rain fell in torrents; it actually poured, fairly drowning out those who were not so well provided as we were; our little place was crowded full, there was no chance to sleep, neither lay down, and so we huddled together and sat the night away. It still continued to rain in the morning and the water was at least two inches deep where our regiment lay. Being so short of provision and the water in the creeks and rivers rising so rapidly and Stonewall having slipped back up the Valley, the Gen'l, fearing that the bridge would be carried away over the Shenandoah (which was only a temporary structure), ordered us back at once, and we taking the railroad track moved at a quick step; the creeks that but yesterday were only of the ordinary heights were now as large as rivers. When we reached the bridge we found it weighted down with great stones, and with the weight of the troops and Artilery had been kept in place; the river was rising rapidly and running like a race horse, [but] the troops all passed over safely but about one hundred that stragled from the Brigade; before they came up the force of the water carried away the bridge leaving them behind. The next day two of them, men from Co. B, undertook to cross in a boat, but the current was then so strong that it took them down stream; the body of one was found several days after, impaled on an Oak in the vicinity of Snickers Gap, or Ferry; the other was never found, at least we never heard that it was. We were taken into the woods about a mile from the river on an elevated piece of ground where there was no danger of being drowned.

Jackson had gone back up the valley, barely escaping the forces of Shields at Port Republic, and Fremont at Cross Keys. All was lovely with us now for a few days. Shields' wounded were brought down to Front Royal. We met here some of our old friends, "the 1st Maryland"; they had been stationed here (Front Royal) and when Jackson made his raid he surprised and took almost the entire command.

Our knapsacks were brought up, for we had been without them about a fortnight, and it had rained almost every day, that is, there had been showers, so it had kept us wet, and my knapsack looked as though it had not been all pleasant weather where that was, but for all that it did seem good to get them.

After a few more days of quiet rest we were loaded into box cars and transported back to Manassas Junction, [w]here we pitched a regular camp about a mile out towards the north of the depot. We spent the time in drilling, by Brigade, Battalion, and Company. K Co. was as good a drilled Company as any in the Regiment. We had spent considerable time in drilling with the bayonet and were now quite proficient in it's drill.

Cap't Hovey with commendable pride used to like to show us off before the rest of the troops. I remember on one occasion, after being out all the forenoon, when we came in that he halted us on the parade ground and drilled us in bayonet before the whole Brigade; every movement was with precision and after drilling us about five minutes he dismissed us amidst the cheers of the assembled Brigade.

News of the movements of the "Grand Army" under McClellan[7] were received and freely commented upon. While some believed that they were meeting with success,

7. Maj. Gen. George B. McClellan's Peninsular Campaign, April to July 1862.

others shook their heads and failed to see where the success came in.

All the soldiers were very patriotic, and all wanted to believe in success, but on the whole, from what we could gather, the news was not of the most promising kind and victory did not sit upon our banners.

On the "Fourth day of July" we broke camp and took up the line of march for Warrenton town, stopping one night on the way; when we were fileing into the field, news came that McClellan had taken Richmond, that while he had given up and suffered defeat on one wing, the other had gloriously entered into the city, but no other particulars were received. A few faint cheers were given, but the greater portion of the command was choosing to wait till a more reliable report could be obtained. We moved on in the morning and pitched our camp in an open field just out of Warrenton.

The news from the "Grand Army" were very unsatisfactory; while we knew that Richmond was not taken, still a victory was claimed and a magnificent object had been obtained. Viz: "A change of base." What did that mean? In our ignorance of great Military movements we could not understand how anything of advantage had been obtained or realized, unless it was that from being within eight or nine miles of Richmond they had changed to thirty or more; if that was the object attained, a few more such victories and we could all go home with a Southern Confederacy fully established. Such was our feelings in regard to this magnificent movement of the great "Army of the Potomac."

The water at Manassas was extremely bad and many were sick; almost all were not feeling well from its effects, but at Warrenton it was splendid, nice cool spring water and as clear as crystal. Cherries were in abundance, the woods even were full of them, and blackberries in some localities farely covered the ground; with such fare the boys soon recovered their usual good health and spirits.

An amusing incident happened at this place which for a long time was a sort of by-word in the regiment, and to this day is often alluded to with many good laughs when we have our reunions. It was this: the orders were to have all lights out in camp at taps, the guard-house and head-quarters alone excepted. The boys for some time had grown negligent, and in many instances kept their lights burning till long after the regular hour.

Orders had been issued to enforce this order, and com-manders of companies were to be held responsible for the compliance of their respective commands. On this particu-lar night Capt. Hovey was "Officer of the day," and on him rested the whole responsibility of seeing this order obeyed. Taps sounded at the usual hour, and about a half hour after, the Col. wishing to ascertain how the order was obeyed, went out; all the lights were out except in K com-pany, Hovey's own, and their lights were burning brightly in every tent. He immediately went to the Captain's tent and, calling him out, showed him the lights. Hovey, taken wholly aback by the sight, immediately roared out, "Lights out in K." It came like a shell into the slumbering camp, awakening all, who, starting up and realizing the situation, immediately repeated the echo of "Lights out in K." It was too good to joke to be punished and was overlooked for this time.

Gen'l Banks, who had marched to this vicinity with his command, visited our camp one evening, [and] when it was known that he was in the camp the boys all assembled in front of the Col's tent, each provided with a lighted candle hid in his cap; an officer entered the tent and requested the presence of the Gen'l at the door. When he came out the lights were uncovered and all had a chance to see him, and three good old Massachusetts cheers were given. The Gen'l acknowledged the compliment and spoke a few words of cheer. In alluding to his retreat from the valley, he said "the thing would never have happened if he had had his old brigade," and we all agreed with him.

I was one of two detailed from the company and twenty from the regiment as a guard for brigade headquarters, where we stayed till we moved again. I visited Warrenton during our stay here, quite a pretty place for Virginia; it was the home of Ex Gov. Extra Billy Smith, a noted man before the war, but I have forgotten whether he was living at this time; if he was, he took no active part in the political world.

Hartsuff's headquarters at Warrenton

One day at Brigade headquarters there came along a Negro who was sick; the Brigade Surgeon who was out walking was the first to see him and looking him over pronounced it a case of Small Pox. It was lucky for us that the surgeon was the first to see him, for if he had gone on down to camp there is no knowing what might have happened; as it was, he was placed in an old negro shanty that belonged to the plantation and a guard placed over him, with orders to shoot him if he undertook to leave, and to warn all others to keep away.

The surgeon, who had had the disease, visited him every day, carrying food and water, and all the medicine he required. I had not seen him for two or three days before we left, and thought him dead; the shanty was burned the morning of our moving.

We stayed at Warrenton about three weeks when we changed our camp and moved on to a place called Waterloo, where we halted at night on a side hill so steep that we had to tie ourselves down to keep from rolling down into the creek below.

Joseph Martin of K company said "I'll pitch my poncho just three times more—a promise he faithfully kept, for he deserted in a few days and we heard afterwards that he reached Canada in safety.

8

Let's Be Jolly

*T*he "Army of Virginia" was now organized and John
Pope,[1] the hero of "Island No. 10,"[2] a western Gen'l,
was appointed to the command. One of his first orders was
that the army should subsist on the country through which
it passed. Some of the boys, construing the order to mean
an indiscriminate plunder of everything that could be
found, went out in squads of two or three and took whatever they could lay their lands upon, [but] they were soon
reminded of that state of things and [that] that construction
of the order would not be tolerated. A patrol guard was appointed, of which I was one, to patrol the country and ar-

---

1. Maj. Gen. John Pope, USA.
2. A fortified island in the Mississippi River near the Kentucky-Tennessee bor-
der, captured by General Pope on April 7, 1862.

rest all found outside the camps without a permit to forage, [and] this soon put a stop to all such proceedings.

Patrol Guard

It was about this time that Ex President Van Buren died,[3] and the regiment paid appropriate honors to his memory. The Chaplain also preached a sermon that was the occasion of some talk and more merriment. He took for his text a character from Dickens, who could at all times and under all circumstances say "Lets be jolly."

The failure of McClellan on the peninsular was perfectly understood by the boys, and the outlook was not the most flattering for the little army commanded by John Pope down in the heart of the Old Dominion, when the great army of McClellan had so signally failed. Consequently the spirits of the boys drooped, and the Chaplain, seeing the gloom settling down, departed from his usual custom and chose as the subject of his discourse a character who at all times could say "Lets be jolly." He spoke of the many happy homes we had left; of the many days of toil; the many long and weary marches; and the privation that we

3. July 24, 1862.

had endured, and all so patiently up to this time, the end
of our first year of service. But then [he] said "Men of Massachusetts, what came you out to see? Was it an immense
picnic? Was it a gigantic spree? Was it a day of sunshine
without clouds? Or was it rather for the purpose to accept
the stern realities of war. Whether if victory perched upon
our banners, or defeat leaned upon our side, were we not
to be the same good soldiers, always ready to do our duty
whenever, where ever and under whatever circumstances
we should be placed?" And above all he urged us to remember the words of the text. He told us that gloomy won
no battles, conquored no foe, that it was best for us to look
the danger calmly in the face, to trust in the God of battles,
and under all circumstances "to be jolly." After listening to
the cheering words of the Chaplain, the faces of the men
brightened and the regiment marched to quarters with
cheers, and ever after remembered the council of the Chaplain.

The time was now soon to come that was to be big with
events with us. The rebel army had released itself from
McClellan's grip (or in the popular phrase of that day, "The
folds of the Anaconda") [and] had nothing to fear from him.
The "On to Richmond" had been changed to "How can we
get away," and Lee[4] was left free to move in whatever direction he chose. Pope's army of less than forty thousand
men seemed an easy prey for his "One hundred thousand
Veterans." Consequently Jackson was started again with his
corp flushed with victory to operate against Pope. Pope in
the meantime had been ordered to advance down into the
heart of "Old Virginia" so [as] to draw the attention of Lee
from the renowned commander of the "great Army of the
Potomac," who had his headquarters on a gun-boat so as to

4. General Robert E. Lee, CSA.

be able to get away in case he was again atacked, [to] save his own skin no matter what became of the army.

Pope crossed the Rappahannock and moved down to Culpepper and vicinity. Pope's army at this time consisted of one Corps, the 1st, McDowell's, Banks division, and a division commanded by Gen'l Siegel,[5] in all about thirty eight thousand men. The thirteenth was in Hartsuffs Brigade, Ricketts[6] Division, McDowell's Corps. Hartsuffs brigade was composed of the 12th and 13th Massachusetts, 83d New York Volunteers or 9th State Militia as they were better known, and the eleventh Penn Vol. The Col. of the 12th was Fletcher Webster, a son of the great Daniel. S. H. Leonard the 13th, Styles the 9th N.Y., Richard Coulter or as he was better known "Old Dick Coulter" the 11 P.V. Now I do not wish to boast, or to detract from any brigade (for I have but recently read of quite a number who claimed to be the best of all the good brigades in the whole army), but I do claim that "Hartsuffs old brigade" was just as good as any, in the camps, on the march, or in the face of the foe, and in point of drill was as near perfection as any other in all the armies of the United States, that they never suffered themselves to be surprised but were ever on the alert, and were always looking out to take advantage of every opportunity when it did not conflict with a straight forward line of duty. And I think the unbiassed historian of that brigade, could it's history be written, would fully concur with what I claim for it. It is not my purpose to write a history of the war, so I shall confine myself simply to the regiment or brigade, with an occasional glance around.

After staying about a week in the vicinity of Culpepper we were ordered down through the town towards Cedar Mountain. I think it was the afternoon of the eighth of Au-

5. General Franz Sigel, USA.
6. Brig. Gen. (later Maj. Gen.) James B. Ricketts, USA.

gust. As our regiment marched along with colors flying and band playing, many of the citizens (mostly female) stood in their doors or at windows to see us pass; none were glad to see us if we except the colored. Many were crying. And I shall never forget one person as she kneeled at the window with eyes and hands upturned to Heaven and with an expression on her face as though she was calling upon the Almighty to send down the most dreadful punishment it were possible upon our heads. I could not keep my eyes off from her as we passed, and a chill of horror ran through me as I looked upon her.

On the ninth of August we moved a little to the right, where we lay under arms; we were about two miles to the south of the town and near the road that led to Cedar Mountain. Banks division [had] passed down this road, and soon firing was heard in that direction, and we knew that the enemy was not far away.

I do not question why we were suffered to remain here all day while a battle[7] was being fought within hearing, but I do know that it occasioned considerable talk with us; perhaps it was to prevent a flank movement. However that may be, we remained till about four o'clock, then we were ordered to fall in, and we moved down the same road that Banks with his division had moved in an earlier part of the day. We had not gone far before we commenced to meet those of Banks command who in a later period of the war were called "Bummers," "Coffee boilers," those who never under any circumstances or consideration would be found in a battle. When danger began to appear, and occasionaly a minié[8] would come singing over, followed by a hoarse shriek of a shell, they would be suddenly taken sick, fearful

7. The Battle of Cedar Mountain (Slaughter Mt.) on August 9, 1862.
8. A bullet invented by Capt. Minié of France. The bullet was conical in shape, with a hollow base, and was used in the muzzle-loading rifles of that period.

pains would come upon them, their legs would become weak, and there would be a great desire in them to turn around, or to lie down till the main part of the army had passed, and then they would go at a double quick for the rear. After the fight was over, these men would come up, and such heroic deeds as they had performed, hair-breadth escapes as they had had, and the wonder was how they could have lived through it all. I distinctly remember at this time one great strapping fellow who probably had not been very near the scene of conflict, who had struck a two-forty pace to the rear, and when we passed shouted "Give 'em h--l boys, we got 'em started"; that was a by-word with us for a long time. Whenever we saw a crowd of straglers making for the rear, someone would sing out "They have got them started, give 'em h--l." Soon the wounded were met and we began to hear some of the particulars of the fight; we piled up our knapsacks in a field and left a guard over them. On we went till we had almost reached the scene of carnage, when we were halted and stacked arms.

We heard that Banks had got the worst of it and had fallen back. It was almost dark and as there was no immediate prospect of a move, we began to prepare for the night by eating our scanty meal and getting some straw from a neighboring stack. When we were about laying down for a nap, Carroll's[9] West Virginia brigade came up with a band playing their favorite tune, which was "West Virginia is Union Still." When the band was about up to where we were (for hearing the band coming we had delayed laying down), a shell came shrieking along and exploded just over our heads, quickly followed by another, and another; the music ceased on the instant and the members quickly beat

9. Col. Samuel S. Carroll, USA, commanding the 8th Ohio Regiment and later appointed General for his outstanding services in the Wilderness Battle in May 1864.

a retreat, followed by the bummers and the officers servants. It was getting to get a rather bad place for ones health, as the shells continued to come. We were ordered to "take arms," for every man had fallen in without orders, and we moved directly towards the place from whence the firing came.

It was a bright moonlight night and the Col. gave orders to "Trail arms" so the light of the moon shining on the bright barrels of our guns would not reveal our presence to the enemy. We passed to within a few rods of them unharmed, but the twelfths, who had not taken the precaution we had, were fired upon and lost several men, amongst whom was Capt. Shurtleff, son of a former Mayor of Boston. We crossed a slight ridge and then moved to the right a short distance and went behind a little hill, where we halted and supported a battery that now came up, and soon it opened fire. Report said that Gen'l Hartsuff sighted the first gun; be that as it may, it was to us a terriably grand sight, to watch the cannonieers, and the firing of the gun, and to mark the shells as they went shrieking through the air followed by a bright light from the burning fuse.

The duel, I should judge, lasted about an hour, when it gradualy died down with only an occasional shot. We slept but little; I think towards morning I slept a few moments.

In the morning we moved back before light and formed a line of battle in a large cornfield to await the movements or attack of the enemy. Stonewall, finding a larger force in his front then he expected (although I have every reason to believe that his army fully equaled Popes in men that he could fight; if not in men, he certainly had this advantage, that he was in a friendly country and could fight every man, for he needed none to guard his trains or his rear, while Pope, being in an enemy's country and a long ways from his supplies with no reenforcements near and none soon expected, had to be very cautious. McClellan had been so very reluctant about leaving the Peninsular, had very near sacrificed Popes little army in addition to his own by his long delay), withdrew to the other side of the Rapidan, knowing that delay increased his strength, while it weakened Pope, for every day of McClellan stay was worth more than a hundred men to him, awaited only to make surer of his prey.

We lay in line of battle till into the afternoon, when having heard of Stonewall retreat, we went back and brought our knapsacks up and pitched a camp about a mile away from the battlefield.

The next day, with Henry Gassett, without leave, we stole over to view the field, for we had a great curiosity to see how a battlefield would look. Details of men were there burying the dead; in the centre of one field was a long trench filled with Union dead; in a stubble field we saw several bodies that were still unburied. At first I thought them Colored, they were so black and swolen, and I wondered how Negros should be wearing the blue coat of a soldier, but I soon discovered my mistake; the stench of the bodies were fearful.

Farther on we saw where the rebel's had buried quite a number of their dead, and not buried either, for they were laid on the top of the ground with some dirt hastily thrown over them; here an arm, there a knee, and then a foot protruded from the ground to tell of the ghastly sight beneath that only awaited the first rain to be revealed.

On our way back we passed the place where the battery was planted that first night and opened fire upon us so heavily. We talked with a few captured rebs and they told us that in that Artilery fight the Cap't was killed and some twenty five or thirty men killed and wounded, and that so many of his horses were killed or disabled that the infantry were called upon to help draw off his guns. Be this as it may, I counted ten dead horses all within a few feet of where the battery stood, and saw several more that were badly wounded.

When we got back to camp, having been gone the greater portion of the day, we found the brigade out, the Gen'l having ordered them out to fire off their guns, and finding so many men absent (for we were not the only ones), had ordered all of those absent to be put on fatigue duty to police up the camp. This was my first and last time that I was ever put on fatigue duty for punishment, but there were so many of us that the duty was quickly performed and I think we had a much easier time then those who stayed in camp. But that is not the idea; a good soldier is ever at his post, shirks no duty, fears no hardship, and is prompt to obey all orders, that was what I ever tried to do, and the idea of being put on fatigue for punishment cut pretty close.

Mike O'Loughlin of our K company, who was out, told me that he was standing looking at some rebs when one of them says "Hello Mike what brought you here?", and going up to them he found an old acquaintance, one he used to work with in the coal mines of Penn. Together they sat down on a log and each tried to convince the other that his side was right. After an hour of pleasant conversation they seperated and each went to his command; he belonged to a New Orleans regiment. As we were not actively engaged, there was no casualities in our regiment. In a few days we marched down the west side of the mountain and pitched our camp close up under the south side. At our first halt and before we had taken rest Col Leonard said: "Men of Massachusetts have you heard the news? R. Morris Copeland and Cap't Schriber have been dismissed from the service."

Of what particular offence Copeland was guilty [of] I do not know, but Schriber could have fraud wrote after his name and not over express it. And so they weeded them out, but not as fast as they deserved to be.

9

Minié Balls Become Disagreeable

*Military movements on the Rapidan and thoughts
suggested by the same—Retreat of Pope's army behind the Rappahannock—Skirmishing—Falling
back—Stonewall in Pope's rear—Pope's last
hope—Recruits—The Chaplain's advice—Heath
the recruit—Mr. Turner—Thoroughfare Gap —
Stragglers put to use—Bristoe and Manassas—Nearing the battlefield*

F or the next week there was a lull in military movements with us. Stonewall remained quietly behind the
river until such times as he thought Pope would be an easy
prey. Lee,[1] having shaken off the great "Army of the
Potomac," turned his undivided attention to the little army
of Va. in hopes to bag them before the legions of McClellan
could join them, for they were now on their way. Consequently Stonewall was ordered to gain Popes flank and
rear, and how nearly they succeeded we shall see.

Let me here say, that to execute a movement, no one,

1. General Robert E. Lee, CSA, in command of the Confederate Forces in
Virginia.

north or south, could do it with such rapidity, could turn up in such unexpected places and at times when least expected, as Stonewall Jackson. His name was a terror in the Union army, and with us expressed more fear than all the other names put together. Of his treatment to his men I have nothing to say, but of my own personal experience I think that the greatest and best generals to their men are those who move with . . . celerity, and having moved, strike. Success is what the soldier wants; it gives him courage, buoy's up his spirits, and [for] an officer that gives success, they will march with unbroken ranks, will suffer all the privation incidental to long and arduous campaigns, will even go to the cannon mouth, and all so cheerfully, [though] not without grumbling, for it is a soldiers priviledge to grumble; deprive him of that and you deprive him of half his life.

That Stonewall was a great General none can deny, and the whole secret of his success was his ability to move troops, and after moving, using them. All the men that served under him knew that their labor was not in vain; after long and weary marches, after hunger, came rest and feasting on the good things that Uncle Sam's commissary furnished them. It was a prize to them worth striving for. Oh! that we could have had a few such generals on our side in the first year of the war, generals that thought more of winning victories than they did of their nice cloths.

There were good officers then, but they held subordinate position; occasionaly, if one did appear to gain victories and was working himself up, many of the others would combine to pull him down, using all means to accomplish their purpose, and so the poor soldier was permitted to suffer through the incompetency, or jealousy, of officers high in rank.

Pope, learning that the army of Gen'l Lee had joined

that of Jackson, and knowing the peril of his own little army down on the Rapidan, but daily hoping that some of the divisions of McClellan would reach him, waited till all hope was gone, and then retreated behind the Rappahannock.

How well I remember that day, of how when we came back through Culpepper the ladies came out with every indication of joy, waveing their secession flags and heeping indignities upon us, but few men were seen and they held themselves aloof and took no part, knowing if they should do or say one tenth of what the women did, it would be all day with them; as it was, it was hard to restrain from doing them harm, and at times we had to make it appear as though we would run the bayonet through them.

It was an exceedingly warm day, and Old Soll poured down upon us his hottest rays, water was scarce, and the dust was in clouds, filling everything; we farely ate it.

After a short halt Gen'l Hartsuff addressed a few words. Thanking the command for the way we were accomplishing this most difficult march, he said "we were in the middle of a long line of troops, and that much depended upon the celerity of our movements, and that he had faith in us that we would perform all that would be required." We had faith in Hartsuff and were much gratified of his faith in us. At last long after dark we reached the Rappahannock at the point where the Orange and Alexandria R.R. crosses it and, going but a few rods beyond, lay our weary selves down to sleep. At Rappahannock Station (the name of this place) there is on the south side of the river two little hills each distinct from the other, about an eighth of a mile apart, the upper one wooded while the rest of the country for a mile or more is level, with only here and there a tree; then comes the timber streching around from river to river.

Directly across the river and behind the little hills is quite a ridge completely overlooking them. We lay during the night just beyond the ridge, and in the morning when I got up (for I had not slept much for there was so much commotion moving troops, and Artilery getting into position, with the rumbling of heavy moving trains, the cracking of whips, and loud mouthed oaths of the teamsters as with their "Yea Mule" they tried to hurry forward their patient beasts, made it a night of not much sleep)—when I got up, the sun was just beginning to make his appearance above the horizon, [and] I saw quite a number of the boys on the top of the ridge looking over the river and on going up myself I saw what attracted their attention. Coming over the plain at the full run was a goodly number of Union soldiers, those that had stragled during the march had got tired and lain themselves down to rest, and were now making it up by a good run, choosing rather the union lines then the prisons of Richmond; those that were the fatherest away were trying their best to reach the friendly shelter of the little hills. Soon there burst out of the woods riding at full speed . . . the rebel cavalry, brandishing their sabres and firing their pistols and calling for the soldiers to stop; a few were taken, others would, in groups of three or four, form and make a brave resistance. The battery on the ridge on which we stood sent a few well directed shots into the rebels, which soon caused them to withdraw within the shelter of the woods. The sun just shining over the treetops, the fleeing union soldiers, the rebel horsemen, the sword and gun flashing in the sunlight, and the puff of smoke from gun or pistol, and above all the deep mouthed cannon and the bursting shell, was a picture in real life such as I had never seen before, and one that today comes fresh to my mind and I can see it almost as fresh as I did on that beautiful 21st of Aug morning 1862.

A few moments later and Hartsuff brigade was ordered to fall in, and we moved briskly down and over the bridge up

on the other side and occupied the two little hills, the 9th
N.Y. and the 13th holding the first one near the bridge,
and the 11th P.V. and 12th Mass with a section of battery
the other one. We threw up a slight earth work and remained in this position the remainder of the day and that
night; the enemy made a demonstration against us just at
night, showing their infantry without the woods, and for a
time there was every prospect of a battle, but the ridge behind the river was well manned by our batteries with infantry supports, and an unfordable river made them withdraw
after they had made a feint and drawn our fire. After we
recrossed the river we lay behind the ridge and experi-
enced quite an artilery fire. I. H. Beals was hit on the head
by a piece of shell, wounding him so as to take him out of
the service. Popes position was a strong one, and Lee, ever
unwilling to be the attacking party, concluded it was best to
attempt a movement by the flank and thus draw Pope from
his position. Popes army, after the casualties of Cedar
Mountain and incidental to so severe a campaign, was fast
diminishing in number, [and] besides, there were skirmish-
ings every day with more or less loss, although a part of
Gen Burnsides command had reached him. Yet, by skilfull
manuvering of his small force, he kept the enemy at bay for
over a week.

Lee was working his way up the river, and our corps
moved from Rappahannock Station to near Warrenton, or
between that place and Sulpher Springs. Stonewall was
now detached from Lee and ordered to go around and
strike Popes rear. The baggin part had now come. Pope
was yet miles away from his base of supplies, and if Jackson
could strike Popes rear and stop his supplies from coming
through, it was only a question of a little time and the
game would be bagged. Pope had nothing to place in his
way, for every man of his little army had been strained to

their utmost for over two weeks, and there was an army of double his number still in his front.

Where all this time from the middle of August was the "Grand Army of the Potomac?" What was keeping it away from the place of danger? Why was it not sent as fast as it could to help extricate the little "Army of Virginia?"

These are questions I will leave unanswered, for the present at least. Stonewall succeeded in his movement, striking Popes rear at Catletts, a station on the Orange and Alexandria R.R., and capturing and destroying all he could find between there and Manassas Junction.

The only alternative left now for Pope to do was to abandon his present line and by forced marches and continual fighting establish his line at some place nearer Washington. And yet there was one chance more that promised success if he could rely upon, and obtain the cooperation of, some of the divisions of the Potomac army that were now beginning to arrive, and that was with those divisions, and such portions of his army as he could spare from his front, strike Stonewall before he could escape or form a junction with the other portion of Lee's army. The thing itself was feasible, but would the commanders of those divisions obey his orders? He had reason to expect they would, consequently he laid his plans and again urged that the reenforcements might be hurried up. Of those that were near and gave him their hearty support were the divisions of Hooker,[2] Kearny,[3] and Burnside[4] from North Carolina, officers who on every occasion where there was danger, were found, and gave their services without stopping to question the policy of whether it was this or that who commanded.

I have forgotten to say that when we were lying at the

2. Maj. Gen. Joseph Hooker, USA.
3. Maj. Gen. Philip Kearney, USA.
4. Maj. Gen. Ambrose E. Burnside, USA.

south side of Cedar Mountain, there arrived an instalment
of recruits for the regiment, about one hundred of them;
they were enlisted for certain companies and joined those
companies on their arrival. K received none, if we except
one Walter S. C. Heath, or "Old Heath" as he was familiarly
called. Co B being full, he was sent to K. The Chaplain,
also seeing the recruits had nice clean dippers, warned
them that if they wanted to keep them, they must keep
their eyes open all the time, for if there was one thing that
a 13th man envied, or wished to get possession of, it was a
nice clean dipper. The warning was not wholly without results, for on one occasion I tried to borrow one to strain my
coffee in; he refused to let me take it, thinking, as he afterwards confessed, that I wished to confiscate it for my
own use. When we arrived at Warrenton or it's vicinity just
at night, in the field where he was to bivouac there were
several hogs, and while we were speculating how we could
capture them as the line was being formed, Old Heath, our
new recruit, up with his gun and fired, and such a squeal
as that hog set up is seldom heard. He was mortally
wounded and soon yielded up his hogship.

Old Heath, when cautioned by the Cap't about doing so
unmilitary an act, pleaded that he did not know the rules
yet that governed soldiers. We ate pork that night for supper.

As Heath had no blanket or tent, Dorkham had kindly
shared with him both tent and blanket, and had carried
them on the march and pitched the tent at night. The
ground was not at all times as even as a house floor, but
many times it was rough and hard to lay upon and again we
could not always pick out our own place, but had to lay
somewhere near that we were put. On this particular night
or in the morning Heath was mad with Dorkham because
the ground was so uneven, and he told D- that he would

not sleep with him again unless he picked out an evener piece of ground for him to lay on. Dorkham told him that it was no honor for him to sleep with Heath and that after this he must provide his own shelter and blankets. We used to laugh at Dorkham for a long time for the priviledge he had of sleeping with Old Heath.

Heath and Dorkham

Mr. Turner of Westboro Mass., father of Corporal M. G. Turner, visited the reg't and staid over night with his son. The next day when he started on his return, his son got permission to go with him as far as the village; he forgot to come back and the next we heard of him sometime afterwards was, that he had been discharged by order of President Lincoln.

Pope, having ordered the divisions of the Potomac army to cooperate with him, ordered McDowells corps to fall back through Warrenton towards Manassas Junction. We marched all night, although it was a very dark night and there was considerable mist falling, yet we marched and covered quite a good number of miles. In the morning we reached Haymarket about half way between Warrenton and Manassas, where we cooked and ate our breakfast and awaited events. Somewhere about noon Hartsuff's brigade was detached from the division to go to Throughfare Gap and if possible prevent the enemy from coming through, or delay him till Pope had finished up Jackson.

The brigade, regiments, and companies were ordered to reform, and all who were not able to march were ordered to keep on with the rest of the division. When the company was reformed Heath was not there and could not be found, so the company was formed without him. When all was ready we started with a quick step towards the Gap. After going a short distance Heath came up and tried to crowd Dorkham out of his place, claiming it as his own. This Dorkham resented, telling him that the company had been formed anew.

The Cap't, hearing the fuss and comprehending it all at a glance, told Heath to get out of the ranks, thinking he would fall in at the rear of the company, his proper place. Heath did not so understand the order, as we shall see bime by.

Hartsuff, who was sick, occasioned by the breaking out of old wounds, was not in command, but Styles of the 9th.[5]

We marched in close order and at a rapid pace, for if anything was to be accomplished, the sooner we were at the Gap the better. On the way up we could hear the guns of Pope and Jackson[6] almost in our rear, and we hoped that enough of the old army was with him to make victory sure.

On nearing the Gap a regiment was formed in line of battle on each side of the road, with skirmishers in front; we advanced in this order through a piece of woods and over a large piece of level ground clear up to the Gap itself. We captured a Johney Reb near the entrance who belonged to a Georgia regiment of Longstreet[7] Corps who had just

5. Col. John W. Styles, USA, in command of the 9th (N.Y.) State Militia (83rd Infantry Regiment).
6. The Battle of Second Bull Run (2nd Manassas), August 29-30, 1862.
7. Maj. Gen. (later Lieut. Gen.) James Longstreet, CSA.

arrived on the other side. The 11th P.V. entered to the right, or held the right just within the entrance. Between the railroad and the creek stands a large stone flour mill. "K take the mill" were the orders from the Col. "Forward K," repeated Capt Hovey, and K proceeded up the railroad and took possession, the rebs who were just entering from the other side firing briskly down at us. There were some pretty narrow escapes as I can tell from my own personal knowledge. And I can truly say that in all my army life I never heard the Miniés when they had such a disagreeable sound. Some of the boys [who] climbed up to the second story windows to get better shots saw large quantities of the rebs farther up the Gap. We stayed in the mill but a few minutes when we were ordered to the other side of the creek; we left the mill and went down side the creek to the bridge, where we crossed and came up the other side into the road. Here lay the body of a young soldier of Co. D., killed outright. We were pushing ourselves well up into the Gap, the miniés whizzing all around us, [and] it was getting to be hot work, when we were ordered back behind a wall and [to] prevent the enemy from coming through till dark at least. Even now we could hear the guns of Pope and Jackson far in our rear. Looking away up through the Gap we could see the shining barrels of some Brass "Napoleons." The battery with us shelled the heights on either side of the entrance. We held the gap till almost dark, when we were ordered to the rear in quick time. We did not run but we took some pretty long steps and we took them quick; we were expecting every moment to get a volley, but the darkness coming on saved us.

We did not halt till we had again reached Haymarket, where we halted for a rest and a short nap; we were all pretty glad to get away from Thoroughfare for it was rather a dangerous place for a single brigade, with the whole of

Longstreet Corps in our front and Jackson with Stuart's[8] cavalry in our rear. We left Haymarket at light, going towards Bristoe Station; grass did not grow under our feet on the way, and there was continual skirmishing in the rear.

Tom Gassett and Duke Wellington of K and some others from the regiment, getting tired, thought to take a rest, and sitting down by the road commenced to take their ease; in a moment the brigade had passed, when down the road at full speed came the rear guard of cavalry, [who,] seeing the group of straglers, reined up their horses. An officer in a voice and tone that was not to be disobeyed said "Up, men, and form here in the road"; every man (for their was a dozen or more) was on his feet in an instant and formed according to orders with the union cavalry in their rear. Down the road now came the rebel cavalry riding at the same speed, and when within a few rods the same officer said "Now men, ready, aim, fire! Now men," he said, "run for your lives or the rebs will have you." Without stopping to see what was the result of their fire, the boys started on the run and soon caught up with the brigade. That officer was John Buford,[9] commanding a cavalry brigade in the army, but now with a small squad was helping Hartsuff's brigade out of a tight place.

Tom said that he saw one of the rebs fall when they fired, but they were only too willing to obey the order to get away to stay and see the results; they were satisfied during the remainder of the march not to stop and take rest till the whole brigade did.

We reached Bristoe, where we halted and made some coffee, and had breakfast, or dinner, then after drawing rations we started up the railroad towards Manassas; all along

8. Maj. Gen. (later Lieut. Gen.) James E. B. (JEB) Stuart, CSA.
9. General John Buford, USA.

the road was signs of Stonewalls handiworks in burnt cars and torn up tracks. We reached Manassas in the afternoon, where we hoped for rest, for all day long we had still heard the guns of Pope and Jackson and had hoped that something was decided, but after halting long enough to take on an extra supply of ammunition, we took up our line of weary march towards where we could so plainly hear the continual roll of the guns of Pope and Jackson. Speculation was rife as to whether we should be taken in to the fight in our wearied condition. That no decided advantage has been obtained we all knew, and by the way we were hurried forward it seemed as though our presence was wanted on the field. When within two or three miles of the field, we passed the division of Fitz John Porter[10] quietly resting in a pleasant grove, with guns stacked, boots blacked, and equipment clean as though on inspection. When we saw these evidently fresh troops, we were pretty certain that we should not be called upon to go into the fight. As we tramped wearily along some of the men remarked in a sneering way, "They look as though they did not wish to go," and I dare say our looks did not belie us in the least. It did seem strange to us then that so many fresh troops should lie idle within so short a distance of a field where there was so fierce a battle being fought. Time told the reason why.

It was after dark before we reached the field, and the battle for the day was over, save an occasional shot now and then, when a noise was heard that indicated the movement of troops and the changes of position; that and the fire of the picket was all to disturb through the entire night. We were halted in the rear of the line of battle and were or-

10. Maj. Gen. Fitz-John Porter, USA.

dered to make ourselves comfortable for the night, [so] after cooking our supper and making some enquiries of what the results of the fighting had been, and getting nothing satisfactory, we rolled ourselves up in our blankets and lay down to sleep.

10
Defeat and Retreat

*Preparing for the battle[1]—The battle—Separated
from the command—Tom Gassett and myself
retreat—Capt. Bates and the "Provost
Guard"—Still retreating—Crossing Bull Run
Creek—Coffee-making—Bivouac for the night —
Finds the regiment—In Centreville
—Thoughts on the battle—Pope's fate.*

We were roused up early in the morning and after
having made our coffee we were ordered to fall in and
taken down into a piece of woods, where we piled up our
knapsacks and left them under guard of a man from each
company. We were then moved to the front and centre,
where we remained but a short time, then we were ordered to the rear, and from there went away up to the
right of the line. Here as at the other places, our stay was
short, for I think without stopping to rest we were again
marched to the centre. Troops were moving in other parts
of the field, going in all direction. A part of Siegel's corps
passed by us and one man from a regiment was straglin

1. The Battle of Second Bull Run (2nd Manassas), August 29-30, 1862.

[105]

along by himself when the Col. saw him and went for him. Grasping him by the shoulder he said in his broken English, "What for you stragle here for? Return to your regiment immediately"; and giving him a good shake, they went on.

It was somewhere passed noon when we were ordered to the left, McDowell leading in person. We had moved along quite a distance when an aide came riding down at the full gallop with an order for McDowell; after reading the order he gave the orders to "countermarch," and going back a short distance the order came "On right by file into line, guide right, double quick march," and down we went through a field and up a slight elevation and there was a sight to behold.

Longstreet corps was advancing in line of battle or in lines, for there was three or four, and to our eyes the field was full of men. Firing immediately commenced, not only with us but all along the line by both sides; men commenced to fall; if badly wounded they remained where they fell; if only slight they went to the rear. In the formation of the line, room enough was not taken and a regiment lapped over us, and we were somewhat mixed together; the order was given for our regiment to move more to the left, and those that heard the order obeyed. I with others did not hear the order and was soon left with those I did not know. On, still on, came the heavy lines of Longstreet command; no single line could stop them long, and gradualy our line was being forced back, although we gave them a brave resistance and contested every inch on ground; still, after their first check when they made their second advance, our fast weaking line could not hold them back. Our lines did not break, but as the enemy advanced fought their way back step by step.

When I found that I was mixed with another regiment I

The advance of Longstreet Corps

started to find my own. I had gone but a few steps when I
met Cap't Palmer of Co. I wounded; he asked me if I
would give him my help and assist him off the field. I
locked in arms with him and we started for the rear; just
then a solid shot came over and struck the ground but a
few feet from us and the dirt was thrown upon us, the shot
ricocheting far away in the direction we were going. Cap't
Palmer said "I can't stand this," and bounded away like a
deer, leaving me far in the rear. I had gone but a few rods
from where the line was formed when we commenced firing, but could not find the company. I searched around and
went back a few rods and found Elis Bruce, and we started
and went a little farther to the left; we there found Tom
Gassett and he said the regiment had moved still farther to
the left then we had yet been, but that now the line had
fallen back so far he did not know where it was. We were
full of fight and wanted to have another turn with them and

as there was another regiment just advancing into the fight, we asked the Cap't of the company on the right "if he wanted any recruits"; he said "Yes, fall in," and we took our place on the right of the line and again advanced into the fight. While we were fighting, Bruce disappeared and Tom and myself thought it best to be looking for the brigade as it was getting late. We looked around to see how the thing was going, and I must say that there was a most discouraging look; where we had fought at the first was now in the hands of the enemy; batteries that at noon were under the union flag, now had the stars and bars[2] to wave over them.

Everything to our hasty glance seemed in confusion. Batteries were going at a breakneck speed and taking positions farther in the rear, and the infantry was moving in all direction. Wounded men were everywhere; some were being helped away, others were striving with all their strength to get away to a safe distance. A wounded man begged piteously for us to take him to the rear; he was wounded in the neck, or head, and the blood flowed freely; everytime he tried to speak the blood would fill his mouth and he would blow it out in all directions; he was all blood, and at the time I thought he was the most dreadfull sight I ever saw. We could not help him, for it was of no use, for he could not live long by the way he was bleeding, so we turned away, and went over a hill where there was a stone house. To the right as we went along was a brigade of Burnsides men. On the farther side we found Cap't Bates of the 12th with his company; they were the Provost Guard of the division. We enquired of him if he knew where we could find the brigade, but he could not; he told us to fall in, in the rear of his company, which we did. Pretty soon the shot

2. The Confederate States Flag.

and shell began to come over and fell thick and fast. Cap't Bates moved his company so as to get out of range, we going with them, but instead of getting out we seemed to be getting more and more into it, the shot and shell seemingly to come in every direction, bursting overhead, striking the ground, and whizzing past as though they would like to take a fellows head along with it. Cap't Bates ordered his men to "double-quick," and away they went over the fields and out of sight of us who were too tired to run. We again took a hasty look, being left again on our own resources, and by the general appearances of things concluded to retreat, so we started over the fields in a somewhat different direction from that of Cap't Bates, bearing more to the left.

We went along not entirely alone, for there was a goodly number of soldiers to keep us company, not going in the same direction however, but all having the same object in view, viz, to get out of the range of the shells. I have no idea how far we went, but should think it was more than a mile and perhaps two, when we came to a road, and such a sight as we saw there I shall never forget, for there, regardless of any order, or organization, but going pell mell, as fast as they could possibly go, were all branches of the service in inextricable confusion, intent only upon one object, and that was to get to the rear. Tom and I had been quite calm till now; we had been close up to the front, and did not know what was going on at the rear; but the sight we saw fully confirmed what we had feared, that the rebels had gained the day, and that the union army was retreating. There were heavy army wagons, Artilery trains, and all the mighty paraphernalia of war, with mounted men, and footmen hurrying back. I should think the train had been parked and when the panic came they had driven, or tried to drive into the road regardless of the ground, consequently many of the wagons in going down the bank, which was from two to four feet, had tipped over; the traces were cut and the drivers went on with the mules alone; boxes of hard bread and barrels of pork lined the way and were trodden under foot.

Tom and I, catching the spirit of the occasion, hurried on but, keeping on the bank, we had not gone far before we came to a creek spanned by a stone bridge. We saw soldiers fording it, and came to the conclusion that it was too deep for us, so watching our opportunity, and when a chance offered, we ran over with a battery. It was now dark, and on going a short distance we came to a piece of woods in which were a lot of soldiers cooking their suppers; being tired and hungry we concluded to stop and get ours, [since] the fires were already kindled, and water was soon procured from the creek, and our coffee was soon made. All kinds of stories were being told by the soldiers; some had performed "Herculean deeds of valor" that day, and I remember one in particular, who had his supper eaten when we arrived, and who seemed to take a particular fancy to us, told us of some wonderful achievements that he had performed, and Tom and I wondered how the rebel army had escaped annialation at his hands. The facts of the case were that he had not been in the fight at all. Having ate our supper, we thought we would have a nap and had just stretched ourselves on the ground when an officer came in and told us the army had fallen back and we were liable to receive a shot at any moment. Our hero disappeared in an instant, and we, not having a relish for any more shells at present, shouldered our muskets and with a goodly number of others started on for we did not know where.

The night was very dark and we could not see where to go, but kept stumbling along. How far we went I don't know, but coming to a house where there were other soldiers resting, we thought we would too. I had just fallen asleep when an officer came and woke us all up and told us to move on, saying he was one of the rear-guard, so on again we moved, but at a very slow gait, for the road was all cut up by the heavy teams, and so dark it made it terrible going over the rough roads. After going a short distance we concluded to come to a halt and wait for daylight, let the consequences be what they would; so, going a few rods away from the road behind some brush, we again lay down and slept soundly till morning.

It was broad daylight when we awoke, and being we did not know whether in the enemies lines or not, we concluded to push on without delay. Going back to the road, we started on, feeling somewhat rested. We saw a few soldiers by the way, but none knew any more than we did about the battle, or where the army was. After going about a half mile, I should think, we saw ahead of us quite a squad of soldiers just getting up and falling in. We hurried on and coming near found them to be all 13th men with the colors and under the command of the Major; there were men from all the companies there. Their first questions were "Where have you been?" and "Where is the rest of the boys?" The first question we could answer with some qualifications, but the second we knew nothing about.

The Major, unwilling to waste time, told us to "fall in" and we marched on towards Centreville. When within a half mile, the Major halted us in an old barn where we could keep dry, for it had commenced to rain, while he went forward to find the brigade; he came back directly, having found it up on the "Heights." We were soon there, for we were anxious to know who were killed or wounded. K had only two men killed, and their bodies were left on the field—Thomas Copeland and Hollis Fairbanks. I have forgotten how many were wounded, but quite a good number.

Thus ended the baggin of Popes army. Was it [a] success?

Or was it a failure? These are questions that the impartial readers of histories must decide for themselves. I can only give my opinion amongst the many others. It was failure, miserable failure. And in the time to come, the unbiased historian will give to Pope and the little army he commanded a proud place in the galaxy of gallant deeds performed. For three weeks Popes little army held the victorious legions of Lee at bay.[3] And there is no other account where there was so much fighting done by so small a force in all the war.

2d Bull Run was a most disastrous defeat for the union army, and for the country as well. But why so disastrous to the army? when in reality it was not near so bad as McClellan defeat before Richmond? It was this. McClellan had a great name; almost the entire army worshipped him and whatever he done in the eyes of a great majority of the privates, and officers as well, was right, simply because McClellan said so. He would suffer defeat, and then issue a pompous order claiming a victory, and, poor fools, the privates would throw up their caps and hurrah and beleive every word of it. Such was McClellan hold on the army.

I have been called by all manner of names, and been threatened to be licked, because I dared to say that McClellan had been licked in his seven day's fight before Richmond.

McClellan had a plan, or he pretended to have, and on that plan he was going to fight, and he would fight on that plan and no other. (What that plan was, no one ever found out).

When John Pope, who was a young officer of growing renoun from the west, was appointed to a command in Va.,

<hr>

3. Various sources indicate that at the Battle of Second Manassas the quantities of troops were as follows: General Pope—64,000 to 73,000; General Jackson—55,000.

McClellan said "It interferes with my plan". So Pope must be got rid of someway, and as the President was inclined to retain him, the quickest way was to suffer Pope to get whipped, even if it does take a few thousand men, McClellan knowing that, whatever he said, the army would sustain him.

So Lee was let to turn his victorious legions, after the little army of Pope had helped extricate him, upon them. Pope, knowing his danger, appealed to the President for help; McClellan was urged, yea, commanded by the President to go forward, use any means, take every means, but to go forward and save the little army, and gain a victory if possible. When ordered to Washington, not daring to disobey, [McClellan] commenced with a snail like pace to execute, throwing the blame if any should arrise on the good President, who said "he would cheerfuly assume all." Precious time was lost.

Lee's guns were thundering in Popes front. Large bodies were discovered on his flanks. Weeks had passed, and yet no help. And at last when the tardy troops did arrive, in some instances they refused to obey Popes orders. Consequently defeat. McClellan plan to get rid of Pope had succeeded. A few thousand men, more or less, had been killed, but the aim had been accomplished. A scape goat must be provided, one on whom to throw the blame of defeat, and as Pope was the least known, he was chosen, and being relieved of his command, was sent away to the Northwest, bearing the ignominy that justly belonged to another.

Now this is the point, this is why the defeat was so disastrous. This monstrous, devilish scheme was so barefaced, that all who were not McClellan blinded could see through [it], and the consequence was that the men began to have no confidence in their officers. The men had no relish to be taken in and slaughtered by detail because one officer did not like the other. Men in our command Hurrahed for the Southern Confederacy, and said "If this is the way we are to be used, lets go home and give the South what they want." A bad state of affairs for an army to be in. The country at large was strongly tinctured with McClellanism, and so when the defeat of the army at Bull Run was announced, and that Pope commanded, the country sympathied with McClellan, and no apologies could be offered in Popes favor. Even the good President influence could not save him (for I haven't a doubt but what he understood all) and Pope had to go, disgraced. McClellan [was] magnified, appointed to the chief command, the same officers that suffered the defeat [were] retained in command, but the army, and the country as well, demanded it, and there was no other alternative for the President to do. Again the army with its snail pace could crawl its way through Maryland at the bidding of the "young Napoleon."

But tardy justice, long delayed, came at last to some of them. They merited more, and in any other country but ours they would have received punishment according to their deserts. But our country chose to be lenient with its officers high in command, and to let the poor private suffer on for a season longer. The life of a private soldier was not of much account with some of the officers.

"Save the life of a mule for they cost money, but let the soldier be killed for he costs nothing." "Two mules and another soldier killed," said another.

11

New Commanders, New Men, New Hopes

Departure from Centreville—Drawing rations—"Fighting Joe Hooker"—Chantilly—Still retreating—On the outlying defenses of Washington—Again on the march—Getting breakfast—Visitors from Westboro— Promoted—"Maryland, My Maryland"— Frederick—Cotoctin Ridge and Middleton valley—South Mountain—"Major Gen'l Hooker Sir"—Rations—"16th Maine Sir"

When we reached Centreville we found the brigade all ready to march and, greeting the boys, we were soon marching towards Washington. After marching about two miles, we halted for the remainder of the day, and night; the orders were to make ourselves as comfortable as we could, it had ceased to rain but the weather was cloudy. We had lost our blankets and knapsacks, and all that pertained to them, and I doubt if there was a blanket or piece of tent in the regiment, consequently our preperation for the night were soon made. As usual we drew rations, and amongst other things we drew some molasses; we had nothing to put it in but our cup, or canteens, and if we put it in our cup we had nothing to make coffee in, and if in our canteens we could bring no water. I drew mine on my plate; we laboured under some disadvantage, but for all that, it was good. How we licked it down on our hard bread[!] Some of the boys were always satisfied with what they received and went and ate it; others were so happy that they danced for joy, while others were never satisfied, never received what they ought, what in their own eyes belonged to them; if they had received the whole then they would not have been any more satisfied.

Our stay here was short for we were making history fast in these days. So moving on we tramped towards the defenses of Washington. We hadn't gone far when we heard firing on our left, and we were turned down a road and marched towards it. Seated there on a white horse and quietly looking us over as we passed along, was an officer that would have attracted our attention anywhere, but more so now, for rumor had it that we had a new Corps Commander, and this officer was the man and his name was "Joe Hooker,"[1] more familiarly known as "Fighting Joe Hooker." McDowell had been relieved and he was appointed to fill his place. Look out now, boys, for more fighting, for Hooker is always ready when there is rebs around. Going on a short distance, we turned off to the left and formed a line of battle and awaited events. There was sharp fighting directly in our front by the way the musketry rattled, but our line there was strong and we were only needed for supports. What the results might have been, had there not come up suddenly one of those terrific storms where the elements seem to be at war with themselves, where the wind blows, and the rain is turned to hail, and the cold cuts even to the bones! For about an half hour the

1. Maj. Gen. Joseph (Fighting Joe) Hooker, USA, commanding the I Corps, Army of the Potomac.

elements did war, and rage fearfully, completely putting to shame mans feeble attempt at warfare. The Almighty did by His vivid and constant flashing of lightning and terriable peal on peal of thunder, show His displeasure at the utter waste of life going on here below.

It stopped the fight, save only an occasional shot during the night. We were wet through to the skin, and as no fire was allowed, we huddled together and tried to keep ourselves warm; at length a hay-stack was discovered and it was soon confiscated to make bedding for soldiers. The morning dawned bright but cold, and we were allowed to build fires and cook our food and dry ourselves, which we were not long in doing.

The army was falling back, for we had heard the rumbling of teams and artilery all the morning; about noon the order came for us to join in the moving mass. We marched along through Fairfax C.H., and late at night, hungry, tired, and very cross, we drew our weary selves up on to what some of the boys called Halls Hill, one of the slight elevations out-lying the fortifications of Washington. The next week was one of the most disagreeable weeks of all my army life. Sorely smarting under our recent defeat, tired, hungry and cold, and lying on the site of one of McClellan old camps but, added to our discomfort, without tents, or blankets, [and] some of the boys without coats, made it indeed a week long to be remembered, and one that tried our patience to the utmost.

Looking over the fields towards Washington, we could see the great dome of the capitol rising above everything. Somewhere about the 10th of September just at night orders were received to march. I was out on picket at the time about a mile away, and as we had nothing to pack up were soon ready. We marched immediately towards the great dome, but as night soon came on it was hid from our sight. We crossed the Potomac on the long bridge and through a portion of the city, going out and up from the river. It was a long and weary march; they gave us no rest. I was not feeling well, being obliged to stop several times. At last, when well into the small hours of the morning, I fell out for good and lay down besides a wall and slept till daylight. I started on feeling much better after my rest, and soon found my brother John, Tom, and Henry Gassett and the Duke Wellington, who had also fallen out and been a-sleep. We started on in company and went perhaps a mile when we thought it time for breakfast, and coming to a farm house where there was all the conveniancies for the same, we halted. A good well of water, a woodpile, and a large field of potatoes were not to be passed by, even if we were in Maryland; while one brought the water, another built a fire, and I over the wall dug some potatoes, which were soon boiling in our cups. We fried our pork, and had a good square meal of fried pork and potatoes with a pot of coffee to wash the whole down. Other soldiers coming up and seeing our fare, fell to, and when we came away there was at least fifty there cooking and eating their breakfast.

Again on the march we soon came up with Cap't Hovey with a small portion of his company, and soon after with the remnant of the brigade. We lay here two days and nights. We drew knapsacks in place of those lost at Bull Run, also blankets and tents. I remember the blankets we drew were so short that when we covered our feet our heads were bare, and if we covered heads our feet were exposed, and let me here say that a soldier wants his head covered as well as his feet.

Here we received another installment of recruits, those companies receiveing them that had none at Cedar Mountain.

Also Mr. Marshall and B. B. Nourse visited us, looking

after the interests of the Westboro boys. On the morning of
the 12th of Sep't. after we had fallen in and were ready to
move, Cap't Hovey ordered Privates Willard Wheeler, A.
C. Stearns, and Charles Drayton to step one pace to the
front and then and there made us Corporals, "to be obeyed
and respected accordingly," again ordering us to our places.
We filed off to the right and took our place in the line, and
commenced our march up through the pleasant land of
"Maryland, My Maryland."

Lee with his victorious troops, after driving the Yanks
into the defences of Washington, turned up the river, and
crossed the Potomac at the upper fords into Maryland, and
was now in the valley, with Stonewall at Frederick.

McClellan, at the head of the union armies, was now
going up to head him off and drive him back.

It was pleasant marching up through the country. Although we were not allowed to forage here as we had done
in Va., nevertheless, we could manage to on a small scale.
As I always contrived to have a little money, I always could
find plenty to eat. I remember one night at Ridgeville,
where we bivouacked, of getting some apples and having
some fried pork and apples, always a favorite dish with me;
some of the other boys brought in some hot biscuits, of
which I bought a share.

The night of the 13th found us just out on the east side
of Frederick Md., where we slept as sound as though there
was not a rebel on this side of the Potomac.

Stonewall held Frederick on the night of our arrival, but
when the morning of the 14th dawned he was on his way to
join Lee in Pleasant Valley. We entered the city early and
marched through in close pursuit of him; five or six miles
away to the west is the Cotoctin Ridge, with the pike road
in full sight, and how beautiful it looked on this pleasant
sabbath morning, the 14th day of September 1862, to see

the army winding up the ridge, the Sun shining brightly, flags waving, and bayonets glistning. If that was a glorious sight, how much more so was the sight when we had reached the summit of the ridge and could look down and across the valley, to see the fields and farm-houses in all their quiet stillness extending up and down in this "garden of Maryland." Looking straight across the troops could be seen, winding their slow length along, the advance of the union army contending with the rear of the rebels, the rugged slopes of South Mountain in the not very far distance.

Down the west side of the ridge and across the valley we pushed. All thoughts of our recent defeats was for the moment forgotten, for in our front were the enemies of our country, and the old thoughts and feelings, and love of country, flag, and home came back, and how eager we all were to again measure our strength with the enemy, and wipe the stain of defeat away. Most of us privates knew that if there was concert of action amongst the leaders, that we could whip the enemy upon any field. So we marched on down the ridge, across the valley and through the village of Middleton on that sabbath day.

We were halted by the side of the road with our guns stacked, waiting for the division of Gen'l Reno[2] to pass, when an officer approached surrounded by a brilliant staff. The Col ordered us to fall in and "give three cheers for George B. McClellan, Commander in Chief of the Potomac Army." Of course we cheered, for a good soldier always obeys.

McClellan in acknowledgement of the compliment raised his cap and rode on. Soon we followed, and on coming to the foot of the mountain we turned to the right and went a half mile or so, when we halted and orders were given to

2. General Jesse L. Reno, USA.

"pile knapsacks," and leaving them under a guard we formed a line of battle and commenced the ascent. The battle[3] in the meantime was going on, Cox's division being engaged at the pike road and at the left of it, while Reno's division was engaged at the right of Cox's. We formed on the right of Reno's, when about two thirds of the way up the left of our brigade became engaged; we being on the extreme right were not actively engaged, although the left of the reg't was where there was some firing, and the bullets sang merrily over our heads. Darkness coming on, the troops halted then and there with orders to sleep on our arms, without any blankets, and not allowed a fire, not even to strike a match to light a pipe. We shivered through the night.

How my teeth chattered with the cold. We huddled together and tried to keep warm. The officers were as cold as we were; a group of them was standing but a few feet from where we lay when a stragler coming up in the dark addressed them: "Can you tell me where the 11th P.V.'s are?" "Do you belong to that regiment?" said Col Coulter. "Yes sir," meekly replied the soldier, and recognizeing his Col. and not daring to say anything but the truth. "How did you lose your regiment then?" said the Col. "I fell out," he replied. "Well, do you see that black line," said the Col., pointing towards a black line that could be seen through the darkness. "Well, that is the 11th P.V.'s, and do you double quick to it in no time, or I'll put you in a place where you cant stragle." The soldier, knowing the metal of his commander, left his presence in quick time for his regiment, well satisfied to escape so easy.

Morning at length dawned and our lines were reformed and preperations were made for an advance. Hooker was

3. The Battle of South Mountain (Boonsborough), September 14, 1862.

there directing the movements. Gen'l Meagher,[4] of Richardson division, with his brigade was forming on the right of us, and not taking room enough overlapped almost our entire regiment. "Move those troops farther to the right," said Hooker. "By whose orders?" said Meagher, turning towards him. "Major Gen'l Hookers, sir"; no more was said, Meagher moving the troops. Companies D. and K. were deployed as skirmishers and sent forward into the woods, taking our places on the line of skirmishers; the order "forward" was given and we advanced to find no enemy in our front, for they were discovered to be in full retreat. Immediately we were filed off to the left through the woods, and coming out on the west side of the ridge near the "Mountain House," we halted for breakfast. Our rations were running low, for we had marched so fast that the commissary had not been able to keep up; two hard bread to a man was issued, a scant meal to march and fight on.

Dan Warren, in looking over the premises, found two eggs and a half dozen potatoes, I found a few onions, and we put them together and had quite a meal out of the whole. After halting a few hours we decended the ridge, pushing on after the retreating rebs, their rear and our advance fighting all the way. We went down through Boonsboro, a place we had visited in our earlier life as a soldier, and on towards Sharpsburg.

The sixteenth Maine, a new regiment, had been assigned to our brigade when we were near Washington, and being unused to marching had stragled fearfully on the way up and had finally been left behind. While halting beyond Boonsboro, one of the boys of the 9th stragled off over the fields to find something to eat. Orders were very strict

4. Brig. Gen. Thomas F. Meagher, USA.

against straglin, and all commanding officers were held responsible for their men. Capt Miller of Hartsuffs staff, seeing him, rode out and asked him "to what regiment he belonged too?" "16th Maine, sir," he innocently replyed, forgetting that he had a figure 9 a foot long in red paint on his Knapsack.

"You lie, sir," said Capt Miller. "You belong to the 9th New York and you return to your regiment immediately." He came back without a second invitation, glad to escape so easily.

How many such tricks were played and things eaterable taken and then laid to the 16th Maine, report does not say, but I think more than once.

12

Hayfields and Cornfield

Resting—Getting into position—Night before the battle—In the morning—The advance—In The Cornfield—Hit the battle—Henry Gassett wounded—Getting him to the rear—At the hospital—Who I found there—Incidents—Rejoins the reg't

Again moving on, we halted at Rohrersville, where we bivouacked for the night in open field by the side of the road, and here we remained the greater portion of the 16th. Having drawn another scant ration of hard bread and pork, and finding some more potatoes, we again had a good square meal. Troops were moving in all directions, and there seemed to be no end to their coming, and rumor said that on the ridge but a short distance away, even now in sight, stood the "Veterans" of Lee's army waiting for us to attack.

Towards night Hooker appeared mounted on his white horse. We were ordered to "fall in" and commenced to move through the fields up towards the right. Antietam creek was crossed and still farther to the right we went.

Hooker, easily discerned by his horse as usual, was everywhere directing the movements.

At length we were within range of the enemy's guns, and when we showed a good mark they quickly let us know it. Nearer and nearer we crawled like a great snake, winding in and out between the little hills and through woods to keep out of sight, wishing to get as near as possible without losing many men. Darkness settled down before we were in position. How well I now remember of going through a piece of corn whose stalks towered far above our heads, and how the enemy, hearing and wishing to let us know with what a reception they were prepared to receive us, would fire a gun, and a shell or solid shot would come schreeching over to warn us of their presence. I remember of how one struck the ground but a few feet away and threw the earth up on to the Major. "Get up, get up," said he, speaking to his horse, "that was ment for us, get up, get up." At last we were in position, and were ordered to remain every man in his place. I was tired, and sitting down soon lay down, falling asleep immediately; the last thing I remember was some horses of a neighboring battery stamping and their shoes striking fire on the rocks. The skirmishers[1] were busy all night, so twas said, but I did not hear them, and as there was no alarm given I slept soundly till morning with the many that slept for the last time their earthly slumber.

A foggy morning was the 17th of September 1862, and each army was astir early and was preparing for the deadly struggle[2] that the lowest private knew was to take place, without building any fire to cook our coffee or anything else, but simply eating our dry hard bread. We were pre-

1. Troops who were spread in a relatively thin line forward of the battle lines and acted as an "early warning system."
2. The Battle of Antietam (Sharpsburg), September 17, 1862.

pared for what was to come. Hartsuff in the early morning was out in front of his brigade reconnoitring, when he was wounded by a sharpshooter. Styles of the 9th was absent, and so was Leonard[3] of the 13th, and the command devolved upon Coulter[4] of the 11th.

The sun coming up soon drove the fog away and we were quickly in line and advanced out of the friendly shelter of the woods into an open field; the stubble had but just been turned in. Directly in our front and but a short half mile away was the rebel line of battle awaiting to receive us. The ridge behind their line was crowned by their batteries and I remember one planted near a stone church[5] that opened fire on us as soon as we showed ourselves. The first shots went over our heads, the second came nearer, but on we went, and were soon up to the fence that seperated the fields. I remember of looking back when a shell came screeching past and seeing it strike in the midst of the brigade following us; we were quickly over the fence and advancing through a mow field. The skirmishers of both armies were here having a regular give and take fight, the rebs falling back as we advanced.

The next field was a large cornfield[6] and we were soon going through the corn. Our batteries, as well as the rebs, kept up a continuous shelling, making music for our advance. While going through the corn I was struck by a piece of shell on my right side that tore my blouse and shirt, and scratched my side a little, just drawing blood; it completely knocked the wind out of me, and I doubled up like a jack-knife and sank down on a corn-hill.

Sergeant Fay seeing me drop asked "if I was hit?" and Cap't Hovey coming repeating the question, as soon as I

3. Col. Samuel H. Leonard, USA.
4. Col. Richard Coulter, USA, assumed command of the 3rd Brigade.
5. The Dunker Church.
6. Now known as "The Cornfield" at the Antietam Battlefield.

In the cornfield

could regain my wind I told them "I was not hurt much only lost my wind." The Cap't told me "to sit there till I would be able to follow on," and went on with the line. I had not sat there half a moment when just behind me, where the ledge cropped out of the ground, a shell struck not a rod away and went into a thousand pieces, causing me to evacuate that place rather suddenly.

I went on and soon joined the company and we left the cornfield for another grass field and at the farther side were the rebels in line of battle; the skirmishers had all disappeared. Still on we went and we boys thought we were to go for them with the bayonet, and we fixed the same. Neither side with the exception of the skirmishers and batteries had fired, but now it was time for the infantry to take their turn, and we were getting uncomfortably near. The rebs fired first but we being so near, many of the balls went over our heads, but still many took effect. We halted and commenced firing immediately. Men now commenced to drop on all sides; I remember now, as I stood loading my gun, of looking up the line and seeing a man of Co. D. who I was quite intimate with throw up his hands and fall to the ground; one little struggle more and then all was still.

Being intensly engaged in loading and firing, I had not noticed in particular all that was going on around me; I knew that many were hit and had left the ranks, but how many I did not know, when Cap't Hovey gave the order to "close up to the right." Looking to the right, and left as well, I saw that there was quite a space between me and my right hand man; at my left stood Henry Gassett, and repeating to him the Cap't order, [I] stepped to execute the same. Just then Henry said "Jim, I'm hit," and throwing his gun down, ran to the rear perhaps a rod and fell. I went to him as quick as I could and, kneeling down, enquired where he was wounded. Before he had time to answer me Cap't Hovey came up and said I had better try and get him to the rear, for he thought the whole line would go back soon. I asked Henry if he could walk and he said he would try. So I helped him up and, putting my right arm around his waist and having him put his left arm around my neck, we started for a piece of woods that was but a few rods away at our right. Before we reached the woods Henry was hit again in the left leg, a flesh wound; the other was a shot clean through the right shoulder. On reaching the woods and going in a short distance, we stopped behind a large Maryland Oak to rest. I gave him water to drink and tried to cheer him up; his wound pained him some and he was faint from the loss of blood. I asked him if we had not better make another attempt to get farther to the rear but he said he could go no further, all he wanted was to rest. All this time the battle was rageing fearfully; the solid shots and shells came tearing through the woods and, some of them striking, those large oaks would drop down cords of wood at a time.

Wounded men were continualy going to the rear, and some that were not. I asked several if they would give me a lift and help Henry to the hospital, but they all declined, saying they had as much as they could do to get back themselves. None were of the 13th though. They told me if I wanted to save my life I had better be getting away from there as the rebels were advancing, and I could see them almost up to the edge of the woods. I again urged Henry to make one more effort for life, but he, holding up his hand for me to shake, bade me good by and told me to save myself. I told him I would not go unless he went with me. He then said he would try, and putting his well arm around my neck and I grasping him around the waist, we again started. Fear gave us wings, and strength as well, for we placed a good distance between the rebs and ourselves before I would consent to stop, although Henry wanted to several times. As we advanced into the woods, the ground declined to the east, and as our rear was to the north we must cross up and over a slight elevation, where the bullets were flying too thick for comfort. After taking a good rest and cheering Henry up as best I could, we again started and went over the hill in safety. We rested several times before we reached the hospital. The hospital was only a field one at a farmhouse, where the Surgeons were to bind up the wounds before sending them farther away.

I laid Henry in the front yard with a great many others and went to find a Surgeon or some of the boys, for I knew there must be several somewhere. I went up to the house and round to the back door but it was full of terriably wounded men, and finding none of our regiment there, I went back and out toward the barn and beyond to an immence straw stack; there I found about a dozen of K men, besides others from [the] regiment.

Some had desperate wounds, and others were ministering to their wants as best they could. Going back to Henry, I soon had him on a nice bed of straw near the other boys.

I made coffee and gave him some, although he had not

much of an appetite for anything. I kept his wound wet with water all the time, as that was all that could be done now, the Surgeon said, when there was no danger of bleeding to death.

At the stack were Sergeants Greenwood shot through the shoulder, Fay through arm, Cordwell hit on head with piece of shell, Corp'l Davenport through the foot, and Private Trask with a mortal wound in side and back by a piece of shell. I learned that Tom Gassett and Hollis Holden were killed, Duke Wellington mortaly wounded and left on field, Cap't Hovey wounded and gone on with many others.

Surely we had had a good shaking up. The battle all this time was rageing with terrific power only a short distance away and many shells passed over and beyond.

I stayed with Henry two days and nights, taking the best care I could, and then I left for the regiment.

Incidents: When I was helping Henry off the fields we saw Gen'l Mansfield[7] with Banks[8] old division going into the fight; when we reached the Hospital they were bringing him back dead.

After I left, the line fell back and the rebs advanced till our line was reinforced, when they in turn drove the rebs back, and so it went till the ground was fought over two or three times. The field beyond the cornfield was filled with dead men, both Yank and reb. Dan Warren counted thirty three dead rebs in the length of four fence rails. We were two hours and ten minutes fighting by the Chaplain watch before we fell back.

The results of this severe fighting was a victory baren of results, if I am allowed that expression, for the day after the battle, instead of following up what had been gained, a "Flag of truce" was granted on the plea to bury dead men,

7. Maj. Gen. Joseph K. F. Mansfield, USA.
8. Maj. Gen. Nathaniel P. Banks, USA.

while under its peaceful folds the living were quietly with-
drawn to the other side of the Potomac.

Again the incompetency of McClellan was shown, for
here was a field, a fair stand up fight, and we were the attacking party, and on every side we gained.

Report says, and I think history confirms it, that at one
time during the fight, when the gallant Burnside was sorely
pressed and he was asking, yes, imploring for help, that
McClellan had it in his heart to send him some, and turn[ed]
to Fitz John Porter who commanded his reserves, fifteen
thousand troops. But Fitz John shook his head and the gallant Burnside was left to do the best he could. If the army
engaged were able to keep the enemy at bay, hold them
where they were, fifteen thousand fresh troops thrown in at
any point would have gained a victory the results of which
would have saved thousands of lives and millions of treasures. Another opportunity thrown away. Another move
made in the great crushing down of some, and magnifying
of others, in the great drama of War.

There were four of us to leave the field hospital together,
and as we were hungry and out of rations, the first thing to
be considered was to get something to eat. A little ways off
to the right was a piece of potatoes and still farther a farm
house that looked as if it had escaped the ravages of war.
So, offering to pay for anything that could be procured
there that was eaterble, Dan Warren started and soon returned with a loaf of bread big enough to have been baked
in a milk pan. We in the meantime had dug and were boiling potatoes, and with our never failing pot of coffee soon
made a good square meal.

We passed on over the ground where we had fought, by
the Dunkers Church, and over the rise of ground so lately
held by the rebels. All bore marks of the terriable struggle;
the wounded with few exceptions had all been removed,

the dead were being burried. Hundreds of citizens from all around were coming to view the field and procure some relic, for Antietam was to live in history as a great battle, whatever the results might be.

13

Hard March South

*"Corp" Jones—High living—"Ho Aleck"—
Review—Stuart raid—Again on the move—
"Albion, I'm all mud—In Virginia—A change
of commanders—Again on the Rappa-
hannock—Soup—"Give us a light"—Slatery and
O'Laughlin's pig—In front of Fredericksburg*

W_e found the regiment over the ridge lately held by
the rebels, in a grove; we reported ourselves at headquarters, and went to the company, which we found in
command of "Corp" Jones, for all the other officers were
away wounded. Jones used to sign his name to all the returns "Corp Jones"; Coulter of the 11th P.V., seeing it, said
"Who in h--l is this Corp Jones that I hear so much about."
Jones did not remain long in command, for another commissioned officer was soon appointed.

We soon moved about a mile over the fields into a piece
of woods, where we pitched a regular camp after our knapsacks came up. Here our life was quite easy, for we had but
little to do, only to picket the river and prepare our food;
there was a very large cornfield within a half mile of our

camp whose golden ears were just ripening; [they] being too hard to roast, we contrived to get old tin cans and sardine boxes, and punching them full of holes with our bayonets to make quite respectful graters, thus we grated the corn and made corn cakes and hasty puddings, and if we were willing to travel far enough to some of the farm houses and had any money, we could get milk and other luxuries, which added to our variety of dishes.

The results of the battle were freely discussed. We had come nearer a victory then ever before and the spirits of the boys were in a like degree raised, and although we did not relish fighting, still we could not see why were were suffered to remain idle all through the remaining month of Sept. and Oct., the best months of the year for military movements. We could not understand why Lee was suffered to reorganize, and fill up his army by conscription, and thus prepare himself for another struggle. But thus it was; there were many things happening these days that to us privates seemed unaccountable.

The brigade was in command of Col Styles of the 9th N.Y. He was not at all popular with the men, and the boys used to plague him whenever they dared. He had a colored servant named "Aleck," and when Styles wanted him he would cry out "Ho Aleck."

One day, when Styles was feeling cross and had put several of his men on fatigue duty for punishment, and had raised a feeling of mischief amongst the men, he cried out from brigade headquarters at the top of his voice, "Ho Aleck." Instantly from the tents of his regiment came an answering cry of "Ho Aleck." Styles was mad and started toward . . . where the sound came from, saying he would put any and all under arrest who dared to mock him. Before he reached the place, "Ho Aleck" came from another quarter; the old man turned, rage depicted on every part of his face, and darted towards the new place, when "Ho Aleck" again rang in his ears from still another source. The rest of the brigade had now awoke up to the fun, and "Ho Aleck" came from another regiment, and went on till all the regiments had joined in the cry of "Ho Aleck." Styles, unable to find any of the guilty ones of his own regiment, turned towards the others and, calling to the officers to assist him, stormed up and down through the tents swearing vengence on any if he could but catch them, but "Ho Aleck" coming from a hundred throats at a hundred different places was too much for him, and after threating to put the whole brigade under arrest, he went to his tent amidst the smiles of the command.

While [we were] lying in this camp, President Lincoln came up to review the army; we were drawn up in a long line as far as we could see, with boots blacked, coats dusted, and equipments in the best of order. The President rode accompanied by McClellan and Gen'l McClernand[1] from the western army, and a staff. When I saw the good President I could easily perceive why and how he was called "Honest Abe." Honesty was clearly depected on every line of his honest face. He looked careworn and troubled, and I thought I could detect a look of pity as he scaned our line.

I think his coming down, or up, to see us done us all good, [and] that each soldier felt, after looking into his honest face, of doing his utmost to help lift the load that bore so heavy upon him. I know that I felt that way.

During this inactivity Stuart,[2] a noted Cavalry officer of the Confederacy, made a circuit of the Union army, capturing several towns in Pennsylvania and some few prisoners, and striking terror and dismay into the hearts of some of

1. General John A. McClernand, USA.
2. General James E. B. (JEB) Stuart, CSA.

the commanders of the union army. McClellan, with his ac-
coustomed ideas of rapid movements, ordered out the infantry in pursuit, and to guard all the fords of the river.

We marched all one night to intercept the daring rider,
although at the least calculation he was fifty miles away and
could ride five miles while we were marching one, and had
crossed the river and was safe on the sacred soil before we
started.

At length, after repeated urgeings by the President and
when there was no more excuses to offer, after the golden
days of Oct. had passed, after the rebel army was
thoroughly rested and its ranks filled, then the "Young
Napoleon" was ready to move the grand "Army of the
Potomac," was ready to inaugerate a campaign from the
Potomac if the President would assume all responsibilities.
The good man said he was ready, and would assume each
and all responsibilities if the army would only move. Consequently, at the close of a cold and wet sabbath day in the
gloomy month of Nov., with the winds sighing in the
treetops of our camp, orders came to pack up. We could
hardly beleive that after idling away so many sunny days
that we would be compeled to break camp and brave the
storm of a November night. We boys delayed to strike our
tents hoping there might be a mistake or the order coun-
termanded. But the order was imperitave and "fall in" was
soon given. Quickly striking and rolling up our wet tents
and straping on our knapsacks, we bid adieu to our camp
where we had passed two months comparitively doing
nothing.

We had hardly passed the borders of our camp when
darkness set in and, with the roads filled with men and
teams, our progress was nessarily slow. It was terriable
marching, the mud was deep, and cobble stones were
plenty, adding to a pitch dark night. Henry Vining, hitting
his foot against a stone, fell full length into the mud, and

on regaining his feet again with the assistance of others, he called out to his brother in a most pitiful tone "Albion, I'm all mud"; this served for a by-word during our entire time of service whenever we saw anyone laboring under circumstances that was not at all favorable for them. Vining, however, was hurt quite a good deal and fell out, was picked up and carried to a hospital where he stayed several months. We toiled up the side of Elk Ridge through the dark and rain and down the other side, continualy stopping and then starting till we had perhaps a mile beyond and four or five from our old camp, when the order was given to halt and make ourselves comfortable. We quickly had rousing fires and, sitting and standing around, we tried to dry ourselves, and, smoking, passed the few remaining hours away. The morning was ushered in with a clear sky and a cold wind from the northwest that whistled around and blew the smoke in all directions.

Late in the afternoon we crossed the valley and the South Mountain Ridge at Cramptons Gap, and decended to the east side where we bivouacked for the night, resuming the march the next day for Berlin, where the army was crossing the river on a Pontoon Bridge into Virginia. We in our turn crossed and went on shareing in all the trials and burdens incident to a soldiers life in an active campaign.

We received a new brigade commander before we started, Nelson Taylor,[3] and John Gibbon[4] the division. We were the 3d Brigade, 2d Division, 1st Corps, of the grand old "Army of the Potomac."

As a soldier is always hungry in an active campaign, so we as the weather grew colder had ravnous appetites, eating readily all the rations supplied by the government and still desireing more.

Forageing was resorted to. To a considerable extent Tur-

3. Brig. Gen. Nelson Taylor, USA.
4. Maj. Gen. John Gibbon, USA.

keys, Geese, and Chickens were taken whenever found; corn-cakes, bread, ham, and smoked sides with butter, apple butter, and in fact everything that was eatable was procured, sometimes by paying cash and at other times by promises to pay when change could not be made.

I remember of waiting two or three hours for my turn to get a corn-cake baked, and then after I received it could not make change. I took the cake and gave my promise to pay the next time I came around, but thus far have not been around since. I had a five dollar Greenback which they were afraid to take at that time. In after years we had no trouble on that score.

We marched on into Virginia, Lee keeping well in our front and only retreating when we pressed him hard; skirmishing was frequently. We moved with McClellan rapidity, slow but a little every day; at the rate we moved, the youngest amongst us would be grey before we could reach Richmond, providing there was no battles or other serious obsticals to block the way. When we were well down into Va. the President, heartly tired and sick of the sluggish movements of McClellan, relieved him of his command and appointed Burnside[5] in his place. Though relieved of the immediate presence of McClellan, still it was a long time before his influence ceased to be felt, and then not before other officers had shared his fate.

Burnside divided the army into three grand divisions commanded respectively by Hooker,[6] Sumner,[7] and Franklin,[8] and we continued on our way. The weather at times was extremely cold, and snow began to fall. I remember of one day when near Warrenton, after marching

5. Maj. Gen. Ambrose E. Burnside, USA, commanded the Army of Virginia, not to be confused with the Army of Northern Virginia, CSA.
6. Maj. Gen. Joseph Hooker, USA, commanded the Center Grand Division.
7. Maj. Gen. Edwin V. Sumner, USA, commanded the Right Grand Division.
8. Maj. Gen. William B. Franklin, USA, commanded the Left Grand Division.

in a hard storm, of scrapeing the snow away and lying down on the frozen ground for a nights rest.

Fredericksburg was the objective point, and towards it the army was draging its slow lengths along. Taylors brigade was sent down to Rappahannock Station, and after losing our way and running on the enemies pickets, we fell back and took a new start, arriving there in the small hours of the morning, the snow falling thickly and very cold. Not knowing how long we were to stay, and being very tired, we rolled ourselves in our blankets and tried to sleep.

The first thing I knew was the officers calling us to fall in and all was astir and bustle around, [and] the long roll was being beaten. Jumping up, I tried to get my traps together, but was ordered to leave all and fall in; the brigade was then in motion, or that portion that was awake. I started with the rest and, going about a mile, we came to that same ridge that we had occupied last August under Pope. Over the river near the first of those little hills were the tents of I should think a regiment of rebels; they had fled at our approach, leaving tents and rations behind. We halted on the ridge while some of the boys crossed and spoiled the camp. A quantity of fresh beef was amongst the spoils, which was served out to us. Jim Slatery and myself put our meat together and finding an old mess kettle and digging some parsnips we made a soup, thicking it with pounded hardbread, and filled ourselves full again.

Many is the times I have looked back to that bleak hill side, with the cold north winds blowing, to that pot of soup sitting between us, and with what relish we ate, or drinked it down, and with what satisfaction we felt when the thing was accomplished and we were full. We went back in the afternoon [to] where we left our traps and staid all night, marching in the morning towards Fredericksburg.

I remember what a disagreeable march this was. How it

Soup

did rain, soaking up the earth and making mud, Virginia mud, plenty. How we struggled along through it. How at the close of day, after we reached our place of bivouac, I with others had to go on picket. While toiling along through the mud and rain, we boys had succeeded in lighting our pipes and were thus trying to get solace through the fumes of tobacco smoke.

Col. Batchelder, seeing us enjoying ourselves and having a like desire, rode up and said "Sergeant, give us a light."

Matches were very scarce with us, few had any and those few held them as choice as gold. When we were going to light our pipes we would cry out "Who wants a light" and a dozen or more would crowd eagerly around with bits of wood or a piece of paper to get a fire. Others would come to them and beg a light and so it would go on till many were accommodated.

Officers as well as the privates were as short, and I think at times more so, and many were the favors they had to ask.

On arriving at Brooks Station, on the Aquia & Fredericksburg Railroad, we camped on a bleak hill side but a short distance away, and the few days that we staid here are amongst the most disagreeable of all my army life.

We lay on the northern slope of a hill, in an open field, where the wind had full sweep, it being now about the first of December. All the wood for fuel had to be brought at least a half mile on our backs and was green at that, consequently our supply at times was quite limited, especially when some of the boys were never known to bring a stick and always wanted the best seat at the fire.

Sitting around the green wood fire with the wind blowing hard whirled the smoke in all directions, and made us all have very tender eyes. We were cold and very hungry, could not get enough to eat, and it was a daily study with us how to supply the cravings of the inner man. The greater portion of the army was between us and Fredericksburg, which was about twelve miles away, consequencely supply trains were constantly passing the station. All kinds of tricks and devices were resorted to to procure something to eat. As only a few of the many trains stopped, some of the boys with a forged order for a box of hard bread would try to procure one, but generaly unsuccessfuly; another way was when, a train was passing along (as all trains went slow), to stand ready with long poles and try to push off some of the boxes. This many times was a success, till at last a guard was posted up and down the track, which stopped all raids on the trains.

This was a poor part of the country to forage in; the people as a general thing were poor, and then so many having passed on before us had taken with few exceptions all, and it required considerable tact and skill to get what remained.

On the first day of our arrival here, Jim Slatery and Mike O'Laughlin went out to a house that they saw through the woods, [and] on coming up to it, found an old woman who thought she was enough for any Yank. The old man was out attending to other parties. They asked her if she had anything to sell, [and] she answered with a look as though she wished them consigned to that place that is supposed to be uncomfortable warm, and in her oppinion soon to be the abode of unnumbered Yankees, that she had nothing for them or for herself to eat, that the Yanks had been there and stolen everything she had, and that the Yanks were the greatest theives she ever saw. They started to go away when they met a soldier who had been in the vicinity several days, and they asked him if there was anything to forage; he told them they need not go away from this place if that was what they wanted, for he had seen only a short time before, in a certain closet, half a pig, notwithstanding what the old lady had just said. Have that pig they must, after what had been said and to keep up the name. The soldier was eager to enter into any plan that would give pork for supper, so they agreed that one should go and call the old lady out and get her toward the barn, another was to steal into the house and throw the pig out of the window, whilst the third one was to then take [the] pig and run for the woods which was only a few rods distant, then all were to meet and divide. The plan worked to a charm, and I think the old lady, the next time she expressed her opinion, could justly say that the Yanks were smart for getting pork. I had a rib for my supper.

We lay about a week or ten days in this camp and were then moved into a thick pine woods about a mile distant; here we all thought we were going into winter quarters, and immediately began to build log huts, but before they were completed we moved away.

About this time we were getting very short of clothing; I had not had a shirt for several weeks and was wearing only a blouse. Others were as short as I was. And how oppertune it was for the Westboro boys to receive a box from home filled with warm shirts and stockings, besides goodies, contributed by loving ones at home. How we boys that did not belong in Westboro wish[ed] we did when we heard their name called and saw them donning their warm things.

The morning was a cold one when we left this place, and the ground was frozen hard; how it did ring as we marched over it with a quick step! We were well down towards the Rappahannock bivouacking at night wherever it found us. One night about three inches of snow fell.

While lying around the bivouac fire one night, asleep, rolled up in my blankets, a stick burned in two and fell over the end of my blanket; a hole was burned big enough to crawl through before I awoke, and the smoke of burnt woolen and rubber had well suffocated me, [and] both blankets were spoiled. William Shedd, the same night and laying but a few feet from me, had on a new pair of boots that he had but received from home, and, getting warm, stretched out his legs, ran both boots into the fire, and burned them so he could not wear them.

The 10th of December we lay on the bluffs of the river, while our batteries for miles up and down kept up a cannonade. Speculation was rife as usual with us as to what the results would be, and there was no lack of stories of the most proberable, and improberable character, and when night closed his mantle around us, we lay around our bivouac fire and slept as sound as though the morrow would not usher in a battle.

14

Many Lost, Nothing Gained

Crossing the river—On the colors—Getting into position—Blanchard of B—Gen'l Taylor—Advance of the line—Reb prisoners—Defeat—Who was responsible—What the boys said—Retreat—Winter quarters

*O**n** the morning of the 11th of Dec 1862, in a thick fog, we marched down to the banks of the Rappahannock river about three miles below Fredericksburg; we were the left of the army. While halting a few moments waiting for the troops to cross on a pontoon bridge, Cap't Hovey ordered me to report to the color sergeant as a corporal on the color guard; the boys of K crowded around, some to shake hands, and all to say "Good by," for they said "You are gone up now." At Antietam, all the color guard but one was either killed or wounded, and judging from that, they thought my turn had come.

The color guard is composed of two Sergeants who carry the colors, one the National and the other the State, and eight corporals whose duty it is to guard the colors, and under no circumstances to allow the colors to be lost.

In a battle it is a great honor to take the colors of the enemy, and it is also a great dishonor to lose the colors, consequently the colors draws the hottest fire and some of the most desperate fighting takes place at the colors, and although at times it is a post of great danger, it is at all times a post of honor.

Deploying the skirmishers

We crossed the river, and fileing to the left marched down its banks. After passing a large stone house, the regiment, with the exception of the color company, deployed as skirmishers; the rebel skirmishers were in full view in the large open plain. The fog lifting at this time, and the sun coming out in all his glory, made a grand and beautiful sight; not a single gun was fired on either side, the rebels falling back in slow and even step as our own boys advanced.

At the distance of a half mile from the river ran the Bowling Green Pike with a hedge on either side, and when we were ready to advance and occupy it, we thought they

would dispute our possession, but no they quietly fell back
to the field beyond. So passed the 11th. Troops were getting into position all day long, and far up the river we could
hear the great guns of both sides as they were maneuvering
for position. We could see the signal flags of the enemy,
and the guns on "Marye Heights." Night settled down, our
boys on the skirmish line held the pike, and we of the colors lay directly behind, while the line of battle lay in our
rear. I went up to the right of the regiment during the
night, drawn thither by a bright light caused by the burning of several hay stacks within the rebels lines. The night
passed without any other alarm; to sleep was out of the
question.

The 12th dawned bright and clear; we were cooking our
coffee early so as to be prepared for whatever might turn
up.

The skirmishers advanced beyond the pike, but no firing
in our front. Private Blanchard of Co. B took his gun and,
sticking it up in the ground by the bayonet, went boldly
over to the rebel line to have a little chat with them, and
trade some coffee for tobacco. Blanchard asked them "why
they did not fire on our boys when we advanced"; they said
"they did not like to be fired at any more than we did, and
as we did not fire they had no occasion to." He asked
"when they would," and they said "the next time you advance on us." Blanchard went back to his place, and soon
the order was given to "advance the skirmishers," and the
firing commenced. The rebels had now fallen back to the
woods, and, lying behind the trees, had a better chance to
pick us off who were in the open field without any shelter.
They soon made it hot for us; some of the boys ran back a
few steps to take advantage of the ground. Gen'l Taylor saw
it and rode boldly up to the line and said "Boys why do you
suffer those fellows to creep up on you in that way; your

guns are as good as theirs; use them." The bullets flew thickly around and we expected to see him fall, but he rode back unharmed.

Although he sent his overcoat afterwards over to Lee our tailor to be mended and there was six bullets holes in the cape.

At last all the preparations were complete and the line of battle was ordered to advance, and the skirmishers were ordered to fall back after several hours of fighting.[1] As we had used up about all our ammunition we were ordered to fall back to the big stone house and reform and refill our boxes. As we crossed the pike I saw Gen'l Bayard[2] sitting on his horse; a few moments later and he was instantly killed by a solid shot.

While being served with ammunition I saw a fellow brought in on a stretcher who thought he was desperately wounded, one foot almost off he said; some of the boys examined him and could not find a scratch. A shell had come pretty close and frightened him; the stretcher bearers had found him lying on the field and thought him hit.

After being supplied we again moved to the front, and while going we met a squad of reb prisoners coming to the rear. "What regiment," some of the boys asked; they said "——Georgia." Warner of K asked them "What part of Georgia"; "Macon," they answered. He lived in Macon before the war, but there were none that he knew. While we were talking the shells came over, striking the ground and throwing the dirt over us.

One of the rebs, laughing, said "That is one of Stonewalls pills, and how do you like to take them." "Oh, well enough," we replied, "if they dont come any nearer than that."

1. The Battle of Fredericksburg, Va., December 12-14, 1862.
2. Brig. Gen. George D. Bayard, USA.

Another one of our boys said "We're going to have Richmond now"; "Well," said Johnie Reb, laughing heartly, "You'll find two Hills,[3] a d——d Longstreet,[4] and a Stonewall[5] before you get there." All this happened in less time then it takes to write it.

When we got back to the pike, we found the brigade there, they having been driven back after some severe fighting.

The fighting on the left was over for this day, and we held the same position that we did in the morning, [with] nothing gained, but thousands killed or wounded. Night coming on, we lay in line of battle awaiting the morrow. The morrow dawned and still we lay in the same position; there was no fighting—only an interchange of shots between the batteries.

I remember a battery far away on our left that anoyed us greatly; about once in twenty minutes they would send a shot down our lines that would strike sometimes only a few feet from where we lay, and then richochet and go still farther down the line. Another on Marye Heights, when they thought we were getting sleepy, would send over some just to awaken us.

We changed our general position but little during the 13th and 14th of Dec., only to keep out of range of the guns on Marye Heights, which was on our right and in full view. On the night of the 14th, company K was sent to the picket line. I staid with the colors; sometime in the night the order came for us to get up as quickly and as silently as possible and march. We started and moved back to the pontoon, crossed, and marched up the bluffs, where we were ordered to lay down, the rain coming down in tor-

3. Generals Ambrose P. Hill and Daniel H. Hill, CSA.
4. General James Longstreet, CSA.
5. General Thomas J. (Stonewall) Jackson, CSA.

rents. Just before morning K company returned, being amongst the last to cross the river.

The causes for the disaster at Fredericksburg are several and were freely discussed as usual by the boys, and many were the theories advanced. Some laid the blame to this cause and some to that, and after a free exchange of ideas, it was decided that as far as the left was concerned, Gen'l Franklin[6] was responsible. And these are [the] reasons. The old spirit of McClellanism was still in the army, and of all the old officers, Franklin was the most devoted; he either would [not] or could not give up the idea of McClellan greatness, and [t]hen Burnside ordered him to attack and take the enemies position, and if he wanted more troops, to send for them. Let us go more into particulars.

These are facts, for we were there and saw what I now write and to a certain extent participated in them.

The grand division of Franklin were composed of the 1st and 6th corps. The sixth corps crossed the river and formed their line on the right, leaving one division to guard the bridge, the 1st corps in the following order on the left: the 2nd division, Gibbons, on the right of the corps joining the left of the sixth, the 3d division, Meade,[7] on the left of the second; and the 1st, Doubledays,[8] on the left of the 3d and reaching back to the river.

In front of the old 1st corps commanded by John F. Reynolds[9] stood the veterans, tried in many a battle of Stonewall Jackson, his men partialy sheltered by the railroad and the timber.

When the advance was ordered and the old division of Gibbon, the Pennsylvania Reserves of Meade, with the

6. Maj. Gen. William B. Franklin, USA, commanding the Left Grand Division.
7. Maj. Gen. George G. Meade, USA.
8. Maj. Gen. Abner Doubleday, USA.
9. Maj. Gen. John F. Reynolds, USA.

Iron brigades of the 1st, there was fighting of the highest
order; on they went, driving the rebs from the railroad and
through the woods, advancing the line a good half mile, but
all this had not been done without a fearful loss in killed
and wounded, and so when Stonewall hurried up his reserves, the weakened lines of Gibbon and Meade after a
most stubborn resistance was forced back. The golden opportunity for Franklin was to send the division at the
bridge into the fight; if that had been done the story of
Fredericksburg would have had a different ending. That division thrown into the fight at that most critical moment
would have turned defeat into a most splendid victory.

But instead, he (Franklin), sent away to Burnside three
miles away for reinforcements, which the gallant hero
quickly sent, but before they could reach the field, although they double-quicked it almost all the way, the day
was lost. To show the desperation of the fight, and how our
boys tried to gain a victory, let me tell what some of the
16th Maine said.

One said when they had driven the rebs through the
woods, they could see just beyond the teams parked, and
the teamsters were making frantic efforts to get away, while
farther up the valley a large mass of rebel troops could be
seen coming at the double quick; soon they were upon
them, and as no help was near they were forced to fall
back, fighting all the way.

Another said, when speaking of how near they were, that
"Old Mr. Libbey his chum speared three of them," thus
showing how near we sometimes got.

But such was the fate of war; the gallant Burnside took
the whole cause of the failure upon himself, blameing no
one, and the battle of Fredericksburg passed into history.

After a day or two, we marched to the vicinity of Fletch-
ers Chapel, where we camped on a ridge; not knowing how

long we might stay here, we made no preperations to build houses or fix up our tents, being contented to sleep on the ground.

Seeing or hearing no signs of moving, the boys began to fix up their quarters, every one to suit himself. Dan Warren and myself pitched together, and after a little we commenced to improve our tent. We dug out the earth the bigness of the tent, about a foot and a half deep, and getting some poles, we locked their ends together and placed them around to keep back the earth, banking up on the outside. In the inside we drove down some crotched sticks and placed some cross pieces, and, in turn, on these placed some long, slim, smooth poles covering about two thirds of our room. In daytime this served as a seat, and at night we slept soundly on this our spring bed.

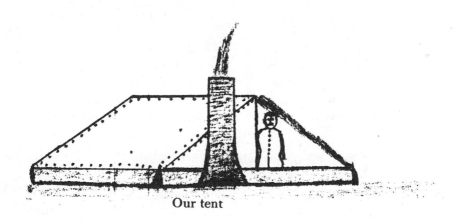

Our tent

In the corner next to our heads we built a fireplace, the chimney on the outside of sticks laid up cobhouse fashion and plastered with mud. The door of the tent was on the same side with the chimney; under the bed we kept our store of wood, while our equipments were stored wherever there was room Here we were snug, and tight, and warm, and done our cooking, ate, and slept the greater portion of our time away. Not all the boys of the company were so comfortably housed as we were. We lived quite an easy life, drilling when the weather permitted, and doing picket duty in all weather. I was out on picket the first day of January 1863, when early in the morning there came in a load of contrabands; they had a yoke of oxen hitched to a cart on which was all their worldly possessions; they were of all ages, from the helpless babe to the old grey head;

Contrabands

they were all smiles wishing us a "happy new year," though fearful of what kind of a reception we would give them. We received them kindly, enquired where they came from and what the news was down the river, and then sent them to division headquarters. I counted twenty one in the company.

At this time the color guard received a new gun, a short rifle with a long sabre bayonet; it was quite an affair.

One morning soon after this I was detailed for camp guard and went out with my short rifle. Now, the color guard is excused from all duty, and only go out with the colors. I had protested against going, but as there was a scarcity of Corporals in the company I had waived my rights and had obeyed orders to help the boys. When we had the old rifle no one had objected, but the other members of the guard had laughed at me for doing extra duty.

The Adjutant, in inspecting the guard, came to me said, "Are you one of the color guard." I told him I was. He said, "Then what are you here for." I replied, "Because I was ordered to." He asked, "Are you in the habit of doing guard duty when detailed for the colors." I told him I was. He told me then, that as soon as guard mounting was over and we had marched to the guard house, to go to my quarters, and tell the Orderly to detail another man in my place, and that under no circumstances was I to go out, only with the colors.

I went to quarters and found that the Adjutant had been there and given his orders, and a man was already on the way.

During the next two months I had an easy time.

15

Protecting the Citizens

Burnside's mud march—Back in old quarters—Hooker in command—Games played by the boys—Promotions in company—Review—Going on picket—On a visit to a safe guard (Haskell) and what I saw there

Nothing of interest occurred till about the middle of January, when we were ordered to pack up and be ready to march; the weather was thick, and every indication betokened rain. With reluctance we took down our tents and made the usual preperation for a march. Some of the boys were careful, but tipped their chimnies over and in other ways damaged their old homes. We were very careful of ours and stood guard over it, allowing no one to injure it in the slightest degree. We marched away about noon heavily loaded with our traps, and bivouacked several miles up the river, the rain falling heavily; it was dark when we halted for the night, and not knowing in what direction to go for wood or water, we lay down in the rain without our cheering pot of coffee. At early dawn the reveillie sounded and, jumping up, I saw that the troops were already begining to march. There was no chance for coffee so, rolling our wet blankets up, we shouldered them and again started through the rain. Where we lay through the night between two slight elevations was a dry brook, or at least it was dry when we lay down at night. In the morning it was a rushing torrent a rod wide and two feet deep. Some of the boys were on one side and some on the other; I was on the lucky side and did not have to wade the stream. All day we strugled on through the rain; the roads were filled with the artilery and wagon trains, we of the infantry in the fields.

How many miles we went I have no idea, but several, and at night we halted in an old woods where we were ordered to make ourselves comfortable; huge fires were soon blazeing and we were in all positions around them. The trains, being obliged to keep the roads, soon had them all cut up; wheels sank to the hub and the poor horses could not pull them out, although repeatedly urged to do so by their driver. Oaths, and curses filled the air while blows fell thick and fast on the poor mules backs. It was all in vain, Burnside was stuck in the mud. We lay in the woods all the next day and night and on the morning of our third day we were ordered back to camp. The weather was still cloudy and it was growing cold, bivouacking one night on the way, and late the next day we arrived at our old quarters. How glad was the sight of our old chimney just as we had left it, although well soaked with rain. Our tent was soon pitched over the hole, a fire was kindled, and with a pot of hot coffee our fatigue was soon forgotten. Many laughable—and stories where the laugh did not come in—were told of this march, and it served to amuse the boys for many days.

Burnside asked to be releived from his command, and his request was granted, while Joseph Hooker[1] was appointed

1. Maj. Gen. Joseph (Fighting Joe) Hooker, USA.

in his place. The appointment of Hooker gave unbounded satisfaction to the boys, and among some of the first of his orders were that the troops should receive a ration of vegetables twice a week, and soft bread every day and if the commissaries could not furnish them, he wanted to know the reason why. Soft bread was forth coming to us every day, and I never knew of an instance where it could not be furnished. The troops had confidence in "Old Joe" and, with the change of rations, were in the best of spirits.

We amused ourselves as best we could. Playing cards was the most favorite. I remember of playing, one stormy day with three comrades, over eighty games of Euchre without going out of our tent. Putting old blankets over the top of a chimney so the smoke could not escape and giving the inmates a taste of smoke was another. Jim Slatery and Mike O'Laughlin tent was the one next to mine. One day when they had a good fire Al Sanborn put a piece of old blanket down their chimney, stopping the smoke completely, and soon their tent was full. Looking out they could see nothing the matter and concluded it was the poor draught, and not wishing to have the laugh on them, went back and thought to stay it out, but the smoke from the green pine wood wet with pitch was to much for them and out came Slatery to look around. The boys, some of them seeing the smoke pouring from every seam, and always ready to laugh at anothers misfortune, came crowding around laughing to see the fun with such exclamations, as "Mike and Jim are going into business smoking sides, and are trying their tent now to see if it will hold smoke." At length one suggested that they look into their chimney, and Jim, doing so, pulled out a piece of blanket; the smoke then came out in torrents. "By Gard," said Slatery, "I knew it was that Sanborn all the time." Mike and Jim, being very honest men, received their full share of games.

John Gliddon, a good soldier and a hard working man, was detailed as a pionier, and was working every day helping to build a corduroy[2] road, going to his work early in the morning and remaining till dark, and in addition doing his own cooking.

One night after coming home, tired as he was, cooking his supper, some one dropped a lump of earth down his chimney, spilling his coffee and making his meat unfit to eat. John was mad, and seizeing his gun rushed out with his war, warrrr (for you could not understand him much better then a blackbird) [and] threatened to shoot the man who did it. The boys, hearing the rumpus, quickly gathered around, and when learning what the matter was, condemned it in strong terms; while enjoying a harmless joke, to spoil a mans supper was too serious a thing to be overlooked, and if the guilty one had been found John would have been permitted to lick him without any danger to himself. It was never known for certain who did it, but we all thought of the same man, and that was Al Sanborn. We contributed of our store and John did not go to bed supperless.

On the first of March we realized again what was often quoted by the boys, as what we were out for, viz, Study, travel, and promotion, this time promotion; Cordwell our Orderly was made a Lieut and assigned to Co. F., Warner was made Orderly, and Wheeler and myself were made Sergeants.[3] After two months of an idle life I reluctantly gave up my short rifle and took an Enfield,[4] and returned to duty.

When we came here in Dec. the citizens asked for a man

---

2. A method of building roads on soft ground. Logs were laid side by side, which resembled a strip of corduroy when completed.

3. See Appendix A.

4. Enfield rifles were made in a number of models both in the U.S.A. and in England. They were a muzzle-loading weapon of .577 or .58 calibre.

to come to their houses and stay to protect their property; they were called safe-guards. Our company furnished three. Bruce went to a widow womans with three grown up daughters, about a mile and a half away, Haskell to a family named Bullard, in the same direction but in plain sight of our camp, and John Stearns went in another direction about a mile away. Bruce and Haskell staid all winter, and John till he was detailed at Corps Headquarters.

Preparetory to the grand review, we had a brigade one and the boys, always wishing to look and appear well, blacked up their boots, scoured their brasses, and to top the whole, put on a paper collar with white gloves procured by the Sutler[5] for the occasion. We were the observed of all the observed, and were looked upon by the rest of the brigade with a jealous envy. They said "we were trying to show off," and gave us the name of the "Band box," or "Paper collar regiment." Some of them took Col Coulters old female dog and put a pair of gloves on her fore paws, and put a collar on her neck and let her loose on the parade grounds; it created a shout and we shouted as loud as any, and as fully enjoyed the joke.

Somewhere about the first of April was the grand review of the "Army of the Potomac." President Lincoln came down and Hooker, with other celebrities, looked us over.

On the day of the review we were up before light, and with the same amount of carefullness in dress and equipments, we started for the Potomac, where the review was to take place, and after a good deal of waiting and standing in line and marching in review, which occupied all day, we arrived in camp about sundown, somewhat tired, and hungry, and a good deal cross, when a detail was ordered for picket and I was one of the unfortuniates. Without any

5. The Sutler was a mobile shopkeeper who followed the army and sold tobacco, canned fruits, and many other items that were not issued to the men.

further preliminaries we started for the brigade parade grounds, thinking that when all the details had arrived we would be marched directly to our posts. But old Col Wheelock of the 97th N.Y. (who was the new brigade officer of the day) thought differently; he wanted a regular "Guard mount," and was mad to think of any other way being suggested. He tried to have the men march off and then march back at the beat of the drum; the men were mad and commenced to yell, but refused to stir an inch. The old man rode up and down the line brandishing his sword and threating dire vengeance on the first man he could catch, but when he was at one end the noise was always at the other, and as there was none that felt inclined to help him catch the guilty ones and it [was] getting dark, he gave the order "Right face, March." The boys obeyed with cheers for "Old Butter and Cheese," as the men of his regiment called him.

I used to go up and see John, and once in a while would bring back a "Pone cake" for my trouble. Pone cake was corn meal rolled into a piece of dough about as big as my two fists and baked in a pot.

I used to go over and see Haskell, but never to eat. I recollect of being over there one afternoon and Haskell invited me into the house. I accepted, and as this is a good representation of a great majority of the poor white establishments, I will give it. The house was simply a log house about fifteen feet square, containing one room with a door on either side; for a window there was a hole about two feet square with a sliding board in the inside to stop it up when needed. The fire-place and chimney were built on the outside of the house of sticks and mud in regular Virginia style. In one corner of the room on the opposite side from the fire-place stood the family bed. In the corner on the left of the fire-place stood a table, in the center of the

room was a bench about four feet long used for a seat, [and]
there was two chairs without backs, or stools, I have forgotten which. When we entered Mr Bullard sat on one, and
Mrs B— the other, while the five children, the eldest a

Mr. Bullard

girl of fourteen, sat on the bench, or floor. On being intro-
duced Mr B— arose, shook hands, and invited me to take
a seat, offering at the same time his stool. Mrs B— arose,
courtesied, and resumed her seat. Declining with thanks
Mr. B— offer of his seat, I said "I would sit with Haskell
on the bench." We sat facing the fire, with Mr B— on our
right and Mrs B— on the left and near the fire; the children were scattered promiscusly around. I now noticed

why Mrs B— sat so near the fire; she was preparing a meal for them, and the pot was over the fire in which was their "pone cake," also a frying-pan in which, swimming in its own fat, was the ever to be found "smoked sides." On the hearth were two old tin cans (such as the boys had bought can fruit of the Sutler in) in which she was making coffee. Mr B— was chewing tobacco, and spitting into, or rather towards the fire, [and] as he sat some distance away, many were the times that he failed of his mark and there was a stream between him and the fire. We entered into a general conversation, for he was quite an intelligent man and was very well informed in some things. Of course he knew nothing about the resources of the rebels, or their condition even, all this was mere speculation with him, but he could talk like a man that knew it all, and he had great confidence in the success of their cause and that they never would be conquered, but would gain all they wanted in the end. To my enquiry of where he based his opinion, he said "that the south would never submit to Yankee rule, they would never be conquered," without giving any reasons. Not wishing to excite him too much, I refrained from talking any more about the war. Mrs B—, with the assistance of her daughter, had by this time set the table with two platters, or deep dishes, and poured the greasy contents of the frying pan into one, and placed the pone cake on the other, [then] announced that the meal was ready. Mr B— arose and politely invited me to a seat at the table with him; I as politely declined, giving as my reason that I had just eaten as I left camp. It was not often that we had a chance to sit at a table and we seldom refused, but the thought of the tobacco juice from Mr. B— mouth satisfied me, without knowingly partaken of it. Mr. B— then drew his stool up, and Mrs B— turning on hers, the children standing around and seeking the most advantageous position. The meal was commenced by each one taking a piece of the cake and dipping it in the fat before eating it. They were not over careful about spilling the fat on the floor or on themselves. While they were at their meal Haskell and myself talked together. After eating everything that was cooked, and drinking the coffee, the old man went back to his side of the fire place, and, producing a dirty looking pipe, filled it, and taking a coal from the hearth lighted it. After smoking away for a few moments [he] passed it to Mrs B—, who, after indulging in a few sweetly pleasant whiffs, passed it in turn to the eldest daughter and son on down to the little younker that was hardly able to run alone.

After staying a few moments longer, I bade the family good night and went out with Haskell. I asked him if that was the way they lived, and he said it was, although they were a little on their good behaviour.

I asked H— where they all slept as I saw but one bed, and I thought by the looks there was no great chambre accommodations; he said they all slept in that one bed. I asked him where he slept and he said on the floor before the fire.

I asked why the old man did not cut his hair and trim his whiskers, for he wore them very long and, by the looks, never combed. He said the old man told him he never shaved, only when he got lousey.

I told Lyman I had a good deal rather he would be a safe guard there than myself, but he thought small favors should be thankfuly received, and he did dislike the routine of camp life so much that he was willing to put up with a good deal. Biding him good night, I went back to camp well pleased with what I had seen and learned, and better satisfied to eat army rations then to sit at the table of a F.F.V.[6]

6. First Family of Virginia.

16

We Are Veterans

Preparing for the spring campaign—March for the Rappahannock—The President's fast—Chancellorsville—Up the river—Casualties—Incidents there—Retreat—Camp at White Oak Church—Again on the march—"The Heights of Centreville"

Winter having gone, and spring having passed a goodly portion away, the army reviewed, and all things were ready for a move. But where, or in what direction, none of us knew; we were still in our old quarters.

Dan Warren, my tent mate, was detailed as one of the cattle guard, as all the fresh beef were driven around on the hoof and killed as we wanted it, an easier way then transporting it on teams.

And somewhere towards the last days of April we received orders to pack up and march the next morning at nine o'clock. As the order did not come till night, there was no time that night to send for the safe guards, and then they did not want to take them off till morning, so I was detailed to start early and bring Bruce in. I went, getting there before sunrise. Bruce had just turned out and was stretching himself before the door. I made known my errend, and he stepping back into the house made its inmates acquainted also. Coming out, we went down to the spring for him to wash, [and] after that being performed we went back to the house, and as its inmates were now up we went in. They were busy preparing breakfast and Bruce told them that I would eat with him.

The family, consisting of a widow by the name of McCarthy and her three grown up daughters, soon had the meal on the table, the old lady sitting down with us but all the daughters declining to do so, the breakfast consisting of army coffee provided by Bruce, smoked sides, and a nice hot corn cake. I really enjoyed it; everything was neat and clean, in striking contrast to that of Mr Bullards; the old lady was quite a talker but the girls said but little. I thought they did not like to have their "safe guard" go away and thought I was in some way to blame for it, and so did not look upon me with much favor. After we had finished, with many thanks for their kindness, I went outside for Bruce to take his leave; soon he came out and [I] helping him carry his things, we started for camp.

Their house was like many others found in Virginia, built of logs, chimney on outside, and plastered with mud, [but] they had what some did not have, a window of real glass. They had but one room, although one end was curtained off for a sleeping appartment, and in there all the ladies slept, Bruce rolling himself in his blanket before the fire. Their sleeping rooms being so small, Bruce when he arose would build the fire then go out doors while the ladies performed their toilet; at night when they retired he would do the same.

Bruce said he had enjoyed himself greatly all winter and

had much rather stay with them then to take his chances in the uncertain fate of war, a point that I was ready to concede at once, after my experiance of the morning, and would even be willing to take my chance with them for the next few months.

Bruce said that none of the young ladies could write, and could read but little when he went there, and that he had spent most of his leisure time in teaching them, and that the youngest, his favorite, had become quite a scholar, and when in camp he had gathered all the reading matter he could find for them.

When we arrived in camp we found the regiment all ready to move, and, strapping on our things, we bade adieu to our old camp with many regrets, for we had passed a very comfortable winter here. Hooker[1] had command of the army, Reynolds[2] the corps, Robinson[3] the division, and Leonard[4] the brigade, while the regiment was under the command of Lt Col Batchelder.[5] Great things were expected. Hooker had the name of being a fighting man; when in command of a division or a corps, would he keep up his reputation in the command of the army? Let us see.

We marched away over the hills towards Fredericksburg, bivouacking one night, and coming near the scene of our last winters fight three miles below the town, in the morning of the second day.

All of our Corps was here, a pontoon bridge was already laid, and the first division was across. We marched down into an open field in the immediate vicinity of the bridge in

1. Maj. Gen. Joseph Hooker, USA, in command of the Army of the Potomac.
2. Maj. Gen. John F. Reynolds, USA, in command of the I Corps.
3. Brig. Gen. (later Maj. Gen.) John C. Robinson, commanding the 2nd Division.
4. Col. Samuel H. Leonard, USA, in command of the 3rd Brigade.
5. Lieut. Col. N. Walter Batchelder, USA, commanding the 13th Mass.

plain sight of the enemy. Here we stacked our arms and laid around, wondering what would be the next move.

A day had been set apart by the President for fasting and prayer, and I think this was the day, but am not positive.

At least, being hungry I had made a pot of coffee and partaken of my army rations when, seeing the regiment on our left formed into a square, I went down to see what was going on.

Col Root of the 94th N.Y. in observance of the day had called his men together and was giving them some good advice as to what would be expected of them in the campaign now opening.

I listened to him till he was through and then turned back to my regiment. He had but just dismissed them, before many had time to go away, when a shell came shrieking over, bursting in their midst, and I think killed and wounded twelve. Another followed, and another, in quick succession, and our regiment this time was the loser. Cap't Bush of Co. F was standing with his men around him when a shell came tearing through, striking him in the side and

Effects of a shell

killing him instantly. Lieut Cordwell,[6] who was sitting near, had his head blown completely off, and Serg't Fay, also in range, lost his right hand and leg, all by the same shell. Many of the boys who were cooking their supper tipped over their coffee pots, spilling their contents, and saying "Why dont they take us out of this." The order soon came to fall in, and marching by the right flank we soon were out of range; none of our company were hit, if we except Cordwell, who had but lately been promoted. While we were lying here, Hooker was not idle, but with three corps was marching up the river, crossing, and coming down on the other side, completely surprising the enemy, who thought he was reviewing an army corps in Old Stafford. An order from Gen'l Hooker congratulating the army was read to us, and also stating what was expected. The enemy, on discovering Hooker on their flank, quickly turned and marched out to meet him, contrary to the expectations of the union leaders.

The two armies met in the interminable woods and swamps near Chancellorsville,[7] where the enemy, being better acquainted with the ground, hoped to make quick work of Hooker and whip his army by detail. The 6th Corps was ordered to remain at Fredericksburg, the others to join Hooker at Chancellorsville. We started in the early morning and toiled all day long and, just as the sun was sinking in the west, we crossed the river on the pontoon and in one sense were joined to the main army.

We were halted but a few rods from the bridge, and had thrown off our knapsacks and were preparing to make coffee, when a most unearthly yell and the sharp roll of mus-

6. Lieut. Cordwell had been a Sergeant in Company K until March 1, 1863, when he was appointed Lieutenant and transferred to Company F. (see chapter 15).
7. The Battle of Chancellorsville, May 2-4, 1863.

ketry caused us to stop. Officers cried "Fall in," and the men, seizing their guns, awaited events. We thought to see our men come running back every moment, to be followed by the enemy. Orders now came to go forward and we started towards the fight, which I think must have been two miles away, although at the time it didnt seem a quarter of the distance. We kept on through the woods, going as fast as possible in the dark, but the firing ceased while we [were] still a long way off.

A new line had now to be established, and we were placed on the extreme right, and ordered to build breastworks, as an attack was liable to take place in the morning. Without a pick, or shovel, or even an axe, it was an exceedenly difficult task to perform.

But with bayonets for picks, and tin plates for shovels, when the morning sun dawned upon us it found us behind a bank of earth as thick and as formidable as the renouned fortifacations at Centreville. The men worked briskly all night, for we had learned the advantages to be gained by being behind a bank of dirt, and had rather have that stop part of the bullets then to stop them all ourselves. In the morning we moved a short distance still farther to the right, the extreme part at the right turning round like a fish-hook. Early in the morning our pickets sent in quite a number of rebel prisoners picked up by them during the night; some had been engaged in the fight of the evening before and were wounded.

One had a bad wound in his neck. Sanborn, wishing to sympathize with him a little, said, "A bad wound that, you've got." The reb, a lean, lank specimen of humanity on which all sympathy would be lost, replyed with a look, sour and ugly enough to satisfy the evil one himself, "Yes: but I wish it was through my d——d heart." "So do I," said Sanborn quickly, and I think it was the feeling of all the boys that his wish had been gratified.

About the middle of the forenoon there was some very heavy fighting on our left, [and] the expected charge was made, but we were so far to the right that it did not reach down to where we lay, although the left of our division was engaged. We lay behind our works and heard the yell of the rebels as they charged our line, and the sch'w's, sch'w's, of the grape and canister[8] as our batteries poured it into them, and the continual roll of musketry, which told of wounds and death. Then came the cheers of our boys and we knew the rebels were getting the worst of it; the firing at length ceased, with only an occasional shot from the picket line.

The next day two regiments of our brigade with a section of a battery under the command of Gen'l Robinson went out on a reconnoissance. We went a mile or more when we found them and, after the skirmishers exchanging a few shots and we losing two or three prisoners, came back.

Just at night Gen'l Hooker rode down the line, and Col Leonard called for three cheers for the "Commander of the Army," which were given with a will by the brigade.

An amusing event occured here one night, which for a time was not so amusing, at least for us. A regiment of new troops had just arrived, and they were sent around to the point of the hook, and were directly in our rear. During the night something start[l]ed them and they, springing up, seized their guns and most of them jumped over their works and commenced to fire directly at us. The most of us

8. Grapeshot was a group of metal balls usually held together with discs of wood and a large bolt. When fired from cannon, the group of balls would break up, having the effect of a very large shotgun. Canister was of the same principle, except that the balls were smaller, and were contained in a metal or leather can (canister).

were quietly sleeping and, being suddenly awakened and hearing the bullets whistling around us, thought we were attacked, [so] quickly seized our arms and jumped into our works. The bullets coming from the rear, we looked and could see the flashes of their guns. Quickly comprehending what might be the matter, we laid low for a few moments till things could be quieted down, which their officers soon accomplished, and peace soon reigned in our rear.

A heavy rain now came on, and the ground being swampy made it a very disagreeable place, the river rising only added to the general discomfort, and the disaster of the 11th corps were the many things that induced Hooker to retreat, which was done without loss.

Chancellorsville is generaly considered as a disaster to the union army, but we boys looked at it in a different light. I should call it a drawn battle with the scales turning in favor of the union. And this is my reason. The rebels lost one of their best, if not the best officer they had; they could have better spared an entire division of their army than Stonewall Jackson.[9] And the union cause gained more in his death than an army corps, and from this time can be reconed the downfall of the confederacy.

We left Chancellorsville in the early morning in a heavy rainstorm, crossing on the pontoon, the river running like a race-horse, and marched down into old Stafford again.

We bivouacked at night on the site of one of the old camps of last winter, not a tree or a stick of wood in sight, save some old brush shelters that had been used for horses. The rain coming down in torrents, we pitched our tents and, very tired and wet, were preparing our coffee when

---

9. Lieut. Gen. Thomas J. (Stonewall) Jackson, CSA, was wounded at Chancellorsville on the night of May 2, 1863, by Confederate Troops who mistakenly thought that they were shooting at Union cavalry. His arm was amputated; however, complications set in and he died on May 10, 1863.

the order came to send a man for a ration of whiskey. Canteens were freely offered and Warner the Orderly went for it.

While he was away for it and dealing it out, I made his coffee and mine, and when he came back our supper was ready. Pouring our whiskey into the coffee we ate our hardtack and pork, and drank the mixture down, then rolling ourselves in our blankets, we slept soundly till morning.

On waking up the sun was shining, and unrolling myself I came out steaming, feeling good all over. We quickly continued the march, going down the river some four or five miles from Fredericksburg, near White Oak Church.

Nothing of interest occured at this place. We pitched our camp in a fine grove, and rested, picketing the river and drilling occasionly. Here we passed the remainder of May and June was upon us. Orders were received to hold us in readiness to march at a moments notice, and day after day passed by and we were ready, that is, we kept our tents pitched and lay around doing nothing. The third division of our Corps, who was camped near, received the same orders that we did, and while they had, when we first came here, filled their camp with all kinds of impliments conducive to their comfort, things that could not be taken on the march, and things their officers did not approve of, such things as tables, chairs, and stools that they had made themselves out of cracker boxes and sticks, kept moving them from day to day. After a little we would go over to their camp, the old one, and come back bringing whatever struck our fancy, whether we could put it to use or not.

About the middle of June orders were received to march immediately. We obeyed, and marching up to the vicinity of the last winters camps, we halted for several days.

The whole army was in motion, but where we were going or where the enemy were we could not tell. At

length we started and moved up the river, bivouacked at
night near Bealton Station and resuming the march at daylight, this time going down the railroad towards Manassas.
The weather was excessively hot, sweat poured off of us
like rain, and the dust covered everything; water was
scarce, good water could not be found, the creeks were
low, and near all the fording places were filled with dead
horses or mules. I remember of coming to a creek and,
being very thirsty, thought to fill my canteen before leaving, so I started up creek to find clear water. After going
quite a distance I looked and thought I was above all im-
purities, for I could see none above, and took a long
draught and was filling my canteen when a comrade asked
me "how I liked the water." "Firstrate" I replied. "I
thought so," he said, "when I saw that dead mule there,"
pointing at the same time to a bunch of bushes just above
me in which lay the swollen carcass. The water being down
and canteen filled, I thought it as good as any I could find
so, saying nothing more, I went on my way.

It was not the first, and neither was it the last, that we
boys were obliged to drink during our three years, but then
we liked to laugh at one another when we had the laugh on
our side, and many were the jokes and hearty laugh we had
around the camp fire in recalling just such things as this.
The stories never lost anything in the telling.

We reached Bristoe Station late at night, where without
stopping to make coffee we lay down for a few hours rest,
but were called up and on the move before light—down
the railroad, through Manassas, across Bull Run Creek, and
up the "Heights of Centreville" before we rested.

How well I remember those long June days, the sun
pouring down his hottest rays, through an unclouded sky
upon us.

How hot and dry the earth; huge clouds of dust could be

seen far away to tell where the army was marching. Dust was upon everything; we sweat, and the dust settleing on our faces encased them as though in a mold.

How glad we were when the order was given "to rest," and, throwing off our traps, we stretched our weary selves on the grass and drank the delicious water of that cool spring in that little clump of trees. We had covered over ninety miles in three day.

The boys did not speculate much about what was going to be done, or the way to do it—that with many other things did not thrive after the first year. We were willing to let the events turn up without anticipating them; we were veterans, and as such were willing to do our duty, go when ordered, and obey even the minutest detail. We knew that Lee was marching his army through Virginia towards Maryland, and here from our elevated position could hear the guns and see the clouds of dust of his army. We knew that a collision was inevitable, but whether on Virginia or Maryland soil we could not tell; whether few or many days should intervene was a veiled picture to us. We had confidence in our officers and the whole spirit of the army was changed from one year ago, then we were boys, led by boyish men. Now we were men, tired men, and led by those who had been tried in many a battle and had not failed. Men and their officers worked together (that is those that were in the field), and the "old army of the Potomac," from Hooker down to the little drummer boy, was working together; it was a Unit, and in unity there is strength. So the old army, though small in numbers, was strong in the strength to win.

17

Taken Prisoner

A*fter* resting a few days at Centreville, we moved on toward Leesburg, in Old Loudon. The weather was extremely warm, and many of the boys stragled by the way.

We kept up by short marches until we were in Loudon, where we lay about a week. One Sunday afternoon I was detailed to go out on picket, and under the command of the Officer of the day we marched out to where he thought the picket post was, but when we got there, there was no picket to be found anywhere. Ordering us to rest, he rode away to find the post. In the near vicinity was a house and as a natural consequence we drifted that way.

There was nothing to be obtained there, if we except the three young ladies, and they sat at their chambre window and entertained us by singing the "Bonnie Blue Flag,"

"Maryland, My Maryland" and a number of other such pieces. They were downright secesh and thought to plague us by singing some of their airs, and in every way and manner showed their contempt of us. We had been so long out that we didn't care what they sang or said, for they couldn't get much ahead of us, not that we used them ungentlemanly, or said things that we ought not to say, but we had good singers that could sing good patriotic songs, and in relation to war matters, we could boast as well as they; after all, we enjoyed their singing. A shower came up just at night, and darkness; we lay down to sleep while we could.

Somewhere about twelve o'clock the Officer came back and, ordering us to fall in, we marched away for the picket post, arriving there at early dawn; the pickets had been moved out five miles, and the officer had not been notified of the change. I was sent with [a] squad of men about one half mile further on to releive the picket there.

This part of the country had not been overrun by troops very much and there was a good chance to forage.

I went to a house, and paid fifty cents for a good square meal, sitting down at a table; the old lady drew a thriving business that day. I also procured a dozen biscuits and took them to camp.

Jack Hall, a reckless fellow of K company, while on his post let a young fellow who was hanging around there take his gun, and when he thought Jack was not looking [he] slipped off the cap and spit in the tube, putting the cap back on. Jack, who had his eye on him all the time, now took his gun, and putting it at the fellows breast threatened to shoot him unless he owned up; the poor fellow was frightened and told Jack he done it. I happened along at this time and enquired what the matter was. Both telling me, I cautioned Jack to be careful about his gun, and to prime it over anew, and the fellow, I told him he was under arrest, and if he tried to run away we should shoot him. He sat down under a tree and kept quiet all the afternoon. When we were releived at night I told him to get out and not come fooling around a picket guard again. It might have been a serious thing for Jack if the Officer of the day had found out that he had let a citizen take his gun while on duty.

While we lay at this place, we heard the guns of the Cavalry fight at Aldie,[1] were put under arms but were not called upon.

Towards the last of June we moved away toward Maryland, hearing that Lee was crossing his army at Williamsport and going straight towards Pennsylvania. This was astounding news—the audacity of the rebs in leaving their base and going so far into the enemies country, we could hardly beleive it. There is no doubt that Lee's army outnumbered the union by a good many thousand. The reason for this was that the two years and the nine months men's time was about out; some had already left and others were only waiting to go. Lee officially reported when he crossed the Potomac 105,000 men, Hooker 68,000,[2] with ten thousand more at Harpers Ferry under Gen'l French. Hooker crossed his army at the lower fords of the Potomac and marched up to the vicinity of Frederick Md. Hooker now asked that the ten thousand men at Harpers Ferry be placed at his disposal, Halleck[3] replying that they might, but on no consideration could they be removed from that place. Hooker remonstrated, saying they could be of no use

1. The Cavalry Skirmish at Aldie, Va., on June 17, 1863.

2. Various sources indicate that the Troop Strength at Gettysburg was as follows: General Meade—88,000 to 104,220; General Lee—70,000 to 77,500. When General Lee crossed the Potomac he had a greater number than the quantity listed above, but lost many due to straggling, sickness, and the like. The range in quantities is due mainly to the different methods of counting and losses just prior to the battle.

3. Maj. Gen. Henry W. Halleck, USA, General in Chief of the Union Armies.

there, while he could use them to a great advantage in the field. Lee had passed on into Penn. and Harpers Ferry was of no account. Hooker told Halleck so, and more, tried to reason, saying, if he was whipped Harpers Ferry would fall of itself, and then if he was victorious the place could be occupied again before Lee could get there, even if he was disposed to do so, which he very much doubted.

Halleck again told Hooker to go on without them; if he could not, to turn his command over to Gen'l Meade[4] and report himself at Trenton, N.J. Hooker, finding himself in the way and his services no longer wanted, done as he was ordered. Gen'l Meade took command of the army at Frederick Md. and as far as practicable carried out the plans of his predecessor. One of the first orders from Halleck was to give Meade the ten thousand men at Harpers Ferry if he wanted them, which offer Meade availed himself of and from that time forth they became a part of the army.

This was one of the mysteries of the war. Why the troops should be witheld to-day from one, and the next day given to another, is one of the inextricable things of the many that happened that we could not account for.

Hooker proved himself, in other times and places, the general that he was.

Rumors were rife. We heard that Lee was far away up in Pennsylvania, that the country was thoroughly arroused, and that troops were hurrying from all quarters to repell the invaders, that the Old Keystone State was one grand camp of union troops. We were even led to beleive that our presence would not be needed, and that this march through Maryland, and Penn. would be one grand Picnic. It was indeed an ovation, but the old army was the one that saved the country.

4. Maj. Gen. George G. Meade, USA.

We left Frederick on the morning of the 28th of June and marched up the east side of the Blue Ridge towards Penn.

We marched at a rapid rate, otherwise it would have been very pleasant. The citizens came out to welcome us, and added to our comfort by placing barrels of water within easy reach; the young ladies with baskets of goodies were nigh, offering us to eat, and with waveing flags cheered us on. We bivouacked at night just beyond Emmittsburg, and marched at early dawn, halting at the State line. Here we remained that night all the next day and night. Where all this time was Lee and his army? Somewhere in Penn, we heard, but where we did not know. We had reached the State line; could we go much farther and not fall in with them?

We did not get any papers and all we knew was obtained from the citizens, by observation, and instinct.

We talked the matter over in a quiet way in the morning, wondering if the day would pass without battle, and at night thankful that it had.

On the morning of the first day of July we marched, the first division in the advance. We had not gone far when we heard an occasional shot, but without thinking much about them, for they were of daily occurence. As the day advanced and we drew nearer Gettysburg,[5] the firing had a nearness that betokened mischief. When about a mile from the village, and at the place where we turned into the field, we heard with sorrow that our beloved corps commander Gen'l Reynolds[6] was killed, and that there was every prospect of a fight. We moved down across the fields, leaving the town on our right, to a grove in which there was a bat-

5. The Battle of Gettysburg, Penn., July 1-3, 1863.
6. Maj. Gen. John F. Reynolds, USA, was killed by a sharpshooter on July 1, 1863.

tery posted; going just beyond, we halted near the Seminary.

In the meantime there was firing going on quite briskly in the front of the first division. We were halted but a few moments when we were ordered to cross the ridge to the other side of the buildings and to build a breastwork. We commenced to work with a will when an officer rode up with an order for Col Leonard. "Fall in" was quickly given, and again throwing on our traps, we moved off to the right. On the double quick we went on over the fields, through a grove and a gap in the fence at which lay an officer of the 12th Mass wounded, next a stouble field where John Flye was hit, [and] the bed of a railroad to another field, where we formed a line of battle, our brigade forming the right of the line, and our regiment the right of the brigade. Here was indeed a sight, for away off over the fields in our front, partialy hidden by a large brown barn and an apple orchard, was a long line of men. I thought at first that they must be our men, for I could not beleive that the firing which was growing in fierceness on our left would be extended around so far in our front. If these were union men, all was right, but if rebels, where was the men to oppose them, for surely our little short line could not do much in that direction. All doubts were soon set at rest, and that long line began to move directly towards us; we could see their colors, and their dirty uniforms.

The skirmishers in our front commenced a brisk fire when we were ordered to advance into a piece of woods; this we did, and the firing became general in our front.

In advancing up, being near the turn in the line, the farther we advanced the greater would be the gap between the two regiments until there was quite a space, the other regiment partially facing the other way. On our left but a little ways off was a little hill, or knoll; this was occupied by the rebels, [who] seeing our exposed position fired directly down our line. This was a most fatal fire for us. Many of our brave boys fell at this time; we being so briskly engaged with those in front we had not noticed them till we received their fire. My place being near the right of the company, I turned to see what had been the effect on old K. The first thing I saw was Sergeant Wheeler laying on the ground but a short distance away. There being so much noise and din, I could not tell by looking at him how bad he was hurt, for I could hear no sound. I went up and spoke to him, but received no answer. I saw that he was shot through the head, the bullet striking him in the left temple, and the blood and brains were oozing out. While [I was] looking at him he took his left arm and put it up to his forehead and tried to wipe it, [and] made a low gurgling sound with his lips at the same time. There was no time now to be wasted on dead men, so leaving him, I turned my attention again to the fight and the boys who were firing away at a rapid rate. The artilery had now opened on all sides and cannon balls were flying from all direction. How the battle was going none of us could tell, for we had all we could attend to in our front. Just at this time I was hit on the left shoulder by a bullet that cut through my coat and the skin enough to start the blood, and paralyzing my arm completely. I could not lift my arm at all; it hung lifeless by my side. As I was of no use, I gave my gun to one of the men who said his gun had got out of order, and went back and sat down trying to make my arm work. A man of Co I—wounded in both wrists—could not get his knapsack off, and, as he was bleeding considerable, he was afraid he would not hold out to get to the rear and carry it. I helped him off with it.

That great long line had been advancing, and when I came out of the woods on my retreat, the plain on our right

Death of Wheeler

was filled with them, and they were slowly gaining our rear. On our left our men were getting the worst of it and were being driven back. Things looked gloomy enough.

I had noticed as we entered the fight, directly on the other side of the town, quite an elevation, and now as I came out of the woods I saw with delight that the hill was crowned with batteries who were speaking in thunder tones and holding back that same long line on our right. Gen'l Howard,[7] on taking command after the death of Reynolds, had ordered a portion of the 11th corps to hold and fortify, and that was what they were doing. This hill is now the

7. Maj. Gen. Oliver O. Howard, USA, who was senior, assumed command of the field when General Reynolds was killed. Shortly thereafter Maj. Gen. Winfield S. Hancock, USA, was ordered by General Meade to take command of the field. The command of the I (Reynolds) Corps devolved upon Maj. Gen. Abner Doubleday.

famous "Cemetary Hill." I could distinctly hear the peculiar yell of the Jonnies as our boys fell back before them.

The victorious legions of Hill[8] corps, outnumbering our boys four to one, were not only driving back the sturdy veterans of the old 1st, but came well nigh annihilating them, they offered such a stubborn resistance.

At a glance I saw that it was almost like running the gauntlet to get back to the town and the hill, beyond which seemed to be, as indeed it was, the only place of safety.

I started back. The field was filled with wounded men and those who were not, all trying to escape the "Anaconda" that had almost entwined us in its folds. I took what I thought then was the direct route to town, by the Penn College which had been turned into a hospital. I did not stop there, but had to turn more to the right to gain the town. On entering the village from the west, I saw a barrel of water standing by the way and I paused a moment to take a drink. I then hurried on, and came to a street running at right angles to the one I was on. I turned up the street and had not gone far before I became aware that there were rebs at the end to which I was going; the bullets came singing down past as though they wanted to hurt someone. Thinking I must be taken prisoner, and seeing our division hospital flag hanging out in front of a church, I dodged in there to clame the right of being wounded. I went in at the main enterance and proceeded up into the body of the house; there was quite a good number already there, wounded in all conceivable ways, rebs as well as union men. I passed up the main aisle and took a seat in an empty pew about half way up. I was hardly seated before a shell came tearing through, scattering the plastering and splinters around. After being seated I was touched by

8. Lieut. Gen Ambrose P. Hill, CSA, commanded the Third Corps, Army of Northern Virginia, at Gettysburg.

someone from the seat behind, and on looking around I saw a reb who was wounded on the arm. He wanted to know how the battle was going; I told him I did not know, and to be truthful I did not, although it had a very bad look, but just then I did not feel like telling him what I thought. He enquired to what regiment and Corps I belonged. I told him and then put the same questions to him. He said he belonged to a North Carolina regiment and was in Hills corps, and was amongst some of the first to be wounded. He was a very intelligent man and we entered into conversation immediately, he doing most of the talking. He said he was a union man before the war, and done all he could to prevent his state from going out. He was one of the delegates to the convention that carried the old State out. After the secession of his state he said he went home and said he would have nothing more to do with politics. He carried on his farm and tried to live a peacefull life. The first year passed, and in the second year more men were wanted, so they came and without saying "by your leave" they took him and put him in the army. Since then he had tried to do his duty as soldier.

He said according to his ideas there was no cause for war, but being a Southern man, with all his interests, home, wife, children, and property there, he should continue to fight till the end, if not for his own sake, for those left behind who were dependent upon him.

The noise that had been in the street in front of the church had now passed on, and comparitive quiet reigned instead, when the North Carolina man arose and, looking around for a few moments said, "I reckon we've changed boots," bade me good-day, and went out.

Two rebel soldiers came in and going down the aisle picked up everything that struck their fancy. When down in front of the desk, they both saw and at the same time seized hold of an Officers haversack, each claiming it as his property, and getting very angry over it. After cursing a good deal and trying to pull it away from each other, they were proceeding to blows when an officer stepping up, took hold of the strap, told each one to let go, and then threw the strap over his shoulder [and] walked off with his prize. The real owner, a wounded union officer, [was] sitting in one of the pews.

A rebel officer now came around and took the name and regiment of each one, and cautioned us all not to go out of the church.

I now went through the room to see how many of the boys I could find, and see if I could help them. I found quite a number of the regiment but only one from company K, Harvey Ross.

He was lying up in front of the desk, and had been for an hour or two. Nothing had been done for him and his wounds began to feel sore; he wanted me to look and see how bad he was hurt. I looked and found that he was shot through the left arm above the elbow, the ball then entering his side. I could not get him over enough to see if the ball went through; he asked me what I thought of him, and I told him I would go for the Surgeon. It was now dark and it was with difficulty that I made my way around. At length, going down into the vestry, I found him busy and quite a number of K men. I asked him if he could just look at a man up stairs; he said he would but he must attend to his own men first. I told him this was one of his men. It being dark he had not recognized me at first. We went up stairs and he looked at the wound and told me to keep it wet with cold water, as that was all he could do till morning. I had already wet it. Some tallow dips had been brought in and we had quite good light.

There was another wounded man laying near, whose

wound had become dry and sore, and in addition he had a bad diarrhea; there was no one to wet it or look after him in any way. I wet his wounds and turned him around and placed him in as comfortable a position as I could, and thus the night passed away.

In talking with some of the rebels, I enquired how the battle had gone, knowing by their looks and actions that things were looking bright for them, and indeed they were feeling good and were free to talk. They said they had driven our boys ten miles, and in the morning were going right straight on to Washington.

Not knowing how much of our army had been engaged, or even where it was, I did not know but it was so, from what I knew of the fight and the licking we got.

With the rebs all around us, and wounded men taking on, with the uncertainities of what was to be on the morrow, [it] made it an exceedingly gloomy night.

18

Guns Shake the Earth

*The morning of the 2d—Taking a walk—Searching
for rations—John Flye—The rag-tag and bob-tail of
the rebel army—The wounded—The fighting of the
2d—The morning of the 3d—The fighting qualities
of some of the men—Their manners—The
drunken Quartermaster—The fighting of the 3d*

O_n the morning of the 2d I was astir early, and did
what I could to make Harvey comfortable, then went
down and saw the other boys, and with Charlie Fay started
out on the street to see and hear what we could and if possible get something to eat. It was still quite early, but there
were soldiers moving around. We went to several houses
and rang their bell but could raise no one. At last we saw a
lady cross the street and enter a house, [so] we knew there
was someone there and went directly and rang the bell. An
elderly lady came to the door, and we asked her if we
could get anything eatable there. She said [we] could not.
Seeing a pump near, I asked her if she could loan us a
towel. I dont know what she thought of that request, for
without saying a word she went and brought one for us, but

her actions showed that she thought us cheeky. Perhaps she thought us rebs, and if so her actions are very excusiable. We went to the pump and gave ourselves a good wash and wiped ourselves on that clean towel, then, going to the door again, we rang the bell and with many thanks returned it to the lady.

There were rebel soldiers everywhere, in the streets, backyards—all around you could see them.

Going up a street that led by the court house, we came to a line of rebels with their guns stacked. Not thinking but what they told us last night was true about our army, we kept right on through their line, going about a rod, when one of them with a gun in his hand said: "Hello Yanks; where you at?" We told him "We're going this way just a little." He said with a smile, "If you Yanks dont wish to get shot, you hadn't better travel that way any farther." We told him we wished to keep within our limits, and were sorry that we had passed them. As he seemed inclined to talk, we felt to take the liberty to ask a few questions, and the first one was: "Where is the union army?" He laughed again and pointed to the hill, said "Look there." We looked in the direction he pointed, and there, sure enough, was the old stars and stripes waveing in the morning sunlight, with a battery its muzzels pointing directly at us. We said, some of your fellows told us last night that the union army were ten miles away, [and] he said "he wished they were, but he thought the fellows had not been where he was." Thinking that the locality might under certain conditions be extremely unhealthy, and not careing to stay so near, or as we were outside their lines, we concluded not to stay there longer and started to go back. We crossed the street and just then a reb came up with a barrel about half full of little crackers; the crackers were an inch square. He turned them down on the sidewalk and cried out as loud as he could yell, "Fall in for rations." The rebs jumped up from all around and came running for their share; other rebs were coming bringing barrels. As they did not extend the invitation to us, we thought it best not to help ourselves, so we passed on.

When we got back to the church we made an examination of our haversacks to see what they contained. In mine I found a piece of pork and about a double handful of hardtack crumbs. Fay could find nothing in his. We fried the pork, and then the crumbs in the fat, and made a pot of coffee using the last we had. We ate this with a relish.

I then went into the church to see the boys. I found there in addition to Ross, Serg't M. H. Walker wounded in foot, Privates G. E. Sprague in chest, M. O'Laughlin in knee, Frank Gould in hip and back, Horatio Culting in head, Albion Vining in foot. Culting, Gould, O'Laughlin, and Sprague all died in a few days. All the boys were in as good spirits as could be expected, and were all pleased to know that the old flag was still in sight. With the exception of Ross they were all in the same room, the vestibule of the church. In the vestry proper was the amputation room. I went in there for a few moments to see how they were doing the business, but it was so full, and the weather so warm, and such an unpleasant odor of ether that I was soon glad to come out. While there I saw a stout young soldier, whose arm had been taken off near the shoulder, just as he began to realize what had been done to him—the puzzeled look, and then the tear that filled his eye when he realized that his good right arm was gone.

While out behind the church in the yard cooking our breakfast, there were rebs and union men, and there two brothers met, one dressed in blue, the other grey, and with the exception of their uniforms both looked just alike. Both were little, red-faced, red-haired, stubby Irishmen, and both blubered, and cried, and hugged each other as only Irishmen can who have a "drop of the sweet cratur in." The union man wanted the reb to go with him and leave the cause of the south, while the reb didn't see how he could go when the union man was a prisoner and would perhaps have to go south whether he wanted to or not. How they decided it I never knew, for I left the yard and never saw them again.

I went up the street to the "Diamond," as they called it—we at home would call it the "Square"—to see and hear what was going on. As I was going along I saw a door open, and thought I would just look in and see how trade was, as it was a country grocery store. As I stepped in I saw it was in posession of a half dozen rebel soldiers, and they were having things all their own way. Some stood on the counter, others were behind, and all were busy; such things as they wanted they laid aside in a pile and the others they gave a toss on to the floor. One of them looking up said, "What does that d——d Yank want?" Thinking my presence might not be agreeable to them, I turned to go out, while they gave one of their peculiar yells.

On going back towards the church I saw a rebel ambulance standing before the door with several of our Surgeons standing besides it earnestly talking. On getting near I heard they were talking about some one in the ambulance. On looking in I saw there, dressed in a rebel uniform and very weak from the loss of blood, John Flye, the first man of our company hit. I told the surgeons that I knew that man, that we were of the same company, and they immediately ordered him to be taken in. Flye was left on the field, and the rebs finding him, and seeing his cloths covered and growing stiff with blood, had exchanged his pants for one of their own, and brought him in. The surgeons, seeing him in grey, could not believe he was a union soldier. Flye died in a few days.

The rag-tag and bob-tail of the rebs came straglin along down the street, and they composed almost every nationality and were of themselves quite an army. I was surprised to see so many in the southern army, for I had thought they had none; this army that I saw I suppose comprised some of the officers servants, for their talk and appearance indicated it. Their outfit comprised almost everything you could think of, from the great Penn farm horse that they [had] stolen from some farmer, and then loaded with whatever pleased their fancy, and almost invariably mounting on top of the whole there were bed blankets, and all kinds of articles, useful as well as ornamental. Tin dishes and straw hats they seemed to have a great liking for. I saw one fellow that had his horse almost loaded down with tin dishes, and another with straw hats, and several that had from one to a dozen. One darkey had three black silk hats on his head and as many more under his arm. One fellow that had an eye to ease and comfort had a horse and wagon and seemed to be taking comfort. I talked with a few of them, but they were very insolent, and were full of the braggadocio, so I refrained from talking and simply looked on.

In the afternoon while [I was] in the church with the boys, the surgeons came around to make an examination of Mike O'Laughlin wound; he was shot through the knee, and the bone was badly smashed. They gave it a pretty thorough looking over, and concluded it must be taken off. Mike cried like a baby when the surgeons made their decision, and plead his poverty and an aged Mother that was dependent on him as a reason why he could not part [with] it. I pittied him, as did all the surgeons, and they promised to wait a few days before taking it off, but poor Mike, he lost his limb and his life as well. We had found out now that the union army was but just outside the town, that from some points we could see the old flag, and indeed our experience of the morning had shown it to our view.

Bullets came whistling over and around, to tell that there was life in the old army still and that they were but a short distance away; but what an insurmountable barrier lay between.

The firing through the day had not been very heavy, only occasionaly a shot being fired to feel the enemy, till just at night it broke out like a tornado in the vicinity of Cemetary Hill. Being wholly unprepared for such a storm, we were taken by surprise and awaited with anxious hearts the results. We knew not how many, or what condition the old army was in.

We could not know whether the new levies of troops had arrived and were taking part, whether it was our men who were attacking or the rebs. All we knew was, that there was a terriable struggle going on near. Our suspense was of short duration for soon the rebels came swarming back down, even as far back as we were, and as I was out on the street at the time, I saw them as they came along and a madder set of men I never saw. They cursed their officers in a way and manner that showed experience in the business, and one that would completely eclipse the best endeavors of a union soldier. It was simply fearful.

I enquired the nature and cause of all this outburst of feeling of some of the quieter ones, and this is the story they told me. They belonged to Hays'[1] brigade of Texas troops and were laying close up under Cemetary Hill when they were ordered to the charge. They said they went up the hill before the gunners had time to depress their pieces

1. Brig. Gen. Harry T. Hays, CSA, in command of a Brigade in Lieut. Gen. Richard S. Ewell's (Second) Corps, Army of Northern Virginia.

to fire at them, and drove the gunners away and were trying to turn the pieces, when the infantry supports of the
batteries came up and they had a short hand to hand conflict. But our boys were too many for them, and they, not
receiving any support, were driven back with considerable
loss. They said it was always so; if there was to be any hard
fighting, they were always the first to be brought in, and
then there was no help given them. They said their officers
didn't care how many were killed, and especially old Hays,
who was receiving his share of the curses. The truth of the
story I cannot vouch for; I only tell it as it was told me by a
crowd of rather excited Texan soldiers at the close of a hot
July day. At any rate, it was a sharp fight with no advantage
to the rebs.

I stayed up and was around on the street a considerable
portion of the night. I slept but little, for the time was filled with big events, and I wanted as far as possible to find
out all I could. There were plenty of rebel officers and soldiers about, and with few exceptions [they] were all free and
willing to talk. I thought the great majority were as anxious
to find out the resources of the North and the feelings of
the people, and about how long we thought the war would
last, as the most homesick union soldier. Of course when
they gained a victory they felt confidant and cheerful, but
as no lasting results were obtained and as a general thing
the Confederacy was losing ground, they were as anxious as
we were for the war to close.

The morning of the third was a most beautiful one, and
as I had nothing to do, no dressing, no breakfast to get or
eat, I was early on the street to get the news and see if
there was any change, but could hear of none. All the
movements of the rebels were kept from us; all we knew of
their contemplated arraingements were what we saw.

Up the street but a few steps was an old, unoccupied
house, and as I passed by it I heard some talking, and

stepped in to see what was going on. There was about an equal number of rebs and union men, and they had found some concentrated water, and having imbibed quite freely, each was trying by argument to convince the other that he was in the wrong. Argument was fast failing and they were about to try the only other way known to them. I took it all in at a glance, and was glad to get out from such a rable. A rebel officer happened to ride by at this time, and as some of the disputants had reached the sidewalk, he stopped and ordered all the rebels to their respective commands, and the union soldiers to keep within their limits. Later in the day the same officer, who was of the Provost Guard, rode down the street, and found one of the rebel soldiers who had not received as much satisfaction as he wished from the morning's debate trying to get up a row with some one. None of the union men wanted to have anything to do, or say to him, and he, thinking that we were afraid of him, had become very insolent and abusive, and was insulting everyone he met. The officer saw him, and rode down so he could hear what the fellow was saying. Finding none of the union men saying anything, but rather trying to avoid him, he spoke up sharp and told the fellow to go to regiment immediately. The soldier, not fully comprehending who or what was being said, seized the horse by the bitts and commenced to run him back. The officer told him to hold on, at the same time using the spur, but the fellow, with a fearful oath, still persisted. The officer drew his pistol, and holding it within an inch or two of the fellows head, told him he would give him just one moment to let go his hold of the horse or he would drop him there on the sidewalk. By this time the fellow began to realize his situation, and who was speaking to him, and quickly dropping his hold of the horse he slunk away down the street and we saw no more of him.

We were now feeling as though we should like something

to eat—could, as the saying is, "eat a raw dog"—for we had had nothing since the morning before when we had cleaned out my haversack. Fay and myself were sitting on the door-steps of a house when a rebel soldier came along with his arm in a sling, he having a slight wound. He stopped and commenced to talk with us. After talking a few moments we said "we wished they would give us something to eat." He asked "if we hadn't received any rations yet." We said "no." He put his hand in his haversack and took out two cakes made of flour, such as I have seen my mother make on top of the stove, and said "he would divide with us." We said "we didn't wish to rob him" but he told us to take it, which we did without further urgeing, and, thanking him for his kindness, Fay and I ate it.

The generous reb

In the church where the boys were was another reb who was a nusiance. He was an Irishman, and done every thing he could to make it unpleasant for them. I was in there when he was walking up and flourishing his fife, and telling what they could, and what they would do with them. I went to talking with him to draw his attention from the boys, and asked him why he was away from his regiment, that all good soldiers would be with their command in times like these and not be up in a hospital taunting wounded men, and added that perhaps he might bring up yet in the guard house.

He was mad with me in an instant, and turned on me in a way and manner that a man will when he knows that the other cannot help himself. He said he was never in the guard house but once in his life, and that was not because he stragled behind, but because he stragled ahead, and that he was not expected to go into battle for he was a musician. He flourished his fife in such close proximity to my head, and was so loud and boisterous that I left the church, he following me, for I knew I could shake him off on the street, or that some rebel officer would pick him up and march him off. I relieved them of his presence for only a few moments, when he came back and was more insolent than ever. He was bearing down so hard that it was unendurable, or at least so thought ———of Company G, who was wounded in the breast. He seized a gun and told him if he didn't leave immediately he would shoot him on the spot. The reb had found his match, and took himself away pretty quick amidst the cheers of the wounded men.

About noon an Officer rode through the street, surrounded by a numerous and brillant staff, that we thought might be Gen'l Lee. I asked a reb who was near if he could tell me who that officer was, and he said he didn't know. He was a man about sixty, quite grey, with a closely shaven face with the exception of a mustache.

In the afternoon, about the time the battle began, a rebel Quartermaster rode along pretty drunk and ugly; he was just spoiling for a fight, and said he could lick any ten d——d yanks there was in the town. As there was none that felt like disputing him, even if we would be let—for if we had shown the least desire for a fight, we would have been shot down like sheep—he rode on down the street continuing his abuse.

There was a public house up on the Diamond that was the headquarters for quite a crowd of rebel officers, and they were lounging around in front of the place. Bullets from the skirmishers were coming over constantly, and one of the officers was wounded in front of the house; some of them swore it was one of our boys that did it, and were going in to clear the streets of the d——d yanks, but the soberer portion thought it was hardly a safe thing to do on so sleight an excuse. The Quartermaster was a fair specimen of some of them.

The fighting had been considerable at different times and places all through the day, and bullets had whistled merrily around with occasionaly a shot of larger size, which would strike a chimney or roof and send the bricks and kindling wood around into the streets below. About three o'clock it broke out like a tornado blast. We that were shut up in the town could see and know nothing of the mighty preperation that had been going on, so we were not prepared for the most terriffic yells and deafning noise of the three hundred guns and the continual roll of musketry that suddenly broke upon us. We held our breath in awe while the dreadful work went on [and] hardly dared to speak to each other, fearing for the results. We all wished for victory, and so we sat, or stood, looking into each others faces, and listened to the dreadful, dreadful noise. I remember now of sitting on a doorstep that hot July afternoon, and heard the roar and din of that mightest battle ever fought on the continent of America. The earth fairly shook, and it did seem as though the heavens and the earth were grinding together. It was simply fearful. Moments seemed like hours, and hours ages, and still the fearful carnage went on. The rebs had

with few exceptions deserted the streets; only one now and
then was to be seen. We in the village were comparitively
safe, being between the two ridges, but the uncertainities that hung over us made it a worse place than if we
could see and hear all that was going on.

But the longest day will have an end, and at length the
fire slackened, and there was only an occasional gun. We
breathed freer, and talked with each other as to the results.
What was to become of us? was the question uppermost in
our thoughts. If our army was defeated, where would we
go, and if victorious, would we be taken away with the
rebel army?

Night settled down upon us without our learning anything of which side had the advantage. I enquired of the
few rebel soldiers seen on the streets, but they could or
would not tell. I thought them bummers, and they had not
been any nearer the fight then we had. When night came
on, most of the union soldiers made themselves scarce, and
the streets were almost deserted. I did not feel like sleep,
although this was the third night that I had slept but little.
I wanted to know what had been the results of all that hard
fighting.

If our army was defeated and I had got to go to some of
the prison pens of the south, I wanted to know it, for there
was an even chance of getting away through the rear lines
of the enemy, and I should take that chance. On the other
hand, if we were victorious and the rebs were going to retreat, I wanted to be where I could be one of the first to
welcome our boys.

I was hungry and sleepy, but both hunger and sleep
were forgotten in our anxieties for the results.

19

Another Enemy

*The night of the 3d—The two rebel soldiers—The
Morning of the 4th—The Quartermaster
again—Leaving the town—At the hospital—"Fay
are you in for it"—The generosity of the citizens of
York Penn.—Rations—Finding the regiment—Our
losses—Dorkham retreat—Jordan a prisoner
—Fleas—Comstock*

A_s the night advanced and I saw so few of the rebs,
I began to feel certain that victory had not perched
upon their banners. Their very silence was an answer, for I
had seen and heard enough in the last three days to know
that they would have let us know in more ways than one of
their success.

I was sitting alone on a doorstep thinking of the events of
the last three days, and watching a company of rebel soldiers under charge of an officer as they came down the
street, halting every few rods and going into backyards and
other places picking up all the rebel soldiers and all the
guns they could find, loading the guns into a wagon that
accompanied them, when a soldier passed up the street

that I thought I knew. He, seeing me and thinking the
same as I did, stopped and came back, we shook hands,
and each in turn enquired where the other had been. He
was a sergeant in Co. I. I told him I had been on the street
every day, at which he was much surprised and wondered
that I had not been sent away. He said he had been hid up
in a cellar since the 1st, and this was his first appearance
out. He was anxious to learn all I knew about the boys, and
also about the fight.

While we were thus engaged, two rebel soldiers came
along loaded down with things that they had confiscated
from a drug store. Each had a large basket filled to the
overflowing with things obtained there, besides pockets
were filled. One had a large jug in his hand, and the other
a large open mouthed jar under his arm.

On seeing us they stopped and bade us good evening.
My comrade who had not been out was a little uneasy and
said nothing. I wished them a good evening, at the same
time rising. They sat their bundles down, and we commenced to talk about the events of the day. They were very
intellegent fellows and knew more then they chose to tell
us, but gave us to understand that although they had got
the worst of the fight today, they were by no means licked,
and when we hinted that perhaps they were preparing to
retreat, they indignantly denied all thoughts of such a thing
and said we would hear more from them in a few days. All
the time they knew they were making preperations for this
end, and they, being familiar with drugs and medicine, had
come into the village to replenish their stock that they were
in need of. After talking a few moments they asked if we
wished to have something to drink. They said they had
some that could not be beat, in the army at least. We both
declined, thinking they wanted to play a trick on us; they,
suspecting, and wishing to relieve us from all such fears,

took the large open mouthed jar up and drank our health in a good draught therefrom, then they passed it to me with the request that I would not disappoint them but drink their health as hearty as they had ours.

As they had not told what kind of liquor the jar contained I drank rather sparingly at first but still without fear, and passed it to my comrade, who followed my example. Then we sat down and talked as only soldiers can; they passed the jar, and we talked on until they were rested, when they rose to go, and—wishing to empty the jar—they passed it again for a final pledge, and we, knowing it was our last chance, took a good long pull, and after [our] shaking hands and bidding each other good night [they] took up their things and departed. They were young men from New Orleans and had worked in a drug store.

They said the liquor was French brandy. I never drank any such before and am very sure I never have since.

My comrade, being a little uneasy, left me. Not wishing to take any risks, he invited me to go with him, but I declined as I was not quite satisfied with all I had seen and heard.

After he left me I walked up and down the streets till I thought there was nothing more to be learned, so, selecting a place that was somewhat retired, I lay down and was soon asleep. I was awakened early in the morning by the rain coming down in a smart shower, and starting up, went for the street. A union soldier who was a prisoner like myself warned me not to venture too far as the bullets were singing merrily around. We waited a few moments and then, peeking out from behind the building, saw a union soldier with a gun in his hand up by the Diamond, then another and another until there was a large squad marched into sight. We motioned them not to fire, but to come to us. They, seeing we were union men, came slowly down, as the rebs were down the street slowly falling back. Those that had been prisoners now came out from the houses and backyards, glad to think and know that we were free again. Some of the boys knew where there was some rebs sleeping and they were made prisoners. Amongst the number was the drunken Quartermaster, who had been sleeping off his bad whiskey, and a more sheepish looking man I never saw then he was. The boys recognizeing him began taunting him by asking him "how many Yanks he could lick this morning?" and, if he felt like taking a turn with any, they would see he had fair play. But the fight was all out of him; he had no desire, was as humble as anyone could wish.

It was soon noised around that Lee had given two hours for the citizens and the wounded to leave the town in, and then he was going to shell it. I did not credit the report, and still did not know but it might be true, so finding **Fay** and going in and bidding the boys good by (for they were not going to be moved), we shouldered our knapsacks and joined the long line of citizens and wounded soldiers over the pike road that leads to Baltimore. One idea of our leaving the town was to see if we could get anything to eat, for we were getting decidedly hungry. In going up a street that led out of the town, we saw an open door, the first we had seen, so we entered in and found an elderly couple seated at a table eating. We asked them if they could spare some for us, offering to pay for all. The man pointed to a few slices of bread, said that was all they had, but we were welcome to a slice; the lady buttered a slice apiece and we ate it, while the man gave some of his experiances of the last three days. Resuming our walk, we continued along until we came to a large barn—about two miles, I should think, from the village. Here was one of the hospitals, and here were hundreds of wounded men of both armies. We tried to get something to eat but there was nothing. Fay said he would go to another farm house that was just over the fields and try his luck if I would furnish the money. I gave him a dollar and told him to get something if it was only salt pork. Fay soon returned without any thing, everything was all ate up. Fay was a hearty eater and needed food more than I did. We again made application at the barn and was told that when some beef that was then boiling was done we could have some. There was nothing to do only wait, so we sat down and patiently waited, if it is possible for a very hungry man to do so.

At last it was announced as done, and those that were waiting were requested to fall into line and receive their ration. We that had dishes fell into line and marched up past the big pot and received about a pint of liquid that a very poor piece of beef had been boiled in. Fay had no cup so as soon as we could we drank the water and Fay fell in and went round, but by the time he reached the pot it was nearly empty and he only received half as much as those first served. It was now well along into the afternoon, and we went and sat down and talked the matter over of what it was best for us to do. We concluded it was best for us to stay and rest where we were and in the morning find the regiment, so we prepared a place behind a fence where we thought we would not be disturbed and at dark lay down. It had rained in showers all day and there were little pools of water all around. I noticed one just behind the fence when we lay down. I was awakened in the night by a stream of water running through where we lay and, rousing up, found it raining hard and we half covered up by water. I said to Fay "are you in for it?" He said "Yes," and we both lay still and let the water go where it would. The cause of our trouble was that some one in the night had hitched a horse to the tree on the other side of the fence and his stamping had loosened the bottom rail which had served as a dam, and let the water down on us.

In the morning we folded our rubber blankets and looked around for rations. The prospects at the barn were not encourageing, so we were turning our attention in another direction when we saw a long string of teams coming up the road and, turning into the field near the barn, we with others went to see who they were and what they wanted. We found they were from York, Pa. and were loaded with food and other goodies contributed by the citizens of that place. After hearing of the victory, they had in a few hours collected enough to load down twenty teams and they had been all night on the way. The food was all consigned to the Surgeon in charge of the Hospital, so there was no prospect of our getting any. I saw one of the drivers eating a big doughnut and, thinking he might have more, asked him if he had any of them to sell. He said he had none, only took those few for a lunch and that was the last. The contents of his wagon he knew nothing about for he only drove the team. Fay and I now thought if we did not wish to starve we must find the regiment, so we started keeping a good watch of everything by the way. We hadn't gone more than half a mile when we saw a colored individual that we knew that belonged to the regiment, [and] we enquired of him if he knew where it was. He said it was up by the village, that the teams had just been up to issue rations and that they were only a little ways from here. This was good news for us, and we went on keeping a good lookout for all teams. At length I saw Dick Wells of the "Commissary"; he saw me at the same time and we had many questions to ask and answer. On [our] arriving at the wagons, he told us to help ourselves, and we soon filled our haversacks with coffee, sugar, pork, and hardtack, the standard articles of a soldiers diet. He told us the regiment was where we fought the first day, and bidding him a good morning, we moved on until we came to a stream of water, where we stopped to cook breakfast. Other soldiers were doing the same, and as fires were already kindled, we soon had a strong cup of coffee with hardtack fried in pork fat. Being very much refreshed and anxious, we put forth extra exertions, for we wanted to be with the boys. We went over the "Hill," stopping for a few moments to see the effects of the shelling in the cemetary, then down town to the Diamond. We were going right on out to the scene of our first days fighting when we were stopped by a union soldier who wanted to know where we were going. We told him, and he said he guessed it was not in that direction, for he was one of the pickets. We returned into the town and went to the hospital, found the boys as well as could be expected, stayed only a few moments, and started to find what it now looked might be a long chase. On coming out I saw Col Coulter of the 11th P.V. and enquired of him. He told me where it was a short time ago, but said the troops were getting ready to move. We went in the direction he told us, and in going out saw a young lady selling onions, [and] bought five or six cents. We went over the fields where the terriable fighting of the 3d had taken place, and on every hand was thickly strewed the effects of the fight. We darst not stop long, although there were many things that attracted our attention and we would like to see. I picked up a sword (and carried it some ways) that I would like to have kept, but threw it away and selected a gun instead. Way down towards "Round Top" we at last found the brigade, or what was left of it. The 13th had 80 men, which was a fair average number. K was commanded by Lt Warner and had seven men; we swelled it to nine. It is needless to say that the boys were glad to see us and hear from others of some we knew nothing of. Major Gould was in command, Col Leonard was wounded, Gen'l Paul[1] lost both eyes. Robinson,[2] our division Gen'l, was wounded, and I dont know how many more were in the hands of the enemy. We had after a tremendious hard-fought fight gained a victory, and there was no doubt of it. The boys were all feeling good over the result, and if the victory were followed up and the fruits reaped, there would be a prospect of peace soon. This made the boys anxious, yes, more than anxious to be on the heels of the fleeing rebels, for it was now known that Lee was in full retreat towards the Potomac. Incidents. Capt Hovey who was on the staff of Gen'l Robinson was badly wounded and Dorkham, when we fell back, found him. Hovey, who was unable to ride, asked Dorkham to take his horse to the rear, an ambulance being provided for him. Dorkham mounted and, as some of the boys said who saw, rode through the streets of Gettysburg at a rate that would have taken him to Baltimore ninety miles away before night. The boys used to laugh at D— for his masterly retreat, but D— was enough for them, for he would say that he saved himself and the Cap't horse, and that was more then some of them did.

Jordan of K, when he was retreating at the full run, a reb in hot persuit, had to jump a little brook. The extra exertion caused his only suspender button to come off and his pants falling down tripped him and he fell headlong into it. While he was recovering himself, the reb came and, laughing at J— perdicament said, "I have a good mind to shoot you." "Show," said Jordan, which increased the rebs laughter, and he took J— along with him. Morris of Co C, who carried the State colors in the fight, was struck on the head

1. Brig. Gen. Gabriel R. Paul, USA, had been in command of the 1st Brigade, 2nd Division, I Corps.
2. Brig. Gen. John C. Robinson, USA, in command of the 2nd Division, I Corps.

Jordan's misfortune

by a shell, and his blood and brains stained the flag and can now be seen in the rotunda of the State House at Boston.

There was an enemy that used to cause the boys considerable trouble and time to keep in a decent state of subjection, and it was no uncommon sight to see many at the same time engaged in this common warfare. One day while in Pa. one of the boys had his shirt off skirmishing when an old citizen came along and stopped to look at him, the soldier taking no notice. "Are they Fleas?" said the old citizen. "Fleas!" said the soldier in a voice of thunder and expressing great indignation. "What do you take me to be, a d——d dog? No, I'm a soldier, and they are lice."

In the fight at Gettysburg, besides being hit on the shoulder, I had a bullet through the inside of my pants of the right leg about three inches below the body, also through the pants of my left leg at the knee. Taking a spear of grass and passing it through from one hole to the other, I had to bend it to get it round my leg. In which ever way I tried, how it could go through my pants and drawers and not injure me, is to me a mystery.

I did not discover the holes in my pants till the next day, and when I rejoined the regiment and showed my wounds (in pants) to the boys, they all admitted a narrow escape for me.

Comstock of K, during the days of fighting, was out on the skirmish line. The officer in charge of them cautioned him when he went out, telling him that there had been several men shot at the post he was going to. Comstock went out, keeping himself well covered behind the banks of earth.

Firing was the amusement of both sides. Directly in Comstocks front was a reb who anoyed him much, for everytime he fired, Johnny Rebs head would peep up and he would fire at him. Comstock, finding out the trick of the Johnnie, thought he would play one on him worth two of the one he was playing; so, taking a gun that had been left there by some one who had been wounded, he loaded it, and putting it over the bank along side of his own, pulled the trigger. Bang went the gun, Comstock having his eye along the barrel of his own; up came Johnnies head to take a look, when bang went the gun, and his head came up no more in sight.

During the 2d and 3d our Corps was not very heavily engaged, although they had to double quick from Cemetary Hill, to the left, during the severe fighting of the 3d.

20

New Men

Again on the move—Rally round the flag—Enthusiasm of the soldiers—The Nine Months men—Lee across the river—Fording Goose Creek—Private Lee—A ration of whiskey —Rappahannock Station—Substitutes—Co. G Man

W_e bivouacked that fifth of July where we found the reg't. Warner, who had been promoted, was in command of Co K. Early in the morning we commenced the persuit of the rebs down over the same road that we had come up. Down past the State Line, through Emmitsburg and many another Maryland village. As we passed through them, the people came out and with water and good wishes welcomed us; if in the advance, pies, cakes, and other goodies were freely given.

At one place where we halted in the afternoon, a gentleman with his family of children came down through the fields from his house which was some distance off on another road, waving the National colors and singing "Rally round the Flag boys, rally once again." It was the first time I had ever heard the song, and coming as it did so soon after one of the fiercest of fights, how it made the blood start with a quickened flow to listen to its soul-stiring strains. Yes, we were willing and more then willing to rally, not only once but many times for its defence.

We marched down on the east side of the ridge and then crossed at Fox's Gap. How well I remember even now of our toiling up that mountain side and then decending into the valley on the other side. It was dark before we halted for the night, and in the morning oh, how it did rain. The first thing I remember was some of the brigade staff officers riding around crying "Fall in, fall in men." How we scrambeled our things together and, without any breakfast, started on the march through the mud, and wadeing the creeks whose waters ran like a race-horse and knee deep. But we were all in good spirits and were anxious, eager, to be let loose upon the fleeing enemy. We crossed the valley and halted a few miles from Middleton near the South Mountain Gap, old and familliar locality. It ceased to rain, and after a few hours rest we crossed to the west side, and fileing off to the right began to build a breastwork, but stopped before they were half done. In the morning we again moved forward through Boonsboro in the direction of Hagerstown. Moving off to the right of the road into a large wheat field, we were ordered to again build breastworks. Why we were here and building works was a topic of considerable discussion amongst the boys. None of us could solve the problem, although there were no lack of sollutions. While on picket one day I accidently overhead the confidential conversation between two of the old citizens living in this vicinity in relation to this mysterious movement of ours. One of them told the other that Gen'l Howard told him that the rebel army would be driven up here and we behind the works would stop them and there then would be the surrender and they would see it. It pleased

A private talk

them much and we had a good laugh over this, an entirely new solution. Henry Wilson visited one day while [we were] laying here. We moved towards Funkstown and at last took our place in the long line of the army, building good and substantial breastworks.

The question was often asked "why were we lying around here ideling away our time?" "Why were we not moving on the enemy?" Were the McClellan tactics to be again used and the rebs again escape? It began to look like it. O how we wished we had "Old Joe";[1] how he would [have] pressed and fought and drove that rebel army! The Lord was indeed on our side, for it rained every day and the "Old Potomac" was running with full banks, which made the crossing very difficult. It was a very critical time for Lee

1. Maj. Gen. Joseph Hooker, USA.

and his army. We thought then, and I have no reason to think otherwise now, that if Meade had pushed as we had a reason to expect he would, he might have taked a large portion of the rebel army and destroyed a vast amount of the munitions of war. Report said that at a "council of war" held at this time, Howard,[2] Wadsworth,[3] and some others of the newly appointed officers were for moving on the enemy immediately, while others and by far the greater part were for delay, and their council prevailed. There is no question but what the rebels would have made a most desperate resistance and there would have been hard fighting and there would have been a long list of killed and wounded on both sides, but in the end would it not have payed; would it not have saved thousands of lives and millions of treasures; for with the army of Va destroyed, the cause of the rebels would have been most desperate. But, say some, how if the Union army had been licked. All I have to say is, that would have been impossible, for the Union army were flushed with victory and reinforcements were constantly arriving, and food and ammunition were in abundance, and from my own personal knowledge had confidence in their officers to an extent never before seen and it would have taken a larger force then Lee commanded to stay their onward march.

On the other hand, Lee's army was a defeated one; they were not on the "sacred soil" but far from their supplies, short in food and ammunition, with an angry river running between them and safety. From my own personal experiance these were most depressing things for a soldier.

While we were lying here, a brigade of nine months troops from old Mass came up to join the army, [and] some

2. Maj. Gen. Oliver O. Howard, USA, commanding the 11th Corps.
3. Brig. Gen. (later Maj. Gen.) James S. Wadsworth, USA, commanding the 1st Division of the I Corps.

of them came up to our works. We were behind a great
bank of earth taking our ease, with the skirmishers in the
woods in front. Some of them, not having the remotest idea
of a battle, asked if we sent men into the field in our front
to do the fighting.

Another told of a great battle he had been in down on
the Blackwater, and how animated he grew as he told how
they sent a whole company around to flank the enemy. We
asked "How many were killed and wounded?" He said
"None were killed but one man had his thumb shot off, but
he guessed he shot it off himself." We laughed and told
them to wait and perhaps they might be engaged in a fight
where a whole army corps would be needed to do the
flanking.

But while we waited Lee was straining every nerve to
get across the river. One day was worth a thousand men to
him. He knew the value of time, so, keeping a bold front,
he pushed forward the means for crossing and soon had the
satisfaction of taking his whole army across, losing only a
few pickets.

If we did not see it, still it was true that a great step had
been taken towards the final closing of the war. The rebs
had been defeated and their prestiege as fighting men had
been broken. They were found, everything being equal, to
be no better fighters then the union men.

Again we were on the move, going down the river, crossing the Blue Ridge, and bringing up at Berlin where we
immediately crossed the river into Va. We went on again
down through "Old Loudon," a good place for forage and
freely indulged in by the boys.

I could relate many amusing incidents of the foragers on
this march. We were few in numbers, all old and tired
men, and disipline was scarcely known amongst us. There
was more or less skirmishing but no results.

I remember of fording Goose Creek one hot summers

day where the water was three feet deep if you could keep
in the right place, but if you turned but a very little to
down stream, to four. Some of the boys plunged right in,
not careing for the wet; others would take off their pants
and, tucking up their shirts, go through dry with the exceptions of their coat tails. I chose the later way as there was
time enough, so strapping my pants and boots on my back
and taking a middle course, I got through all right, but
when I reached the opposite bank could not climb up, for
the banks were steep and so many had gone before that it
was only one mass of soft slippery mud. There was nothing
to stick to; it all wanted to stick to you. Others were in the
same perdiciment, and after vainly trying several times and
slipping back each time, I got a friendly hand and came out
all right at last with dry pants and boots. The Gen'l sat on
his horse and laughed as though he enjoyed it.

Down near Harmony where we bivouacked one night,
Lee of K went out to forage. Night came on and he was
wanted for guard, but he had not returned. Morning came,
and we were ordered to march, but no Lee. Where was
he? but no one could answer. We moved on, some of the
boys taking his gun and equipments, [and] about noon he
turned up and reported for duty. He said he went to a
house and they gave him something that was in harmony
with his feelings and he imbibed so freely that he knew
nothing till after we had moved; when he came to himself
he started without even a look or a smile.

We marched down through old and familliar places until
one morning early we found ourselves down on that ridge
at Rappahannock Station, the rebs holding the two little
hills across the river.

Gen'l Buford[4] with a brigade of Cavalry was waiting for
the first streak of dawn to ford the river and charge their

4. Brig. Gen. John Buford, USA, commanding the 1st Division of the Cavalry
Corps.

camp, while we with our rifles were to aid. The rebs, being on the alert and mistrusting what might be up, left on the double quick at the first sign of movement on our part. Buford crossed, and charging across the wide plane, took a few prisoners. We remained on the hill side for several days and, as it rained, the surgeon ordered a ration of whiskey to a man. We sent for it and when the man came back he passed near the Col tent (Col Batchelder). He called to the man and asked how much he had. He showed it to him. The Col. thought a moment and told the man he had not enough, and stepping inside, wrote that the surgeon had ordered a full ration and he should accept nothing less. The man went and showed the commissary the Col. note and soon returned with a double amount. When he came to our quarters and told his story, we sent him to the Col. with [a] canteen full as his share.

I mention this to illustrate the way in which some commissaries filled their orders. How easy it was to send half rations when full were ordered, and charge for full, not only in whiskey—for that was not issued, only on special occasions such as a long and weary march, exposure to the wind and rain—but in everything that was needed, short weight in coffee, sugar, pork, beef and hardtack and full weight charged to the men, the government paying and the commissary putting the money in his pocket while the poor soldier went hungry.

We moved up the river a short distance and pitched a regular camp. The weather was exceedingly warm and during the day we did nothing but lay around in the shade until we received our first installment of substitutes. I wish I could pass over in silence these men; yes, they were men in form but posessed but few of the traits that govern men. To think that men and town of the loyal north should send down such to be companions and associates of in many instances their sons and brothers and then say the army was corrupting the morals of the young men. Life in the army was very different from life at home. In the one place we could chose our companions and those we wished to associate with, but in the army how different. Here we were of necessity thrown together; there was no choseing. When we took our place in the ranks perhaps it was between two of those desperate characters. We also had to draw rations with each other, and although we need not lay under the same blanket, yet we could not lay very far apart, and is it a thing to be wondered at that the boys should to a certain extent inhale into their system some of this poisonous element when the atmosphere all around was filled with it. And to-day as I look upon the good citizens who were soldiers and went through that trying ordeal, I say they are men who have been tried as few have been and are worthy the best wishes if nothing more of the community in which they live.

How well I remember that morning of getting up and going with Warner out to the vacant space between our tents and headquarters to see the subs who had come in, in the night, and how sadly we went back after looking at them, for of all the worst specimens of humanity, here they were. I dont know as there were any outright murderers, still there were those who had been engaged in riots in New York and had hung Negros to lamp posts, but all other classes of villians were represented, picked up from the slums of the cities. There was almost all nationalities, from the cockney of "Old Hingland" to the "Creole of Cuba." There was two hundred of them when they started from Boston to join us, but about a dozen had been shot or drowned on the voyage out in trying to escape. After breakfast we went up to hear the roll call and see them as they answered their names. Many had forgotten the name they gave when they enlisted, and others would try to make them believe that was their name when one was called and there was no answer. There was less than a hundred men in our regiment and the prospect of having this crowd turned loose upon us was not pleaseing. They were divided into clans, or clicks, and they would steal, fight, and do almost everything to each other clan; a great many had their pants slit open either up or across in the vicinity where a man is supposed to have his pocket book. Our regiment was excused from all other duty but to look after the subs, eighteen [of whom] were assigned to K Co. Their conversation was foul, with almost every other word an oath. Gambling was a favorate ammusement with them; some would gamble all day, and then all night.

They were a little afraid of the old boys, and if we did not leave our things lying too loosely around, they did not trouble them. There was an old Portugese amongst them and one day he got fearfully mad with one of the subs, and slipping his long sheath knife up his sleave and shaking all over with rage, he cried in his broken English, "Go with me to the bush; go with me to the bush," but the sub[s], who were not all brave men, did not dare to go, and the matter was dropped for the time being, perhaps to be taken up at some other time.

Gambling was now a common thing. I remember of lying in my tent one day with the end open and Co G's tents now pitched along side, so I could lay in my tent and look directly into theirs. Soon three men came; one appeared to be pretty drunk and the others were helping him. The drunken man belonged there, but the other two belonged to the 12th Mass. From their conversation I learned that they had been gambling and that the 13th man had won a good share of their money, and they were waiting for him to get sober enough so they could play a few more games and give them a chance to win back some of their money, but the longer they waited the drunker he grew, till at last it was with the greatest difficulty they could make him speak. Finding all their labors in vain with him, and with a promise to see him the next day, they left. The sleeper, after they had been gone a few moments, jumped up as sober as I was, and turning to me with a hearty laugh said, "I wonder how much they made this time." He said he had been out playing with them and having won all their money had lent them five dollars apiece and had won that, [then] concluded not to play any more and took this way to get rid of them.

"The guard house was immediately filled by the most desperate. Some were ironed together and orders were to shoot any that should attempt to escape. We tried to drill them and make soldiers of them, but it was a rather difficult task. I took about half of the subs of K Company down before a board of surgeons to have them examined, [and] they pronounced them old, diseased men and unfit for the service. I was in and saw the examination and I never saw such men before.

They did not stay a great while with us, but deserted as fast as oppertunity offered. Those of our command who had been taken prisoners at Gettysburg and paroled there now rejoined us. The government not recognizing their parole, they had been at York, Pa. having a good time. Heath, the recruit that fell out on our march to Thoroughfare Gap over a year ago, was now sent to us as a deserter and was confined in the guard house.

The last of Sept we moved over the river down towards the Rapidan. Guns were given the Subs and they were put to doing duty; when on the march if they got tired they would throw them away and at night go to the camp of some other regiment and steal them some. Haversacks were continualy lost in the night and great precaution was taken to keep them. I used to pull off my boots and place them under my head for a pillow, with the strap of my haversack and canteen around my neck.

The 16th Maine was a great sufferer in this respect, so much so that complaint was made and the Subs were searched and questioned to find if they posessed anything that did not belong to them. Nothing was found, but orders were issued to arrest all found outside their camp. This order applied more especily to the subs. After marching and halting, we found ourselves down again by the Rapidan.

21

On Unlucky Ground

*Frenchy the sweet singer—The execution—The
story of the Sub—Fording the Rappahannock—Retreat—Centreville—Jordan and the tobacco—Again on the advance—Scenes around
the campfire—Incidents*

*A*mongst the Subs was a Frenchman who was a sweet
singer, and many were the nights we used to sit and hear
him sing; he always sang in French.

One cold night after a hard days march we had made our
coffee and were sitting around our camp fire smoking. We
got Frenchy to sing. The Marseillaise Hymn was a great
favorite with us, and Frenchy could sing it in a way that
only a Frenchman can. I dont know whether it was in the
air or what it was, but we all said we never heard sweeter
singing than on that cold and clear evening in Oct. Before
he had finished one verse the regiment began to gather
around and as he proceeded the men from other reg't's
came, and soon we had nearly the entire brigade around
our little fire. After [his] singing a song or two, the Col. sent
for him to come to headquarters, and Frenchy was there
singing when I went to sleep.

One day the whole division was ordered out into a field and, after forming three sides of a square, we ordered arms to await results. Near the centre was an open graye and a coffin beside it, and coming nearer and nearer was the sound of the muffled drum. Soon a dozen men in charge of officer marched in, followed by an ambulance in which was a soldier condemned to be shot for desertion. Beside him was a priest. They went to near the grave, when he was

The execution

taken out and seated upon his coffin, then blindfolded with his hands tied behind him and legs strapped together. The soldiers were drawn up before him and at the command ready, aim, fire, the fellow fell back and all his earthly accounts were forever settled. We shouldered arms and marched back to camp, having witnessed an event that was becoming common. At another time we were ordered out in a drenching rain to witness what would have been another execution and this time a man of our own regiment.

The circumstances are these. After the subs came to us and we had drilled and we got somewhat acquainted, guns were given them and when we moved they were expected to do a soldiers duty. One night when we were in the face of the enemy, he with others were detailed for picket, and while on his post deserted. He had told some of his chums before that he intended to desert to the enemy. When daylight came and he was between the lines, his courage failed and he stayed between the lines all day hid. At night we moved, [and] he started back, thinking he could reach New York where he knew he would be safe, but after swimming the Rappahannock he was picked up by the Cavalry and sent to the army. As desertions were of daily occurence, examples must be made, so he was to be tried by courtmartial and sentenced to be shot. His friends in N. York, for he had powerful ones, went to Archbishop Hughes to have him intercede with President Lincoln, and the result was a reprieve [that] came after we were ordered out and his grave dug. He served the remainder of his time in a penitentiary in New York.

The rebs were again in motion after the departure of the 11th and 12th Corps to reinforce the western army, consequently they were trying their old game of flanking the army. As we were not large in numbers and a good ways from our supplies, a retreat was ordered; the rebs finding we were on the move quickly followed. I remember how close they followed us as we went toward Kelly's Ford. We were the rear guard of infantry and the cavalry constantly skirmished all the way. We reached the Ford at dusk and as there was but one pontoon bridge and that was being used by the teams and artilery, we had to ford it. The water to a short man like myself came to my waist and I had to hold my cartridge box up to keep it dry. After crossing we were halted on the banks and were not allowed any fire; the nights were cold, and with our wet cloths and no coffee we passed a very uncomfortable night. Towards morning, with others, I went for wood, and after a half mile we found a fence and each taking as many rails as he could carry, we went back and built a fire.

The reason we were not allowed a fire earlier was, they were afraid of shells. We laid at the ford two or three days when one morning before light we started back, coming out to the Orange and Alexandria railroad near Bealeton. Heavy firing had been heard by us all day up at that old familiar place Rappahannock Station. When we crossed a ridge and came in sight of Bealeton, there was a sight that I shall never forget, for in park, covering acres of ground and as far away as the eye could see, were the white covered wagons of the army. The whole train of the army had been in park here, but were now starting and winding their way, not in single file but three or four abreast towards Bristoe, Manassas, and Centreville. I had no idea before that there was so many teams, for we had never been so near the rear before, and it came very near being the front this time and that accounts for our presence here. It was now a foot race with the rebs and us to see which would get to Centreville first. How we marched! The weather was fine, and we were in good spirits, although we could not exactly understand this movement, yet we were determined that no Johny Reb could beat us in marching over such old and familiar ground. We slept a few hours at Bristoe, and then forward was the word. The wagons of the army filled the roads and the troops the fields. When nearing Manassas our regiment was thrown out as flankers and thus we toiled on to Centreville. Manassas, Bull Run, and Centreville were to us unlucky ground; twice had a battle been fought there, and twice had we been thoroughly whipped. Were we again to try our fortunes in a battle that had such an unfavorable omen for us? We formed a line of battle on the western slope near Cub Run and awaited events. No enemy appeared, the teams were being parked at Centreville and beyond, other corps began to arrive, and we breathed freer then we had for several days. The day after our arrival, the rebs foiled of their plans but hoping to inflict some loss upon the army, attacked the rear division of the 5th Corps at Bristoe. The Gen'l formed his line in a cut in the railroad which served for a breastwork, [and] they were repulsed with slight loss. We stood under arms while it lasted. We stayed here a few days and then marched towards Thoroughfare Gap. When we marched away, Frenchy's gun and knapsack were there but no Frenchy; he had deserted [and] we never heard his sweet singing again. Crossing the battlefield of the 2d Bull Run, I noticed many familiar objects but, not stopping, I had not as much time to look around as I wished. As we passed a tree, a grinning skull protruded from the ground—some poor fellow hastily burried and the rain had washed the earth away.

One night just as we were preparing to bivouac, a shower of bullets came whistling over our heads, startling us a little, but it was only a nest of Guerrillas that we had started up. We moved on through the Gap and pitched our tents, forming a regular camp, the first for many days.

The Sutler had not been with us since leaving the Rapidan, consequently tobacco was very scarce with us and those who were fortunate enough to posess the article could get promises to pay of fabulous sums. I had a very small piece about an inch square that I had carefully guarded and used very sparingly. One day, being on brigade guard and not thinking but what the other regiments had tobacco in plenty, I filled my pipe and was commencing to smoke, when a crowd of 16th Maine boys all [began] saying "Cant you give me a small piece? I haven't had a chew for three days," or, "I havn't smoked for a week." I could not resist their appeals, so giving all I had with me to the Corporal, told him to divide.

Jordan, who was detailed as cook for the Col., came to me and said if he had some money he knew where he could buy some of a teamster. Money was almost if not quite as scarce as tobacco. I had a little money, but not wishing to part with all I gave him a half dollar, telling him that he could have half that would buy. He took it and I did not see him for over a week, [and] then he had no tobacco for me or anyone else. I said nothing to him about it, [but] I afterwards found out by some of the boys what Jordan done with my half dollar and after laughed at my expense.

Col Batchelder had no money or tobacco, and being an inveterate smoker, offered Jordan a fabulous sum if he could find him a piece. Jordan, who was priviledged to go back to the teams, found a teamster who had a piece he would sell for cash, but would take no promise to pay, so he came to me, knowing I always had money. He bought the tobacco and gave it to the Col., and at pay day received his pay and then told the boys of the joke he had played on me. I failed to see where the joke came in and afterwards there was trouble between us.

In about a week we moved away, and coming upon the teams, John Hill found a teamster that had a plug of Navy that he would sell for one dollar. He brought the man with him and the tobacco. Hill, Rawson, and Sanborn would each take a piece and pay me at pay day. I was always willing to accommodate, so I paid the dollar and the boys were again happy.

We twisted around and camped a few days at Bristoe near where the fight was a few days before, when we halted here the first night. Heath the stragler laid his coat down near the fire where we were making coffee; some of the boys discovered that pest of the soldier "Army Crums"[1] had taken posession and, not wishing to have them so near, took a stick and pushed the coat into a hole a few rods away. Heath soon returned and missed the coat, declared that some one had stole it. How he tore around and swore he would lick the man that had. After we had plagued and laughed enough for one time, we told him we saw it going toward a hole, and perhaps if he looked quick he might find it before they had time to bury it all up. Heath took the hint and said no more about it.

One day as we marched along we saw Gen'l Custer[2] with his long golden locks.

One windy day as we were resting in a field where the grass was long and dry, some of the boys built a fire for cooking. Some of the sparks blew into the grass and before anything could be done the fire went up through the 16th Maine and down toward the Rappahannock River with the speed of a race horse, throwing up huge volumns of black smoke as it went through the pine forests.

Still moving, we reached the vicinity of Kelly's Ford. The rebs on the opposite bank disputed our passage, but our success at Rappahannock Station caused them to fall back. A pontoon was laid and we quickly crossed after the retreating rebs. Our corps was sent back towards Rappahannock Station, [and] after a hard march we bivouacked at night in a shrub oak lot. As it was growing cold fast, some half dozen of us started off for rails before it got dark, prefering to get rails before we made coffee. Others made their coffee first and trust to luck for a fire. A few picked out a good place and scraped a few twigs and sticks, built a small fire, and

1. Lice.
2. General George A. Custer, USA. He was later killed in the famous Battle of the Little Big Horn on June 25, 1876.

taking the best places, waited our coming. The first to arrive with his back load did not like the way they had planned, so he picked out another place about two rods off, where he threw down his rails and was building a fire when I came in. He invited me to his place and I threw my wood with his; another came in and threw his wood with ours, [and] we were getting quite a pile, and if a soldier likes anything on a cold night it is a prospect of a good fire, and ours was good indeed while the others was decidely bad. Dorkham [was] coming in just now and if they could prevail on him to stop with them, they might get through the night quite comfortably, so they pressed him quite hard to stop with them. Dorkham looked for their rail pile but could see nothing. While their fire was fadeing out, our fire was blazeing brightly in the growing darkness. He threw his wood with ours [though] we had said nothing to him, being busy with our suppers. Dorkham got his cup and was soon making coffee, as busy as any of us, when over came a lump of earth striking dangerously near his cup. He looked up and told them to be careful, but they were not pleased and soon over came another without doing any damage. Dorkham made a remark and some of the boys warned them that possibly they might throw one too many if they kept on.

My coffee was just on the point of boiling and I had it suspended on a stick when over came a root, striking my cup and spilling a little. I was mad, and setting my cup down I told them that was played out and if there was anything over here they wanted they could have it pretty quick. Sanborn, who threw the stick, was mad and he said he could lick any two of us, and if I did not shut up he would lick me now. I told him he had better try it on, for braggin had never licked anybody yet, and I felt to have him try. He started for me and I would have met him half way for I would have fought him then with the certain knowledge of getting whipped, [but] the boys of Sanborns fire caught him and those of my party me, and the whole thing was soon forgotten. Before morning they were all up around our fire, glad to sit or lay on the smoky side.

Three or four of us had chipped in and bought a hatchet, and we used to take turns in carrying it. The one that carried it today used it first at night to pitch his tent, after which it went the rounds. Dorkham and I were tenting together and I sent him to get the hatchet of Vining, who had his tent pitched. He came back and said he could not get it. I started for Vining and wanted to know why Dorkham could not get the hatchet. He said he did not know that we were pitching together so had let it to Rawson, Sanborn & Co. He got it quickly for us though.

Those men always wanted the first and the best, without giving anything in return.

22

There's One in Every Group

Camp at Licking Run—Nig Wilson and some in-
cidents in his army life—Cutting railroad
ties—Old Heath and some of his doings when in
camp

W_e recrossed the Rappahannock and went up the railroad
to a place called Licking Run, where we pitched a
camp in a thick pine grove. The subs of our company had
almost all left us. I think there was no more than a half a
dozen left. The weather was cold and we done nothing but
eat and keep warm. Nig Wilson, one of the subs who had
deserted and was captured and brought back, had by some
hocus pocus arrangement escaped punishment and [was] sent
to the company for duty. One morning after roll call, instead of making his coffee with the others, he went back to
sleep where he lay till about nine o'clock, then coming out
of his tent and finding the fires all out in our street, looked
over and saw one in Co G's where Old Bluler was cooking
a pot of soup. Nig walked over and put his pot on where
Bluler had taken his off for a moment. When B— was
ready to put his on again there was no room. He sat his pot

down and was going to enlarge the fire when Nig told him to stop. Bluler then wanted to know whose fire it was when Nig up and knocked him down, kicking his pot away and stomping him in the face. Nig then ran back to his tent and crawled in under his blanket and pretended to be asleep. Bluler cried murder and the boys were out from every quarter. Bluler knew him and told who it was and the Officer of the day came over to arrest him. Nig denied all knowledge of the affair, said he had not been out of his tent since roll call, and that Old Bluler was mistaken, when an officer of Co G. who had been standing at the head of the street [and] saw it all confirmed B— story. Nig was taken up before the Col., who immediately called a drum head court martial to try him. It was such an unprovocked one that he was sentenced to be tied up by the thumbs unless he owned up. With the most fearful oaths he stoutly denied all knowledge of the affair. He was taken to a large pine tree in rear of Col. tent where he was tied, his feet standing firmly on the ground with his arms up and thumbs tied to a limb. It was about noon when his sentence commenced. His chum made him a pot of coffee and stole up there and thought to feed it to him but the Col. saw him and ordered him away, saying he would serve him in the same way if he caught him there again trying to feed him without orders. Nig stood it all afternoon and when taken down and allowed to come to his quarters was as ugly and defiant as ever, swearing with fearful oaths that he would never give in. The next morning it was cold and the wind sighed through the branches of those pine trees and made us shiver clear through.

He was allowed to cook his breakfast, after which he was taken up to the Col. and a chance was given him to acknowledge his guilt, but he was still defiant and he was again tied up in the old place; he was ugly and defiant and determined not to give up. The Col. asked once or twice during the forenoon if he was not ready to give in, but still a surly no. About noon the weather growing colder and the wind coming down through the trees pierced to the bone. Nig could stand it no longer, completely broke down and begged to be released. He was willing to own up that he knocked Bluler down and kicked him [and] after he was down he cried like a baby. He was released and, after being cautioned about his future behavior, sent to his quarters.

The Orange and Alexandria railroad was now undergoing repairs, and a large force of contrabands were employed in cutting sleepers and laying the tracks. We used to have to repair the roads every time we advanced, and every time we retreated it was torn up, bridges were burned, and for miles the track would be destroyed. If on a fill the whole track would be taken up bodily and thrown down; another way was to pile the sleepers up in a pile, place the rails on them and set fire, [then] when red not, take the rails by the ends and twist them around a telegraph pole. These were called Jeff Davis necktie. If the time was too short, pile stones or other sleepers on the ends and when hot they would bend—anything to make them of no use. As the contrabands were not doing it fast enough, a detail was made from the brigade. I was one of the detail with six others from the company and over two hundred from the brigade. We started in the morning and marched about four miles down the tracks and halted and waited for the axes. After they came we hung them and marched two miles further to the woods where we made a camp and prepared to chop.

We were to cut down trees of a certain size and cut them off a certain length and hew one side. Some of the boys had never cut a tree in their life and knew nothing of falling down a tree. Some would chop all round and let it fall whichever way it would; one hardly knew when he was safe, but there was one good thing, the trees did not fall very fast. Old Heath was taken from the guard house and was one of our number. The boys all chopped firstrate the first day and were tired when night came. Health couldn't sleep any more than an Owl so he was up prowling around to see what he could find.

Sometime in the middle of the night I was awakened by Heath saying in a half whispered tone, "Haskell, Haskell, get up and come with me. I've found a calf," but Haskell was tired and told him to go away. Heath urged but Haskell still refused, until at last Heath took his axe and went away. When I awoke in the morning Heath had the hindquarters of a calf all dressed and was distributing it out to the boys. I had a generous slice for breakfast. Heath came to me while eating and said if I would excuse him [from] chopping he would get a kettle and make a veal soup for dinner. I told him to go ahead for I thought more of the dinner than I did of his work, and if he made a success I would excuse him all day. We all chipped in of our hardtack and went for the woods. Not having the fullest confidence in Heath, about ten I sent a man to help him. He

Getting dinner

found him fast asleep on our blankets and no preperations for dinner save a pot which he had before we went out. He woke him and they both went at it, and when we came in at noon it was nearly done. I have forgot to mention that the hard bread at this time was very wormy—a large white worm, and when eating the bread, if not very careful, they would get in your mouth, and the juice flying up in the roof would cause you to spit immediately. In the top of the soup floating around were several of these not very palitable articles of food; they had at first, when breaking up the bread, tried to pick them out but as the time was short and there was so many of them they had turned the whole in and were now dipping them out with a spoon. We ate our dinner and Heath was allowed to sleep all the afternoon.

At night there was every indication of rain, so four of us pitched a tent and fixed up around to keep the water out. Four in a tent made it crowded so we had to lay spoon fashion; as I lay on the outside it was no easy matter to keep dry. We drew a ration of whiskey that night and saved some for the morning.

It rained in the night hard and those of the boys that could keep dry were in no hurry to get up. Heath who was never sleepy in the night time was up and away telling Jack Hall before he went what a good breakfast he would have, that he had saved four or five pounds of the best of veal and had it in his knapsack. After he had gone Hall opened it and found it, also his whiskey. He took out the meat, drinking the whiskey, and when we got up gave us the steak. We cooked and ate it, not knowing but it was all right. We were sitting around the fire smoking when Heath came back. He had been out prowling around to see what he could find and not being successful was hungry and tired. He went to his tent when he came in, and stayed a few moments, when he came to the fire and tried to hire Haskell to cook his breakfast, offering to share in as good a one as could be found, there at least. Haskell declined and then he tried Hall, but he refused also. Heath was mad and went to his tent growling about what he had done for us being up all night and then we were so d—n mean we would not cook a breakfast. He soon came out boiling with rage and swore that Haskell had stolen his meat. Haskell denied, but Heath was positive; he declared that no one but Haskell had been to his tent. He swore revenge and tore around like a mad man, he started for an axe, saying he would chop Haskell to pieces. The rumpus was attracting the attention of the rest of the detail, so I thought it time to interfere. I went to Heath and asked him what he had lost and the circumstances attending it. He said he had saved a little piece of the meat, enough for his breakfast and laid it away in his knapsack, and that when he came in a few moments ago he saw the meat, but when he looked just now it was gone. I asked him if he was sure he saw it, and he said he was just as sure as he stood there talking. I told him if this was the truth, and I could back it up by every man there, that Haskell could not by any possible means have taken his meat. And I told him more, that if he didn't want to be put under arrest he had better keep a little quiet, for there was an enquiry going around of who had killed a calf, and that a new axe had been found, and that a search was going to be made of the detail as soon as it stopped raining to see who was short an axe, and that instead of quarreling with his friends about a little meat he had better be looking up his axe. This calmed him, for he had a great horror of being put under arrest again. The joke was that we, all of us, had eaten every morsel of his meat an hour before he said he saw it. Heath soon had an axe. An order was issued to search, but as it continued to rain and the men were so badly provided with shelter, it was deferred until we turned in our axes the next day. My men all had an axe. Heath and Haskell were on the best of terms before night. Some of the boys went over to the house where the calf was owned and saw the place where it was killed; there was a safe guard there and how anyone could kill and get away without a noise no one knew, only Old Heath. The next night we were ordered back to camp. The rain had softened up the ground and those six miles were hard ones to march.

We arrived in camp about nine P.M., all but Heath and Haskell, and had eaten our supper and were sleeping soundly when I was awakened by Heath calling out "Orderly, Orderly, for the love of God get up and get Haskell and I some soft bread for we are nearly famished." The orderly told him to go away or he would put him in the guard house, and I heard no more from him that night.

23

A Visit Home

*J*ohn Parra, who was a Cuban, and a sub was in his tent one night, when he heard some one stepping and soon a hand came in and began to feel his person over. He was frightened and crawling out ran calling for the Sergeant. We told him to take his bayonet and if he was troubled again to stick it into them. He wanted to know if he should stick their faces and we told him to mark them no matter where he hit. We soon moved down to within a mile of Rappahannock Station. The Purveyor came up with quite a quantity of provisions and as we were liable to move at any time he was anxious to sell. The next day was Thanksgiving at home, [and] we thought to have something extra, so a few of us chipped in and bought some flour. I bought a lb. of sausage and sweet potatoes to make out the dinner. Just at night the order came to move at six A.M. We then started in on the cooking and what I couldn't eat of my sausage and potatoes I packed in my knapsack. The flour we ate or gave away.

We were up and away before light. It was a clear, cool, frosty morning and when the sun came up how it made things sparkle. We crossed the river and bore away towards the Rapidan, which we reached and crossed just at dark, going but a short distance when we went into bivouac.

As soon as I could lay off my traps and gun, I started for a rail fence that was close by. There were so many of my way of thinking that the rails disappeared faster than I walk. I started on the run and soon had three good rails on my back, troops were still marching in, and soldiers with rails were going and fires were being built in all directions. I could not tell in what direction my reg't was, but after one or two enquiries I came out all right. I cooked and ate the remainder of my Thanksgiving supper, thinking I had well earned it. The night was cold and with some wind before morning, the cold had routed us up, and all the extra rails were on the fire. The reveillie sounded at five A.M. and at six we had again taken [to] the roads or fields. The teams blocked the roads so our progress was slow. We moved towards Fredericksburg until we passed the Wilderness tavern and turned on a dirt road and came to the plank road that led to Orange C. H. While waiting for the teams to get over the dirt road, we heard the sharp crack of a rifle near the crossing of the roads. We stood to arms while the staff hurried to find the cause. How the straglers and bums came out through the woods towards us. The scare was caused by a squad of rebs watching their oppertunity, dashing out at the junctions of road and shooting a few mules and trying to run off some of the wagons.

The road was out of repair, yet we moved at a faster rate. After going several miles and hearing the booming of guns, we turned off and went through the woods. It commenced to rain and we were halted at dark and lay there through the night; no fires were allowed. In the morning the 13th were thrown forward as skirmishers, K company on the left, and my place being on the left I was the last man. We found the rebs in our front posted behind the run called Mine.[1] While out there Gen'l Meade and staff rode up and he asked of me if we had seen any rebs in that direction, pointing to the left. I told him we had not. Just then an aide of Gen'l French[2] rode up and reported the arrival of his corps. Meade asked where French was; the aide replied that the Gen'l had gone to Robinson tavern to report to him. Meade, with a look that expressed supreme displeasure, said with an oath that he had not been there since morning and that he had ordered him to report to him here.

The corps arriving, they were sent to the left and Meade rode away. The corps forming on our left releived most of the men of K company and we got behind a little hill, made a small fire and were making coffee. Dorkham was there and, his coffee commencing to boil, he made a spring and dropped his mitten at the edge of the fire. I saw it and said, "Dorkham, your mitten is in the fire." He snatched it away and straightening himself up turned to me and said, "What['s] that to you, you have been feeling inferior to me for several days." It was not a smothered laugh that went up from around that fire and for a long time it was a querie how anyone would feel if he was inferior to Dorkham. We were soon releived and we drew back into the woods where we slept till morn.

Before light [we] were arroused and ordered to leave every thing that would make a noise, and marched off to the right where a strong column of troops were being

1. The engagements at Mine Run, Va., on November 26-30, 1863.
2. General William H. French, USA.

formed. It had cleared off in the night, and a strong wind was blowing fresh from the northwest. How we shivered and shook as we stood waiting for something to turn up, we did not know what. At length it was announced that we were part of a column being formed to make a charge. We were formed five lines deep; we were in the second line. A gun on the right, another in the centre, and still another on the left, would announce that all was ready, after which an hours cannonadeing and then the charge by the infantry. The signal at right, in the centre, but no response from the left, an Aide rode away to ascertain the cause and we were ordered to rest on our arms. Soon it was known that Warren[3] of the 5th Corps was not strong enough to take the position assigned him; the troops were then ordered to their former position. The 13th went on the skirmish line for the next twenty four hours, where we could look over the ground and the works of the rebs. After leaving the wood the ground sloped to the run, then up a slope to where the rebs had their works; their batteries showed their teeth at every favorable place. Meade was wise not to risk a battle at that time and place, for it would have been a regular death trap, without any gain. The reason that from the time we left the woods we should have been under their fire, and the run lined with briars and bushes with steep banks and water three feet deep and freezing cold was a barrier not easily surmounted. "Descretion is the better part of valor," and so it proved here. After twenty four hours we were releived and sent back into the woods, where the priviledge was given of building as many and as big fires as we had a mind to. We were cold and the wood dry and the boys soon had fires big enough to roast an ox. The rebs were as cold as we, judging by their rous-

3. General Gouverneur K. Warren, USA, commanding the V Corps.

ing fires which we could plainly see. This was a grand old woods. Primeval I think, oaks centuries old and dry as tinder. All day we enjoyed the warmth, and at night the order came to "fall in" and get away as silently as and quickly as possible. We were soon off, going up by Robinson tavern, turning to the left into the woods, and making for the Rapidan. I remember of how we had to wait for the teams to get out of the way and the other things necessary to a large army on the retreat through a country of poor road with swamps and woods, how we at last reached the vicinity of the river with the darkness so thick that it could almost be cut, how I vainly searched for water and wood and had to lay down without my refreshing cup of coffee. In the morning we found both, and after strengthening the inner man were again on the move, crossing the river and moving towards the Rappahannock. [I remember] of how hungry the boys were, eating acorns and picking up the grain and eating it where the mules had been fed. Taking all these things together, my rememberence of Mine Run is not of the most pleasing character. That night when we bivouacked, Fay came and wanted to know if I didn't want to have him cook my supper and let him eat with me. This was a practise much resorted to; some of the boys were great eaters and when we had from three to eight days rations with us, could eat all in half the time, and if there was no chance to forage would go very hungry, unless they could eat in some such way. In camps we had enough and to spare, but on the march in an active campaign where we were up nights, some of the boys would eat all in half the time; besides we had no convenient place to carry so much bread and many times [it would] get wet and spoil. I had already filled my canteen at a nice brook, so I told Fay to get the fire ready and we would see what could be done in the supper line. My haversack was searched and a dirty piece of salt pork was found worth its weight in gold now, and broken hardtack worth a dollar apiece, enough for a good square meal. Coffee was soon making and Fay was frying the pork, while I was pounding the hardtack in the corner of my tent with a stone. This mixed with water and a little sugar stirred in and fried in pork fat made a dish much relished by us.

Each with a pint of coffee, and as much fried bread as we (I gave Fay the meat, which he greatly enjoyed in eating) could eat made us feel good, and how well we sat and

The evening smoke

talked over the events of the last few days and enjoyed our evening smoke. The privations were for the time forgotten, and then rolling up in our blankets the gloomy surroundings were also forgotten in "tired natures sweet restorer, balmy sleep." The next morning we marched for Kelly's Ford. Arriving there, we were assigned to some log huts that the rebs had commenced to build. Our tents were used for roof and we were soon comfortably housed. Here an order came to give furloughs of ten days to some of the best men to go to Massachusetts or anywhere else. I put in my application and in a few days it was returned with granted upon it. It was 12 o'clock at night when an orderly from the General brought it to camp and it was dated to commence then; the Col. sent his orderly to notify us so we could be away. Hastily packing my traps and leaving them in charge of the boys, I reported to the Capt tent, received my papers, and with nine others started about one o'clock under the charge of a teamster who was to pilot us to Brandy Station nine miles away on the Orange & Alexandria Railroad where a train was said to leave at six for Washington.

We tramped along over the frozen ground without a thought of rest, in time to take the train if there had been any to go, but there was none and we could not find anybody who could tell where there would be one. When the Gen'l got ready was all we could learn. So we must wait, and making ourselves comfortable as we could, [sat] around the fire of the guard in front of the tent of the Provost Marshal of the Army.

Just after daylight an officer rode along and attempted to ride between the guard and the tent of the Gen'l. The guard stopped him and told him he could not pass there. The Officer said "that no d——d guard should stop him" and tried to ride by, when the guard brought his gun down on the horses nose. That stopped him. The officer with an oath attempted to draw his sword, when the guard brought the point of his bayonet at the officers breast, [and] cocking it told him to "stop or he was a dead man."

How it would have ended I do not know, for Gen'l Patrick,[4] who was dressing in his tent and hearing the rumpus stepped out and told the guard to shoulder his gun

---

4. General Marsena Patrick, USA, Provost Marshall.

and turning to the officer asked his name and rank, told him he should know better then try to force a guard, [and] ordered him to report at such a place under arrest.

We reported to the Gen'l, showed our furloughs and were given permission to board the train that was now getting ready. We loaded ourselves on some platform cars and at about nine o'clock started.

At Rappahannock Station we waited for a train that they said was coming from somewhere, [and] after an hour or more of waiting we went on to Bealeton. Here, after more waiting, the train went by; we again started. The morning was very frosty and sitting on those platform cars—for we could not stand up over that rough road with the smoke from the engine so thick at times we could hardly see each other, sitting down and holding on when there was nothing to hold on to—we bumped all over the car,[which] made it a not very enjoyable ride. At Manassas more waiting for a train, and after that had passed, a clear track for Washington. It was now past 3 P.M. when we reached the office of Gardner Tufts, to get Soldiers tickets at reduced rates for Boston. Mr. Tufts told us that we had just fifteen minutes to buy our tickets and get to the depot in. $14.00 and some cents were quickly counted out, and we started on the run down the street to catch the train with our furloughs in our hands. We arrived there just in time. The officer of the Provost-guard looked at the first furlough, and seeing we were Massachusetts men, told us to get aboard, as the train was then moving out. At the lower station in Baltimore a soldier came aboard and after looking at our tickets gave us some very useful information. He said we had paid our fare to Boston but that when we reached New York we should take seats in a certain line of coaches and they would transport us across the city, but the driver would demand two dollars apiece, but to keep our seats and, if he still refused,

call the Police. At the upper station he took us to a restaur-
ant where we bought fried pies, doughnuts, cake for our
supper. Our stop was short, and we were away for
Philadelphia, reaching there about midnight. It was snowing hard when we crossed the city. New York was reached
about four A.M. and the coaches were there in waiting; we
took seats and the driver asked for his pay, which we refused. He became angry and threatened to call the Police;
we told him we wished he would and if he didn't we
should. After a few oaths he jumped on his seat and we
were soon in the other part of the city.

A train was in waiting with a car fitted up expressly for
soldiers, with bunks and other conveniances and in charge
of a Hospital steward. At South Framingham I left the
train, promising to meet the boys on a certain day in Boston. On going into the depot I met Col Leonard and Chaplain Gaylord going up to Marlboro to attend a war meeting;
they urged me hard to go up with them, said they wanted
to exhibit a soldier just home from the front. I asked the
Col. if he thought it wise for me with a furlough of ten
days, two already gone, to go around on exhibition. He said
"No," and advised me to go on my way.

I took the next train for Ashland, where I staid all night
with my sister Mrs Clark, and the next morning Mr Clark
carried me up to Mothers. I remained about a week, and
on the morning of the day agreed upon with my old comrade Henry Gassett, went to Boston to meet the boys. To
say I enjoyed my stay but feebly expresses it, and so I will
pass it by in silence.

24

A Home away from Home

Returning to the Reg't—Ox horn pipe—Building houses—Library—Incidents of the picket—The Officer of the day—Nat Seaver

At Natick comrade Frost boarded the train and we went together, failing to meet any of the other boys. We returned by the Norwich route; the boat touched the Jersey shore to land passengers.

We saw a train standing there and asked an employee "what train it was." He said "The express for Philadelphia." We said "Thats our train" and were going aboard when he stopped us and said "Soldiers dont ride on that train." We said "We didn't know as they did, but we were," and got on. Nothing was said and before we reached Philadelphia half the passengers were soldiers. At one of the stations a squad of Colored soldiers got aboard and a more happy set of men it would be hard to find. They kept singing a song, the chorus of which ran thus: "New Jersey, Oh! that the place for me, for there a pretty colored girl kept company with me."

It was raining hard at Philadelphia and continued all the

way to Washington, which we reached just at dark. We
went to the Bureau of Information and were directed to a
place to get supper and breakfast, and to another place to
sleep. In the morning when we went to take the train, a
corporal with a file of men were there to search us to see if
we had any liquor, which was "contraband" with soldiers.
We each had a small bag filled with goodies contributed by
friends, and when in Boston Henry Gassett had purchased
a pint of Whiskey and sent it to the boys. I had it in the
top of my bag, and when the corporal stopped us, he asked
Frost what he had in his bag and told him to open it. Frost
did, and the first thing he found was a pint of liquor, which
he with a grin put in his pocket. I in the meantime had
turned and, stepping behind Frost, had opened my bag,
taken the bottle out, and placed it under my left arm. I
stepped boldly up holding my bag wide open. He put his
hand in and turned some of the things around, [then] told
me to pass on. I think he was in a hurry to get to quarters
to have a drink of that which he had seized.

We took seats in box cars for Brandy Station. I thought
to have a smoke and took out a pipe, a genuine Ox horn,
for I had purchased six in Boston to give the boys as a re-
minder of home. I had just got it well under way and was
letting the smoke out by the mouthful when a Sergeant
Major of a Penn Reg't who had been watching me and
could stand it no longer came up and said, "Pardner I'll
give a quarter for that pipe." I told him the pipe was not
for sale but if he wanted that kind of a pipe I had one in
my pocket I would give him. He urged me to take the
money, saying he was more than willing to pay for it, and
he knew how short a soldier sometimes got. I told him to
do a good turn to some other soldier and I would be paid.
When we arrived at Brandy, before we had hardly stopped,
Lieut Warner ran along side to tell us the reg't had moved

and to stay on the cars until we reached Culpepper. He told us the reg't was near Mitchells Station. He was on his way home on a furlough. We reached Culpepper late in the afternoon and after making some enquiries started, three of us (for we had found Crosby on the train down), for the camp some six or eight miles away. We went down the track and before we had gone half way it was dark.

We came to a creek. The bridge being gone [and] we not wishing to ford it, went up the bank hoping to find a favorable place. We came to a tree blown over and not knowing whether it reached to the other side, for we could not see, we mounted the trunk and crawling on all fours reached the other side. We soon saw some fires and going to them found them to be teamsters. We enquired for our brigade but they didn't know anything about the brigade but told us there were troops camped over the hill in the woods. We went on as directed and after many stumbles we came in sight of the fires, and soon the camp was reached, which was the 16th Maine. Our reg't was the next line of fires. Reporting at headquarters, we were told to go to our respective companies.

To say the boys were glad to see us is expressing it mild. Walker & Slatery made me a cup of coffee and from the contents of their haversacks I had a meal. As it was late they offered to share their blankets and we were soon sound asleep. The contents of my bag I distributed amongst all the boys. The pipes I gave to the boys, passing them out without any thought of partiality for I had only four besides the one I smoked. The pipes were very popular, and some of the boys thought I had ought to have given them one instead of the ones I did. I told them I ment to be fair, and if I had known or thought they all wanted that kind of pipe I would have bought enough to go around. This satisfied all but Henry Vining. He felt bad and I offered to give him

mine; he said he had just bought a "Brick Wood" and paid
fifty cts for it, and that he would swap even for the one I
had paid two cts. I laid the pipes along side and told him to

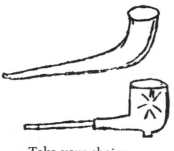

Take your choice

take his choice. He took the clay. That would have been
my choice also.

Building houses were now the order of the day, [and]
Walker, Slatery, Sargent, and myself built us a double
house, that is, we put our tents together and made a splendid one.

As we thought to live here all winter, we would commence and build one both comfortable and convenient, so
stakeing out our lot, we cut the timber the desired length,
notching the end and fitting them tightly together and plastering with mud—the walls were about four feet high—over
the whole spreading our tents, tacking them tightly to the
logs. On the opposite side of the door was the fireplace,
built of stones with a chimney of sticks, plastered outside
and in with a thick coating of mud. On each side of the
door we made our beds by driving four crotched sticks into
the ground and placing one across. On these we placed
poles, and on top of these we placed wild grass, which
made a very nice bed, [and] they served for our seats in the

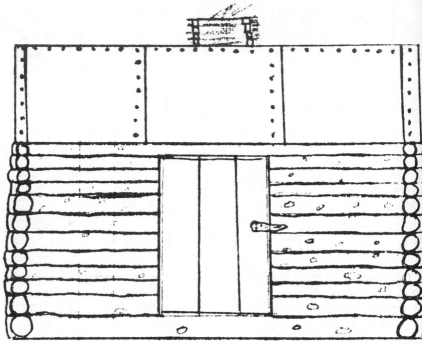

Our winter quarters

day time. Under the beds we stowed our wood. We went to a house about a mile from camp, and got some board, and layed a floor between the beds. We made a bench about three feet long, for a seat for the two who slept at the backside of the beds to sit up to the fire in cold weather. With an extention top to [it], this bench served as our table. We bought a coffee pot and a frying pan, [and] over the fire-place we had a shelf on which we placed our curiosities. It took us several days to build the house, but we never re-

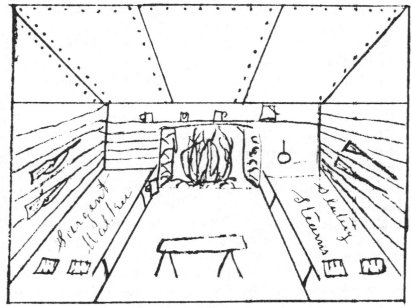

Inside the house

gretted the labor in those three months that we passed so comfortably there.

Our brigade was the out-post of the Army, the main body being encamped at Culpepper and Stevensburg. Our duty was principally picket; occasionally, if the weather was fine, we would drill. Books and papers were in abundance, and we spent a good portion of the time in reading. We had a library, the assistant Surgeon being Librarian, and the library in his tent. All were allowed the privilege of taking out books, and if any of the boys had books sent them, after reading, they would place them in the library for the benefit of the others.

Occasionally, when tired of reading or visitors were in, we would have a game of Old Sledge, or Euchre.

We used to go out about two miles to the picket post and stay[ing] three days at a time. We were divided into three releifs, one on the posts, one held under arms at the reserve post, and the other could sleep at the reserve, but all were supposed to wear their equipments. Our turn came once in about six days, or three days out and six days in camp. Brigade guard mounting was strictly adheared to, which in cold or stormy weather made it extremely disagreeable to us. I remember of being out at one time when it stormed all the time; it rained so hard there was no guard mount but each detachment forming as they arrived, we were of the first and had the right, and on reaching to post were on the first releif. It continued to rain the twenty four hours we were on post. Coming to the reserve we were supposed to rest keeping our equipments on; it was just at night and the orders were to keep a half dozen men awake to give an alarm if there was one. A sergeant of the 90th Pa was to have charge the first part of the night, calling me anytime after twelve. I rolled myself in my blanket and lay down by the fire but a few feet away. The night wore on, the fires burned low; when the sergeant awoke and starting up quick, [he] was completely turned around, and when he started to call me, went the wrong way.

I happened to wake up, but being snug and warm dreaded to get up, so lay and heard it all. He awoke a man and asked him who he was, but he belonged to another regiment. Then he woke up another sleeper, but he was not the one wanted.

He came back to where he started from to begin anew. He went to man after man until I thought he had woke up enough to form a relief for the whole army. He had been cussed and called all manner of names that a soldier could think of, and their brains were quite fertile in that direction.

He was now mad clear through and gave a yell at the top of his voice, "Wanted to know where that d——d 13th Reg't was."

I started up and asked "Whats wanted?" He felt ashamed to think he could not find me when I was so near, calmed down, and said it was time for me to call my men, and then told me what a time he had. I laughed, but didn't say I had heard it all. He lay down by the fire, and I not careing to wake the men, stirred up the fire and smoked the remainder of the night. In the morning it was snowing hard and as the ground was well trodden over and by moving a few rods away it was higher and dryer, we (a few) thought to move and build new huts. We did so and had just got our houses done and were congratulating ourselves when the Brigade Officer of the day rode up and saw how well we were obeying the orders about wearing our equipments. [He] said "What regiment do you belong to?" We told him. He wanted to know "Who was in command of that squad?" I told him I was. He wanted to know if I didn't know what the orders were in regard to our equipments. I told him I did. He wanted to know then "why we had them off." I told him we had taken them off while we were building our huts. He took my name and rank and said he should report me at Brigade Headquarters, [then] rode away. That was the last I heard of it. At another time while out, I had divided my men into three releifs, taking their names and dismissing until wanted. Al Sanborn, full of the devil, went and told Nat Seaver that I had taken his name (Nats) from the 2d and put it on the 3d—that he had looked on my book and saw it. He knew it would make Nat fighting mad, and Al wanted some fun. Nat was a very exciterable man and had no reason. I was sitting by the fire when he came and wanted to know "Why I had changed his name from the 2d to the 3d releif." I did not readily take in what he ment, but looking up, saw Sanborn near, who gave me a wink and I understood. I asked Nat what he ment, if he wanted the 3d releif. He was so mad he didn't know what he ment and cursed and tore round and said I might shoot him before he would go on that releif. He accused me of favoratism and called me all manner of names, the boys laughing and shouting to hear him go on. After we had enough of it, I told him to dry up or he would not go on any releif, for I would send him to headquarters. He muttered some and then went to another fire and sat down, where he stayed until I ordered the 2d releif to fall in, calling their names. Nat, hearing his name called, came forward feeling very cheap and excusing himself by saying it was one of Sanborn old tricks. Poor Nat, he would the next day be just as ready and as willing to believe him.

Orders were received that as many of the boys as would reenlist could have a thirty days furlough to go home, or if the regiment would, they could have the same, but few accepted this offer. Dan Warren (with the exception of old Heath) were the only ones from K.

25

Starting South

H eath, and this is his story, when he was ordered by
Capt Hovey at Haymarket to get out of the ranks, [he]
fell out and with some others like himself, followed along
until they were tired, when they stopped in a piece of
woods, built a fire, made coffee and went to sleep. They
never woke up till the next morning, and then while cooking their breakfast a squad of rebel cavalry rode up and ordered them to surrender. They were kept in the rear until
after the battle of 2d Bull Run was won to the rebs, and
then were sent to Cumberland Md., where they were
paroled and sent to the parole camp at Columbus Ohio.
Here Heath deserted and came to Worcester, where he
said he had a wife and two children living.

Arriving at Worcester Mass. he was arrested for larceny
and sent to the House of Correction for eight months. The
day before his time was out, the Provost Marshall arrested
him as a deserter and sent him to us. We were very busy

moving from place to place and there were many deserters amongst the subs, and this being a complicated one, [he] was not tried until winter. The court could not find him guilty, as he was ordered out of the ranks by the Capt., and then there was no record that he was ever mustered in.

He was captured by the enemy, and his confinement in jail he claimed was beyond his control. The court took the same view and discharged him with full pay for all the time he had been in the service, some eighteen months. His pay amounting to over two hundred dollars, he reenlisted and received three hundred more. Not being satisfied, he went down to the 16th Maine with a fifty dollar counterfeit bill, and told them there wasn't a man in all our reg't that had money enough to change it for him. A Sergeant changed it, and old Heath left on his furlough. We never heard from him again. The next day the Sergeant came up to camp to find Heath; he had tried to pass the bill and found it worthless. If there was ever a downright cunning rascal, that man was Walter S. C. Heath.

Quite a number of rebel soldiers had enlisted in our army and they were afraid of being taken prisoners, so the oppertunity was given them to go west and fight the Indians. John Parra of K company who came to us as a sub and in fact the only one that did not desert, availed himself of this priviledge. His story is quite unique. He said he was from a wealthy family in Havana Cuba, that when he was young he was in the Lopez insurrection,[1] was captured and tried and sent to Spain to serve a life sentence in the chain gang. After serving a few years, through the influence of his family and his youth he was pardoned, but was never to set foot again on Spanish soil. He was engaged in the tobacco business in Vicksburg Miss., was married and had children

1. One of the expeditions led by Narcisco Lopez, an advocate of Cuba's annexation to the United States, between 1848 and 1854.

when the war broke out. Not being a citizen, he thought he
was safe from the army. In the second year they raised a
company in V— and he was urged to go as a cook, which
he did with the promise that he would never be called
upon to fight. After a short time a gun was placed in his
hands and he had to take his turn with the rest. In one of
the Western battles he was taken prisoner and soon after
he took the oath of allegiance to the U.S. Coming to New
York he thought to establish himself in business in a small
way and, finding one of his countrymen, he obtained a loan
of a few hundred dollars and was just ready to start when
he found one of his old chums of the Lopez expedition and
the joy was so great and the liquor so strong that he had no
money when he came to himself. Massachusetts was paying
three hundred dollars bounty, and he immediately enlisted
and sent the money to the friend who had loaned him
some.

Al Sanborn who went out a Corporal and was reduced to
the ranks, then made a Corporal again, & then a Sergeant,
got some liquor, and made things quite lively for a time.
Not being satisfied with the sport he was having in his regiment, he thought to have some with the 39th Mass. He
went over there in the daytime, and was successful in picking up a row: they got the best of him and not being satisfied, he went over again in the evening, and was commit-
ting a nuisance near one of their tents. They heard him and
ran out, calling on him to stop; the Col. was out side his
quarters, and hearing the noise, and seeing a man running
towards him, call[ed] to him to stop also. Al, not having the
least idea which way he was running or who was calling
him, told him to go to h—l. The Col. not relishing the idea
of going there at present, and wishing to know who and
what he was, questioned the men of his command. The
next morning a complaint was entered, [and] Al was ar-

rested, Court-marshalled, and reduced to the ranks for his days sport.

U. S. Grant, having been appointed Commander in Chief [2] of all the armies of the United States, visited this out-post and reviewed us. We were much pleased with his appearance. On the distant hill beyond the Rapidan, on pleasant days we could see the Rebels at their drill. The old army of the Potomac was reorganized, the old First and Third Corps were to be no more. Their numbers were so small that they could no longer be called Corps. The First [was] to be consolidated with the Fifth, the Third with the Second.

Jan, Feb, & March, had gone by, and April had now come, and still the Army was in winter quarters. How much longer would this last was a question asked, but no one could answer. We knew the time had come for action. Action ment fight, and fight was death to some—who, none could tell. Three months longer and our time was out, but how much those three months ment for us. About the middle of April we were ordered out of our comfortable houses, [and we] pitched our tents about a mile away. My recollection[s] of this camp are not the most pleasing. The ground was low and on a wide plain, where the wind had full sweep; an April squall came up one day and all our tents blew over and we were nearly drowned out. On the first of May I was on picket and could hear the bands of the Johnies very plain. I think they must have been having a review.

One day while in winter quarters Walker and Slatery went out and picked a mess of greens. I stayed in camp and boiled the pork, and when they came in it was all ready to put the greens in. They were boiled in a few moments and,

2. Maj. Gen. Ulysses S. Grant, USA, was commissioned Lieut. Gen. and placed in command of all the Union Armies on March 9, 1864.

with some vinegar, we had such a feast as is seldom enjoyed. The Sutler was ordered to the rear, and the boys
were laying in a good store of tobacco. Jordan had been dealing in the article for some time, and having quite a stock
on hand wanted me to buy my supply from him. Wishing
to accomodate, but not liking his kind as well as the Sutlers, I at length took a dollars worth with the promise to
pay him when paid off. The Sutler's was Navy, Jordan's
Cavendish. On the 17th of April Lieut. Col. Batchelder resigned. Major Gould had been promoted to Col. of the 59th
Mass, Capt. Hovey was promoted to Lieut Col., and Capt.
Pierce, Major. From the first of May I kept a diary, and
shall with some additions follow it. I find "Cloudy but no
rain, a lonesome day. The Johnies are quite happy, their
drums and bands can be heard quite distinctly. Was up
under arms half the night."

The 2d "Fair but windy, a squall of wind and rain at sunset.
Every thing is scattered around, was relieved from picket
by the 16th Maine. No drill."

Thursday the 3d "Fair but windy. Company drill in forenoon, after which target practice, battalion drill in afternoon. Signs of a move near, Signal Station broken up and
men ordered to the rear. Drew three days rations, and in
the evening drew three days more."

Wednesday the 4th "Fair, a pleasant day, routed up at 1
A.M. to strike tents and prepare for a march. Marched at
half past two towards Culpepper, turned off and went to
Stevensburg. From there to Germania Ford, crossed and
went to near Wilderness Tavern. Bivouacked at 4 P.M.
Marched about 24 miles. One of our hardest marches." My
recollections of this day are very fresh. The day was warm,
and we were heavily loaded when we started, but as the
day advanced the boys commenced to throw away their
things. Over coats and blankets went, knapsacks were over

hauled, and extra stockings, drawers, old letters that the
boys had treasured up, in fact any thing and every thing
that could lighten the load. At Stevensburg we came upon
the camps of the other Corps, and such sights of clothing as
were there, and all the rest of the way. I commenced by
throwing away drawers, stockings, then tearing my blanket

Lightening the load

in two, cutting off the cape of my over coat, knowing from
past experience that I should need them in a few days.
Some of the boys threw away every thing but their rations.
Thursday the 5th "Fair and warm. Revillie at 3 A.M.
Marched at sunrise, but only a short distance. Firing in the
woods on our right. Was held on the reserve till noon,
when we went to the front. The fight has commenced in
earnest.[3] Sharp fighting both left and right. Was engaged
about sunset, but without much loss. Haskell wounded in
the breast. Four others missing, cant tell what results will
be, hard place for a battle." In coming into the road we
passed by Wilderness Tavern, and saw Grant, Meade, and
other Corps Generals in consultation. We were held in the

3. The Battle of the Wilderness, May 5-6, 1864.

road for a few moments, then move[d] back behind a large mansion that stood on the road leading to Robinson's Tavern. Firing was going on briskly down this road. While lying here, a portion of the Second Corps march[ed] over the fields to the Orange Plank road, [and] a smart engagement of a few moments occurred there. A little after noon we marched down across the road into the woods, sharp fighting going on in our front. Formed line of battle and continued to advance. Nat Seaver fell, and I thought was wounded. I found he was troubled with heart disease; the excitement of the coming battle overcame him. I layed him in a good position under a shrub and placed my over coat on it to shade him and went on. This was a wilderness indeed. There were islands of hard land from a quarter to several acres in extent, surrounded on all sides by low swampy ground, with bushes so thick, and horse briers running to the top of the trees with thorns an inch long woven in and out, [as to make] it almost impassable. After forcing our way through this jungle for quite a distance, we were ordered to move by the left flank, and as we had been moving down parrallel with the road, to move by the flank any distance we must cross the road. The rebs had a battery down there, from which they were throwing grape and cannister, making it exceedingly hazardous to cross. Quite a number of the Brigade were killed and wounded crossing this road; the missiles would come with a swi—s-s-s-h, filling the air full. I chose to run directly after fire. When over, we formed a line of battle almost at right angle from the other, and advanced up to the edge of one of these impassable swamps of a few rods in width. We lay on the ground and soon heard a noise of men breaking through the brush in our front. We heard the order "Halt, front, right dress," and "order arms," then an Officer enquire, "What regiment?" and the answer "South Carolina," the Flower of the South [at] this time. Just before sunset the order came to advance. We tried, but the swamp was a barrier not easily overcome, [and] before we were half way through we were ordered back. The bullets sang merrily for a while. We lay here in line of battle all night. Drew ammunition. The heaviest of the fight was at our right and some of the wounded were laying between the lines. One Soldier there took on bitterly, and every time any one tried to reach him, called for a fresh amount of bullets. The woods caught fire and burned over a part where the dead were.

In advancing through the woods, Co. D was deployed as skirmishers, and when we crossed the road D was left. Soon after, they were relieved and ordered back to the starting point. When he arrived there, he could not find the brigade but was told it was down in the woods somewhere. He started to find it, and was going down the road, meeting wounded men, when they saw a fellow coming at a full run, without a cap, haversack, gun or equipment of any kind. On coming near, Lieut Rawlins, who was in command of D, saw it was the Orderly of K. He stopped him and asked him where the regiment was. He said they had been in one of the worst fights yet and the regiment was all cut up with hardly a man left. He was terriably excited or frightened and immediately passed to the rear. Rawlins hardly knew what to do, but thought if the boys had been so terriable handled, the best thing he could do was to go on and perhaps they could help some of the wounded. Going on, he found one of the Brigade Staff, and found the affair had been somewhat magnified and the Brigade was safe down farther in the woods, which he soon found.

Friday May 6th "Fair and warm. Was relieved at daybreak by the Brigade that had the 9th Mass in it. Marched back to the open ground, and without halting marched again to the front, then back to the reserve. Heavy fighting at Parkers Store, also at the Plank road. Ordered to the Plank Road. Built breastworks, Lieut Stuart killed. Gen'l Wadsworth[4] killed. Saw Col Gould and his reg't." When ordered to the left, we saw the new Brigade of Mass troops coming to the rear like frightened sheep. Gen'l Patrick had three lines of his Turkey drivers[5] (as the boys called them) to stop the straglers. When we were building breastworks, the rebs, climbing into the trees, picked off quite a number. Our boys went down into the woods and they (the rebs) soon came down. Col Coulter of the 11th P.V. in command of a brigade was ordered to the left. Instead of going the way we did, he started his men through the woods, got in the rear of a division of rebs, and after some sharp fighting and tall running, reached our lines. "D—n my heart," said Coulter; "I'd gone through there if it took every man I had."

Saturday May 7th "Fair and warm. Not a great deal of fighting to-day. Remained behind our breastworks. Releived about five o'clock by a portion of the old 3rd Corps. Marched back to the left centre, when we were ordered to build fires, make coffee. Various reports flying around. Is this a victory. Bands were playing, and there was cheering in different parts of the line. Reported that Butler and Smith[6] were near Richmond. Also that Hooker was in the Valley. Marched at half past ten."

4. Maj. Gen. James S. Wadsworth, USA.
5. Equivalent to the Military Police of today.
6. Generals Benjamin F. Butler and William F. (Baldy) Smith, USA.

26

The Work Gets Harder

Spotsylvania C. H.—Incidents—Sedgwick killed—Moving by the flank—Still fighting—Jim Slatery—Fighting and still moving by the flank

Sunday the 8th "Marched in the direction of Spotsylvania C.H., passed Todds Tavern about two A.M., Sheridans Cavalry bivouacked here. Charged the rebs and drove them three miles, when we were repulsed. [1] Dorkham wounded. Rice missing. Gen'l Robinson wounded. The day was extremely hot, several sunstruck."

The march was a tiresome one. We had our dishes and canteens strapped so as to make as little noise as possible. When we passed the campfires of the Cavalry, how good they looked to us tired soldiers. They cheered us on by such remarks as these. "We are glad you've come." "Go on boys you'll soon find them." "They are just ahead." Coming to a piece of woods that had been on fire and in places still burning, we halted; I dropped to sleep. It didn't seem more than a minute before the "Fall in" was heard; daylight

1. The Battle of Spotsylvania Courthouse, May 8-18, 1864.

was just breaking. Moving quickly forward we passed the Cavalry outposts, formed a line of battle on the march, and went out of the woods and into a field towards a wooded ravine. The zyps, zyps of the bullets were coming thick and the prospect of warm work ahead caused me to unhook my knapsack and let it drop. When it struck the ground I heard the old dish rattle and the thought of coffee, soups and the other dishes that had been made in it, and besides it was the same old dish that I had started with, caused me to stop, turn round, and unstrap the dish from my knapsack

Saving the dish

and, taking off my canteen, run the strap through the bail and, slipping it over my head, go on. We went on down through [the] ravine, driving the rebs, coming to a clearing with a house, and to the right a battery which was sending shot after shot at us. One struck the colors, breaking the staff without any injury to the bearer. After leaving the woods we ran and fired as fast as possible. A squad of Cavalry dashed out of the woods on the left, dressed in blue and swinging their swords for us to stop firing. We thought they were our men and slackened fire, when in an instant over the hill went Battery, Cavalry, and all. A parting volley from us brought down the Capt's horse and he was taken prisoner. On down past the house, through the

woods we went more than a mile; the heat was so intense
that many of the boys had fallen out. We halted a moment
to get breath when Gen'l Warren ordered us forward and
on we went towards a pine woods. Just as we reached its
edge came a volley, and then another, and our lines sadly
thinned by the heat and our long run, gave way before the
breastworks of the enemy. Our Division General, Robinson, lost his leg. The fighting was now general. The 6th
Corps came up and charged the rebs at the same place, but
the rebs were too much for us and the whole army was
brought to bay. After the repulse I went into the woods
and made some coffee and had a short nap. Just as I entered the wood I saw several of the boys carrying George
Emery in a blanket. I thought him wounded, but he was
sunstruck instead. Rice we never heard from. We lay at the
left of the line until night, when we were ordered to carry
ammunition to the front, where we stayed all night. Lieut
Whitcomb killed.

Monday May 9th "Moved to the right and built breastworks. Advanced, and built another line, and at dusk advanced and another line was built. Heavy detail for Skirmishers from the regiment. Casualties of the army heavy.
Rawson and Comstock sick, Sedgwick killed."[2] This was a
day to be remembered for hard work. Early in the morning
we went but a short distance, where we halted behind a
battery; the bullets were coming over quite thick. The battery boys had been drawing rations and a box with a few in
it was lying there. Gen'l Sedgwick of the 6th Corps came
along and stopped at the box, picked up one of the crackers
and went on eating it. Within five minutes we heard he
was dead, killed by one of those bullets. We moved off to
the right a half mile or more and in a pine grove we built a

2. Maj. Gen. John Sedgwick, USA, who had commanded the VI Corps.

strong line of works. We had hardly finished them before we were ordered to advance and on coming to a clearing, we were again ordered to build, but before the works were far advanced we were again ordered forward, this time in plain sight of the enemy. It was growing dark and it promised to be an all nights work, as we were ordered to build a strong work for we would receive a shelling in the morning. A heavy detail was made for the skirmish line, which so reduced our working force as to make it doubly hard for those that were left.

May 10th "Kept close in works for the rebel sharpshooters were busy. Moved to the left. All the privates detailed to bring up ammunition. Only the Officers and Non-Com left. The line ordered to advance. Hard fighting but nothing gained. Lee[3] wounded."

As we expected, as soon as it was light the rebs let us know that they were awake, and greeted us with shot and shell. Moved to the left, keeping well behind the works until the woods were reached, which hid us from their sight. The old 3d Corps was massed in a field here to make a charge. We, that is the old 1st, were massed alongside to go with them. It was a grand and glorious sight to see those old and battle scarred Corps, with their tattered flags, waiting the order to advance, and grander and more glorious when the charge was sounded, and the Sphere[4] and Diamond[5] went forward together to meet the foe. We went or tried to go through the thick woods, but the Jonnies were at the other edge and with shot and shell while the Minniés whistled thick around us. After several hours of vain attempts and night coming on, the army fell back to its first position.

3. Private Lee of Company K.
4. Insignia of the old I Corps.
5. Insignia of the old III Corps.

May 11th "Got seperated from the regiment last night but found it early this morning. The rebs, having got the range, gave us a taste of their shells. Moved out of range. Rawson and Seaver came up but went again to the rear. A heavy shower." In the confusion of falling back through the woods, I lost the regiment and came out with the 90th P.V., staying with them all night, finding my reg't quickly in the morning. Heavy shelling, several wounded. Moved behind a little hill to get out of range. Rawson our Orderly and Seaver came up to report, but in reality to get their rations. Seaver was really sick, you could see it by his looks, but Rawson was as well able to do duty as any man we had. A heavy shower of wind, rain, and hail added to our pleasure.

May 12th "A wet day. Went on a reconnisance to find the enemy, found them in force, came back and took up our old position. In the afternoon moved to the left and took up our old position. Clifford wounded, Slatery missing. Report says that the 2d and 6th Corps charged, and took seven thousand prisoners and twenty pieces of Artilery. A good haul if true. Seaver for duty."

The showers of yesterday turned into a storm. Early in the morning went up through the woods to feel the enemy, found them in about as social a condition as a Hornet or Yellow Wasp would be in when their nest is disturbed. While feeling our way along we passed a large oak tree, and after we passed, its hugh trunk afforded a protection for about a dozen straglers from the different regiments. Sergeant Walker of K was sent back to order them forward, but just before we reached there, a shell struck the tree, knocking about a cord of wood in every direction, and completely routing those who had taken refuge behind it. Our object accomplished, we returned, and were moved to the left, changing positions several times. Just at night we

were in a thick pine woods that showed the effects of recent shelling. A few prisoners were taken, and to the remark "that there had been some shelling here," one said,
"You'ns dont know what tis to be shelled as we'uns do."

I thought, not if this was a fair sample of our shells. In
going into the woods I picked up a large blanket soaked
with rain and so passed a comfortable night.

May 13th "Last night was a most miserable night for some
of the boys. It rained, we lay in line of battle: there was not
much sleep or rest: heavy picket firing, moved back to the
right, and took up our old position behind the breastworks.
Shelled by the rebs. Meades order congratulating the army
on the victory of yesterday read, the Cavalry reported at
Hanover Junction. Comstock reported for duty."

May 14 "If last night was a miserable night this one beats
it. We moved about 10 P.M. towards the left, and went
about four or five miles, the mud was awful, half leg deep
half of the way. The boys are pretty tired and worn out;
how much longer we can stand it is a question with some.
Remained in this place till just at night, when we moved to
the right a half a mile, the rebs shelling us smartly but
doing us no harm. Thus far I have passed through the
storm of battle safely, and I pray God he will keep me to
the end." The incidents of this twenty four hours are many,
but a few will suffice. While marching along through the
mud, halting at times to get through some extremely bad
place, some of the boys sitting down, all cross and ugly,
and it was almost as dark as the Egyptian darkness, a squad
of horsemen tried to pick their way through the lines. The
boys did not relish to have the horsemen there and refused
to move, cursing and swearing at them roundly. At length
one said, "Boys I know you are tired, but I am Gen'l Warren, and I must go through." A line was opened quickly for
him. When we halted, I sat down and was asleep in an in-

stant, and when I awoke the sun was rising, a great round ball of fire directly in the west, and all the time we were here I could not make it appear different. As our Division Commander was wounded, the Division was temporarily broken up, and the Brigades were sent here and there to do the hard work.

Sunday May 15 "O for a day of rest, a day that we poor tired & worn out soldiers can lay down and enjoy the quiet of a sabbath. Afternoon—a quiet day thus far, with a promise of its continuance. A shower came up, raining hard. Formed four lines of battle; we were in the third line. All expected a charge but after waiting two hours was sent to our first position; thus ends the day." While waiting, I sat down with my back to a stone heap, and slept the time away.

Monday May 16 "The morning is foggy. All is still and we all hope it will continue so. Slatery came up, and I had the disagreeable duty of stripping off his stripes. Rawson came up; he ought to be served in the same way, but favoritism goes a great ways in the army. Formed the Division in four lines of battle, and after lying round an hour or two went back to our old position." In the forenoon Corp. Slatery and Corp. Gould of Co. H came up, having fallen out without leave. A drumhead Court-martial was ordered, and both were ordered before it, and both were sentenced to be reduced to the ranks in the presence of the Regiment. A Sergeant of H and Sergeant Stearns of K were ordered forward. The sentence of the court was pronounced and they were ordered to take the stripes off each. I hesitated, for I knew Jim was a good soldier and prided himself on his stripes, and was an especial friend of mine. "Sergeant," said the Captain, "do your duty." I knew it was best to obey, so taking my knife I cut some of the stitches, and loosened the ends quickly, tore them off, and told Jim to sit down and we would pick the stitches out at our leisure. A short time afterwards Rawson came up, limping along with a face a yard long, trying to make it appear that he was awful sick. Some of the boys cried out "reduce him," "serve him the same way"; he was ordered to appear before the Commander of the Regiment, and what excuse he had I do not know, only he kept close to the Regiment for some time afterwards.

Tuesday the 17 "This has been the stillest day since we commenced the move. Not a gun has been fired to break the almost Sabbath stillness. The troops are resting after their arduous labors. A rest that we all need. Mike Lynch returned to the Regiment, after sixteen months service in a battery. About 5 P.M. moved down to the left a short distance, building breastworks will be the order for the night."

May 18 "Worked all night on the works, and in the morning moved off to the left about a mile. Heavy shelling in the forenoon, but no one hurt in our Brigade, although we were under their fire all the time. In the afternoon, moved back to our old position. Layed in the shelter of a hill till night, then went into the works. Chamberlain, who was wounded in the first days fight, came back."

May 19 "Burnsides troops changed position and leaves us the first line of battle. All is quite still. The rebs are on the lookout, and are making themselves busy in looking over the works that Burnside has just left. Heavy firing on the right. We thought as it was on our flank and rear, and felt quite uneasy about it. About sunset the Reb skirmishers made a dash on ours, but a smart shelling from one of our batteries drove them back to their own lines." We were indeed startled when suddenly, almost in our rear, there broke out a heavy musketry fire. What did it mean? Were the Rebs up to some of their old tricks? Were Stonewall's games to be again applied? After about a half hour the firing ceased. The cause of the trouble was that the Rebs were hungry and thought to get at our ration train, but the First Mass. Heavy Artilery and other troops were coming to reinforce our army, and the Rebs, instead of getting the train, got a licking.

May 20 "Today has been a very quiet day, no firing on any part of the line to speak of. Extremely warm. Report says that we took last night between four and five hundred prisoners. Received a mail. Was on the alarm guard at night."

May 21 "Still in the morning. About 10 A.M. left the works and started toward the rear. The Rebs discovered our movements and commenced to shell. Crept back and stayed a few minutes, when we left them and marched away. All the afternoon we toiled on, reaching Guinea Station just before dark. This was a very hard march. The boys are pretty well played out. Fay reported a prisoner." The hill beyond the station, which commanded the country and was necessary that we should occupy before the Rebs, was reached by crossing a swamp over a corduroy road about a mile long. When Gen'l Warren reached the hill, there were about a dozen rebel cavalry men who thought to hold the place till their troops arrived. Warren, knowing the importance of the hill, and fearing he would be too late if he waited for the troops, put himself at the head of his Staff and charged up the hill, driving off the Rebs and, by keeping a bold front, kept them off until the tired foot soldiers arrived.

27

Closer to Richmond

*First skirmishing—Jericho Ford—Incidents—
Across Pamunkey—Thirteen miles from
Richmond—Rations—Bethesda Church—The
skirmish Line—Cold Harbor*

Sunday May 22 "Revillie at 3 A.M. to cook coffee, did not
march till near noon. Our advance kept up a skirmish fire with
the Rebs. The Rebs are falling back toward Hanover Junction,
and we are making for that place pretty fast. Bivouacked at
night at Bulls Church in a corn field. There was not grass
ground enough to lay on, a new way to starve the Rebs by
treading down their corn."

May 23 "Routed at daylight and started on the march, following the Rebs. About noon came up with their rear
guard, who where protecting the crossing of the river. Rested till the second Corps came up, when we were
marched up the river to Jericho Ford, crossed the North
Anna on a pontoon bridge. When well over, was attacked
and a fierce fight of a half hours duration took place.[1] The
Rebs were repulsed with considerable loss. Loss small on

1. The engagements at the North Anna River, May 23, 1864.

our side." When we started on the march this morning, some of the Division broke into a smoke house of two old ladies, who had shown kindness to some of the boys the night before, and took all the meat they had. They told the Gen'l. what had happened, and he immediately ordered their arrest. I saw the two soldiers with their guns on their shoulders and their bayonets thrust through the smoked sides going on to join their command. How proud they stepped along with their prize. I saw them when they were returning the meat, and they had not that proud look, but sneaked along, as though they would like to get out of sight as quick as possible. All the boys would justify anyone for taking any thing (when they were hungry) from the Rebs, but after kindness was shown by them, and they had done what they could to help us, was not approved by any one (Bummers excepted). I were glad to see them going back, and the boys were not sparing in calling them names. We were cooking our coffee as unconcerned as could be when we heard firing in our front. The boys said, "They are shooting pigs," when all at once a terriable yell and a musketry fire broke upon us. Coffee pots were emptied in an instant, bummers ran to the friendly shelter of the river bank, and the soldiers were ordered to fall in and move quickly to the front. The first Division of our Corps, who crossed before we did, had entered the woods and thrown up a work, and now it did them good service. We went to the right and protected their flank. It was a short and sharp engagement and ended as it commenced. Rawson, in his hurry to reach a place of safety again, lost his cap and could not stop to pick it up, but instead, for several days wore an old nasty Johnnie Reb hat; as an Orderly he made a pretty figure.

May 24 "Worked all night building breastworks—during the day made a reconnoisance as far as the railroad, but found no rebs. Last night and today took quite a number of prisoners. Heavy firing on the left. Hancock and Burnside[2] are making up things, *'I reckon.'* All kinds of reports as to results. Armstrong and Stowe promoted to 2d Lieut." Last night after the fight when everything was still, while lying in line of battle, a reb who had lost his way came along through the brush, when one of our boys said softly "Who comes there? What regiment do you belong to?" When he answered up promptly "The 16th South Carolina by Gard, and what regiment are you?" "The 13th Mass. by Gard and

16" South Carolina

you drop that gun quick," it is needless to say that the gun was dropped, and he came into our line.

May 25 "Moved early this morning to left, went about two miles where we formed a line of battle and marched into a thick pine wood; heavy skirmish firing in our front. Halted and built a breastwork in double quick time, the minniés

2. Maj. Gen. Winfield S. Hancock and Ambrose E. Burnside, USA.

flying around us thick, but fortunately none of our Regiment was hurt. Cannonading on the right, showers in the afternoon." This was dangerous locality. An Indiana Regiment went on the skirmish line, and within five minutes brought back a capt. and two privates dead; others came back wounded. There were not many long stories while we were holding ourselves.

May 26 "A constant fire was kept up on the skirmish line, some cannonading on our side, but no reply from the rebs. A severe shower in the morning, and several more during the day. Made ourselves as comfortable as we could through the day. Rumors that a night march may be expected, but destination unknown."

Friday May 27 "Started about 9 A.M. to recross the river. The bridge broke and occasioned some delay. Crossed about 12. Halted at 2 A.M. and drew rations. Marched about three hours down the river, then halted and made coffee, after which we continued to march till sunset, then bivouacked, having marched about twenty five miles." The day we layed in the woods, after the severe shower the water stood in our holes about a foot deep; all sat on the bank but Rawson. When I first saw him in the morning, he was half covered up pretending to be asleep. The rest of us made our coffee and sat on the bank and smoked and talked the time away. Rawson roused up and tried to hire Seaver to make him some coffee, but he declined, and so he went without. He was the butt of many a joke and the laughing-stock of the whole Regiment. At night when the order came to fall in as quietly as possible, he kept his place in his hole, and the Capt. formed the Company. When the order came to march and we were actually moving, he jumped up and ran to the side opposite from where the bullets came. The country through which we marched had never been visited by troops before and there was a splendid chance to forage if we could only have had the time.

May 28 "Revillie at 4 in the morning. Started at 5 and crossed the Pamunkey at just 12 M. Went about a mile and formed a line of battle, and commenced to dig; built a splendid work and are all ready to receive visitors from the other side. Cannonading at the front and the Cavalry engaged. The other Corps come up and form on our right."

Sunday May 29 "Routed at day light to prepare for a march but did not march till noon, when we moved to the front[3] about three miles, where we halted till night, when we moved down to the left to Lynden Cross Roads, where we formed a line of battle and threw up a light work. No firing to speak of today. Rumors that Gen'l Lockwood[4] is to take command of our Division. Thirteen miles from Richmond."

May 30 "Did not get up very early, but soon after we moved back to the right and front, halted a few hours in a grove. When the Rebs attacked, the left moved down to strengthen it, formed a line and commenced to dig. Moved still further to the left, and then threw up a work. The Rebs attacked our Corps again on the right, but were repulsed. A good deal of cannonading up and down the line." We were on the flank in the morning while the other troops were coming forward to protect it; then we were ordered forward, halted a little time in the wood. How we did wish that rations would be served, for we were terribly hungry, and the weather was very warm. I who had almost always had enough to eat and to spare, was so hungry that I actually staggered when I marched. A heavy firing on our left caused us to be moved down in that direction. We passed over a plowed field and the bullets striking the ground kicked up clouds of dust. We advanced down into the wood, and soon became engaged. Darkness came in and the fight was ended. A ration of fresh beef was served in the night; as we were not allowed any fire, how to cook it

3. The engagement at Totopotomoy Creek, Va., May 29-30, 1864.
4. Probably Brig. Gen. Henry H. Lockwood, USA.

was a question. At length a small fire or smoke (for there
was more smoke than fire) [was] made behind the trunk of a
fallen tree, and after holding it in there a few minutes, we
ate it."

May 31 "All is quiet in front of our Corps to day. Hard
fighting on our right in the forenoon; the second Corps engaged. The cavalry had quite a fight on our left just before
dark. No particulars received as to results. Our skirmishers
advanced a mile or so, but the line remains unchanged.
Dan Warren returned from his furlough, and reported to
Capt Bucklin."

June 1 "All was quiet till about 9 A.M. when we moved to
the left and advanced about two miles where we found the
Rebs, halted, and threw out a new line of skirmishers. I
was detailed to in command of those from our Regiment.
Advanced as far as a piece of woods and ordered to advance
again; went through the woods and found the rebel line of
battle; firing briskly on both sides, heavy firing on the left.[5]
Division moved to the left, the skirmishers remained the
same."

The Cavalry fight last night at dark was at Bethesda
Church; we pass it in the march of today.

As we passed near the church we saw Grant, Meade, and
members of their Staffs seated there on settees brought
from the church. Just beyond we found the Rebs up and
dressed, ready to receive us. Their shells came screaming
and bursting quite thick. We advanced in line of battle
through a piece of woods and halted at its farther edge. The
rebs were across an open field in full view, throwing up
works in a very lively manner. In the valley between ran a
little brook with a fringe of brush on either side. The skirmish line was thrown out and I was in command of the

5. The Battle of Cold Harbor, Va., June 1-12, 1864.

men from our Regiment. My orders were when I saw the line on my right advance, to start my men on the run and not stop till we reached that little fringe of brush, or until the others stopped. The line started, and away we went over the open field on the full run. Just soon as we cleared the woods the Rebs fired. A shell came so near me that the wind from it whirled me around and whisked my cap off and whirled it more than a rod away. I went and picked it up and ran after the men. The brush was gained without loss, [and] after a little we were strengthened and we were ordered to push on. By moving a little to the left we entered a piece of woods which the rebs were determined to hold, but after considerable fighting we drove them through. I remember now of standing behind a tree, the Rebs firing, and hitting it several times. It may seem as good fun now to talk and laugh about, but there in its reality I failed to see where the fun came in. Had one man killed in my squad.

June 2 "Considerable firing up and down the line. Stayed out on the skirmish line all night and till 3 P.M. the next day. Was relieved by the 6th New York Heavy Artilery, found the Brigade, but the Regiment had been sent down to the left of the Division. Went on and found the Regiment in an open field, without any shelter, the shells flying thickly around. None of our boys hurt by the shells. Rainy in the afternoon. The 18th Army Corps on our left."

Rations about this time were very scarce and, as usual in a long campaign, we were very hungry. Coming in off the skirmish line, I found a large bone, with some shreds of meat still on it, but more maggots than meat. I hit it a blow against a tree, and holding it in the fire a few minutes, with my knife I scraped it and ate the meat. As it was rainy, and the ground low, we were indeed fortunate if we could find a rail to lay on; two rails would do if we could manage not to slip between, but three was a luxury indeed. We were now in the immediate vicinity of McClellan's Peninsula Campaign, and the marks of former struggles could be seen. There were several old chimneys still standing to mark where there had been a village. Rawson, with a keen eye for present safety, although not always looking for comfort, crept into one of the fire places, on the opposite side from where the bullets came, not large enough for a dog, and stayed there until he was obliged to make his appearance.

June 3 "Cloudy with rain. Heavy skirmishing on the right. The 13th lost heavy. Tremenderous heavy shelling on the right and in our front. The air was filled with cold iron: no one hurt in our Regiment.[6] About noon there was a lull in the storm of iron, but by the middle of the afternoon it raged again in all its fury. The Brigade moved to the right, all but the 13th, who were advanced and ordered to build another work. A splendid work. Heavy firing on the left."

June 4 "Moved into our new works at dark; all was still in the morning. Moved at about 10 A.M. and joined the Brigade at the right, and were held in the reserve. It is reported that Burnside is moving towards the left. John Stearns was taken sick and sent to the rear. Dan Warren, who was on the cattle guard, was wounded yesterday. Cannonading in the afternoon."

June 5 "Moved at half past—A.M. a short distance to the right. Raining hard, all is quite still. This is the stillest day for some time; about night the rebs attacked in the old place, but the old 3d Corps was enough for them. Got ready to move when the pickets opened a smart fire. Crept back into the works and waited until all was again still, when we left. John reported for duty."

6. Probably Company instead of Regiment is meant.

June 6 "Marched two or three hours to the right and rear, where we bivouacked. All was quiet till afternoon, when there was considerable shelling, but we were out of range. Ordered to be ready to march at a moments notice. No signs of marching, we pitched our tents, as there were signs of rain; an extremely uncomfortable day. Heard that Alphonso Comey was killed and his brother James wounded. Old school mates of mine. They belonged to the 25th Mass., 18th Army Corps."

June 7 "There was the usual amt of firing today, and as we are out of range we do not mind it. The 9th N.Y. or 83d, our old chums, mustered out and start for home. N. C. Meinard returns from his furlough. Straightening out the camp is the order of the day."

28
Snakes and Frogs

Al Sanborn—Barbers—White Oak Swamp—A square meal—Crossing the James—The advance on Petersburg—Maneuvering in front of Petersburg—Incidents

June 8th "We are still in camp, a thing that is quite remarkable with us. About the same amount of firing. The boys do nothing but eat and sleep, are resting for the work that is still before them." Al Sanborn went down to the teams to see Ira Donovan; Ira gave him a bag of hardtack to bring back for the boys. He had almost reached camp when he met an Officer, who enquired "If he could tell him the way to Bottom Bridge." "The bridge without any bottom," says Al. "Bottom Bridge," says the Officer. "O Yes," says Al, "You keep right along down that road and you'll come to a bottom without any bridge." You d——d rascal," says the Officer, "I'll teach you to make fun of me," and turning he tried to catch hold of Al, but he was to quick and ran for the camp, where he was soon lost to the Officer in the tents. Little Stevie Warren would lay in his tent and blow his fife until we were all tired and sick of it.

John Hill and Henry Vining were the barbers, and at

The way to Bottom Bridge

such times as this they had their hands full, for every one would want a shave or haircut. In shaveing we would lay down on a rubber blanket with a woolen one rolled up and placed under the neck to throw the chin up. Then the operator would scrape away, standing on his knees. In cutting hair a stone or stump would answer for a seat; five cents for a shave, and ten for cutting hair.

June 9th The lull in the storm of battles still continues. I can get no news worth recording, although there is plenty of reports flying around. Occasionally guns are fired on the left. Dove and Cody promoted to Lieut, Wales and Damrell to Captains. Damrell a prisoner."

June 10th "Fair and warm, most beautiful weather, all is quiet with now and then a gun. What an appetite I have. Can eat every hour in the day and then feel hungry. Rumors are flying around that the army will soon be somewhere else." A reporter who had libeled the army was drummed out of camp; the boys jeered and laughed good to see him. A couple of drummers led the procession beating the rogues march, then came the libeler on a led horse, with a large placard on his back on which was printed Libeler of the Army, and a file of soldiers in the rear.

June 11th "Revillie at three A.M. All cooking breakfast. Marched at five towards the White House, went about five miles and turned to the right and went on until we crossed the railroad, then turned to the left and went a mile or more, halted in an open field and ordered to pitch a camp. It was noon before we halted. Dont know the name of the place. Marched 10 miles."

June 12th "All is still. Company inspection by Capt Kimball. Reported that Hooker had routed the rebels from the Valley. Heard that Lincoln had received the unanimous nomination of the convention at Baltimore. Half past five, all packed up ready to move. Marched at seven P.M. and bivouacked at twelve near Baltimore Cross roads."

June 13th "Routed at three to continue the march, arrived at the Chicahominy at light, crossing on a pontoon bridge, and went up the river to White Oak Swamp. Found the rebs. Our batteries shelling the woods. Supported the battery until ordered to the left of the Brigade. Built breastworks, and layed in them the remaining portion of the day. Heavy firing on the skirmish line. A sharp fight on the left and rear. Double quick to the left to strengthen the men." We were now in the vicinity of the Seven Days Fight, and many evidences were seen of those encounters. We lay at the edge of the swamp, near a road that ran through it; our object was not to fight, but to hold the road, while the army was passing on to the James. We lay close to a little ravine that held some of the largest black snakes that I ever saw. We killed four or five of these old residents, and we saw crossing the path that ran from the road to the swamp, a dozen or more. We thought if we staid there that night, we should have plenty of company. The boys that came up from the bridge reported the whole country below filled with troops, and all of the mighty paraphernalia of war moving for the James. Just as night was coming on, a smart fire of musketry broke out on our left about half a mile away. It was some of our Cavalry dismounted, and some rebel Infantry that had broken through the swamp. Our Regiment was started at the double quick for the scene of action, and by the time we reached there it was over; darkness came on and the regiment lay in line of battle. I was sent on the picket. During the night, we heard some one calling in our front. We said "this way," when two men came up. In the darkness we could not tell whether they were Johnnies or Yanks. We asked them their regiment, and they said "4th South Carolina"; we told them that we were "the 13th Mass." They dropped their guns and equipments pretty quick, and one took off his haversack and passed that. We told him to keep it, and we sent them to Headquarters.

June 14 "Left the Front about 10 P.M. and marched towards the James." Passed the 1st Division of our Corps about 12. Marched an hour, and came up with some troops. Upon enquiring who they were, were told it was the 1st Division of our Corps again, having marched that hour in a circle. Came up with the Division at 3, rested till 5, when we were again moved forward. Halted about 11 within three miles of the Charles City Court House and 3 from the James. Still resting at dark, the whole Army reported to be in this vicinity, and that pontoons were being layed across the river. "Good if true." After we halted at 11, I went to bathe and fill my canteen, and then returned to the Regiment. Sawyer, the drummer, went another way and came upon some soldiers who had just shot a young steer. They told him to go in and help himself as there was more than they wanted; he cut off, I should say, more than eight pound of that tender steak, and brought it in. He came back just a few moments after I did. I had my tent pitched for a shade, and was lying under it; he crept in and showed me his prize, and said if I would help in the cooking, I might eat with him. No sooner said than done. We had been drawing rations, and amongst the rest was molasses. I soon had coffee, steak fried, and hardtack with molasses before him, and we made a most substantial meal. After we had eaten every morsel, Sawyer said he could eat a little more if it was only cooked. I told him I thought I could, and we both took hold and another meal was prepared and eaten. Still not feeling quite satisfied, we cooked the remainder of the meat and devoured it. We had eaten enough, and lay down in the shade of the tent and slept all the afternoon. I never felt any bad results from it, but Sawyer, it liked to have killed; in fact I thought he would die before we reached home, and he suffered from its effects for years.

June 15 "Rose at 5 and made coffee, so as to be ready for anything. Quartermaster F. L. Stone and Charles Drayton, both formerly of K, but now of Wilde's African Brigade, called to see us. They were looking well. Report says no bridge as yet is layed, but that the army is crossing on transports. The Cavalry had a smart fight back of us. No particulars. A good rest."

June 16 "Revillie at 2 A.M. but did not march till 4. Marched down and crossed the river on a transport at about 10 A.M. Halted till about 3 P.M. when we commenced the march towards Petersburg. The roads were dry and dusty and water scarce. Marched till near 11 P.M. when we halted till 1 A.M. to make coffee; at 1 A.M. we moved on till 3 when we halted again. Some firing all day. The 7th Mass. Regiment start for home. Saw Chandler Pike

of that Regiment—he was an Upton[1] boy." There was a
pontoon bridge layed, and the trains and Artilery were
crossing at a rapid rate. After we crossed we took a nice
bath in the noble James. We killed one of the biggest
snakes that I ever saw, and he was in the act of swallowing
another snake almost as large as himself. There was an
enormous corn-field, with the stalks as tall as our heads.
The dust was fearful; it covered every thing, away up
through the country we could see the dust rising like a
cloud from the army that was toiling along; the grass, trees,
fences, and even ourselves were covered. Our faces were as
completely covered as though we wore a mask and the
sweat flowed furrows down our cheeks; the dust was in our
eyes, and the sweat caused them to smart intensely. After
leaving the James no water could be found, and the boys
suffered with thirst. When we halted at 11, we were near a
swamp, and thinking I could find water I started into its
depths. After going quite a distance, or what seemed so in
the dark, I came to a pool or what was once, but now I
should say more bull frogs than water. I commenced to dip
it up using my drinking cup, trying to fill my larger dish.
The frogs, anticipating my intentions, tried to prevent me
by saying "aint fit to drink, aint fit to drink." I was one of
the first to invade their dominion and they tried to scare us
away, but after a little, seeing their water disappearing,
they showed fight and the boys had to arm themselves with
sticks to keep them back; at least that is what they reported. After giving the water a good boiling, I drank some
made into coffee. In the morning after our two hours
march, I found more water, that to strike it with a stick it
would crack clear across, the scum was so thick.

June 17 "Started on the march at 9, and went to the front,[2]

1. Upton, Massachusetts.
2. The Siege of Petersburg, Va., which lasted from June 15, 1864, until April 2,
1865.

halted in an open field and was held in reserve, was manuvered around all day. Heavy firing with Artilery, report says with good success. At sunset move again to the left and front."

This night was a succession of starting and halting, moving by the right flank, and then by the left. Moving forward then backward, and the bullets of the Johnnies flying thickly around. We were twisting around, try to keep out of their range and still work ourselves up to the front, when Capt Kimball said, "Sergeant Stearns take the right." I stepped up to that place, and after a little asked Hill, the tall Corporal on the right, where Rawson was. He said he did not know, had not seen him for an hour. The bullets were coming from our left, but as we advanced and twisted, they began to come from the right. Rawson made his appearance and tried to push me from my place. I told him I was there by the Capt's orders, and should stay there until he ordered me away. The Capt, hearing the rumpus, stepped up and asked "What is the matter?" I told him. He then asked Rawson where he had been. Rawson said he had been right there, pointing to the left of the Company. He said he had been turned round & thought we were marching left in front, as though that would change his position. The facts were that he had been keeping a safe place in the rear. The Capt. told me that I could return to my place.

June 18 "Last night was a most disagreeable one. Spent most of the night in getting into position, advanced early in the morning, and built a breastwork. Mike Lynch wounded. Advanced again, and another line of works. A run for the railroad, at dusk another run for a ravine: the minniés flying thick, went on the skirmish line. Eleven wounded in the Regiment."

Early in the morning we advanced and took the front, re-

lieving a portion of Burnsides Corps, who had driven the
Rebs from their first line of works. Advanced through a thin
piece of woods where the rebs had been drawing ammunition. Many boxes of bullets were captured here, all of English make, and they fitted our Enfields completely. We filled our boxes and went on. Halted at the edge of the wood.
Every time we stopped we began to dig, deeming it much
better to let a bank of earth stop the minniés than our
bodies. The soil was light and sandy, and it took only a few
moments to throw up quite a bank that would shelter. The
shells were flying and cracking in every direction. We were
sitting down behind our bank hugging the earth pretty
close. Mike Lynch, who sat beside me, thought the bank
was not quite high enough at his head, and taking the
shovel began to throw up some more dirt. A shell just then
exploded in front of us and the pieces flew in every direction. One struck Mike in the back and he sat down in my
lap, making the most peculiar noise I ever heard. I think I
should have laughed if he had been killed outright. The
Captain wanted to know how bad he was hurt, but Mike
could not tell him. I lifted his jacket and saw a hole in his
back, and told the Capt. so. He asked me if I and Sergeant
Wilson would take him to the rear, and come back as soon
as Mike was in a safe place. Mike thought he was about
dead, and couldn't walk. We put our arms around him, and
half carried and half walking [him], started through the
woods. Before we had gone far, a solid shot came along that
liked to have taken all our legs off. We dodged so that it
caused Mike to laugh and he felt better. After going about
a half mile or more we found a Stretcher bearer and put
Mike on and bid him good by. Mike was not badly
wounded and came home with the regiment.

Burnside's men were burrying their dead, where they
charged the night before. Also the dead Jonnies.

When we got back we saw some new made graves and on enquireing found they were those killed by the same shell. I think it was twelve killed and wounded in the brigade. While waiting for our turn to go ahead, Gen'l Griffin[3] and staff rode up. He stopped and listened a few moments, and turning to one of his aides said, "Where is Col Switzer? I dont hear anything from Col Switzer?" He waited a few moments and then said, "I wonder where Col Switzer is? He should be right over there, but I dont hear his guns." He waited a moment longer and turning to an aide said "Go and tell Col Switzer to push [and] keep pushing." The aide rode off and soon Switzer guns were heard on our right. We advanced on over a ridge, being partialy concealed by an orchard. Gen'l Warren was there and told us that we were to run to a cut in the railroad where we would find shelter. The field we were to cross was a smooth one and in plain sight of the Jonnies. We were to go a regiment at a time. Ours was the second that ran and we lost none;the one that followed us gave a shout when they started and the rebs gave them a volley and they lost twelve in killed and wounded; from the railroad to a ravine we had another run and accomplished it without any loss. Directly in our front was a fort with five embrasures on the face that fronted us, and the muzzels of those dogs of war looked grimly down on us. It was the belief with us that we were to charge it and we were looking for the easiest place to get in. Darkness came on and that stopped the operations for the day. The Brigade fell back to a ridge and built breastworks and the 13th remained on the skirmish line. This was the fort, and it was at this place that they commenced to dig, to blow it up at a later period of the war.[4]

3. Brig. Gen. Charles Griffin, USA.
4. Now called the Crater Battlefield. Eight thousand pounds of powder were exploded in a tunnel under the Confederate Works on the morning of July 30, 1864.

29

Different Types of Heat

Bleuler—Sergeant Mann killed—Clear water—Hot
—K's Commanding Officer—The better
commissary—Incidents of the picket line

June 19 "Not much sleep last night. Considerable
firing on the skirmish line but not many hurt. Great sport
for the boys. The Rebs have a strong position. We came
near charging it last night. Mortar shells were fired during
the night. All day we have kept up a constant fire." Old
Bleuler of Co. E would not come behind the works, but
stood up and with a crotched stick for a rest for his gun,
and kept firing away. We tried to have him come down,
and not expose himself needlessly, and telling him he
would catch it if he didn't, but he still persisted, and before
night poor Bleuler was carried away on a stretcher. There
was a good many guns lying around of those who had been
killed or wounded in yesterdays fight. We took the ramrods
and put them into our guns, and fired them over into the
Fort. They went with a terriable screech, almost frighten-
ing ourselves, the first ones we fired: it was great sport for
us for a while, but the Rebs did not like it, and opened

their great guns, and for an hour or more there was a regular artilery fire duel.

June 20 "Relieved at 1 P.M. from the skirmish line and went back to the line of battle. Drew rations and had a few hours sleep. The skirmishers kept up a constant fire, otherwise there is no firing; the minniés whistled pretty thick all day; five men wounded in the Regiment. Dave Sloss the Color Bearer one of the number. Received a letter from Gilbert."

June 21 "Last night our Regiment moved a few rods to the left, to relieve a part of our first Division. This morning we were greeted with a regular shower of minniés; this is a most dangerous locality, have to keep holed all the time. The dust and sand is awful and the heat is great. One man of the Regiment wounded. Cannonading on the right. No news today."

June 22 "Still in our holes, for it is dangerous to show our heads out of them. Sergeant Mann of Co. H instantly killed this morning. Cary of B Co. in afternoon. An artilery duel on right in forenoon, heavy artilery and musketry firing on the left just at dark. Report says that the First and Second Divisions of our Corps engaged but the results not known. Heavy firing on the right a long distance off." About 4 o'clock this morning as I lay awake, with no thoughts of getting up, I heard Sergeant Mann of H Co. say, "If that is your game I'll try my hand at it," and it hardly seemed a moment before I heard some one say "Mann's dead." The bullets were coming over unusually thick, and Mann, who was wide awake, thought to fire a few shots to keep his hand in. He took his gun and crawled up to the works, put his gun over, and before he had time to fire, fell back dead. His chums took him in a blanket and carried him to the rear and buried him before the sun was hardly up. Cary of B in the afternoon was making coffee, and happening to straighten up a little received a bullet and fell down dead. We had men detailed to stay at the breastwork and fire. The breastwork was a solid bank of earth about five feet high when we stood in the ditch, and from four to six feet thick, according to the nature of the ground. There were little holes or embrasures to fire through, and if we kept close behind the bank, we were in a certain sense safe, but to keep close in the works was an impossibility for us to do, so we dug holes about two feet deep, or if three or four dug together, they dug deeper, and spreading our tent over the hole about a foot above the ground, made quite a good shade. In the hole we would do our cooking, at night going back to get our wood and water. Behind where we lay about eight or ten rods was a little ravine in which was our water of a poor quality. The ridge on which we lay was barren of tree or shrub, with only here or there a tuft of grass, and with the dry sand and suns rays, made it an exceedingly disagreeable place. Everytime that we were obliged to go back to the little ravine, we did it at the peril of our lives.

June 23 "Hot, Hoter, Hottest. Today has been the hottest day of the season, uncomfortably warm; we were in our sand holes, without a breath of air stirring, and every time we stirred the sand would sift down in showers. I dont know but what we shall all be sick, if we stay here in our present condition. We cannot lift our heads up but what a minnié will zyph by. Cannonading all up and down the line. Report says that we lost a battery last night on the left."

June 24 "Received orders to pack up and get out of this. Moved at early light, was relieved by a portion of the 9th Corps. Moved to the left and relieved a portion of the second Corps. Heavy cannonading in Griffin's Division, heavier on the right. Report says that our forces were shelling the town. In the affair of the 22d we lost three guns, and the quarter part of the 15th and 19th Mass. Regiments. While passing in the rear of Griffin's Division we stopped at a pump to get a drink of clear water. The shells were flying around thick, for old Griffin was just waking things up when a shell came through the crowd, instantly killing the man who had hold of the pump handle. I did not stay any longer to get clear water."

June 25 "The heat still continues, and there is no sign of rain. The woods are all on fire, which does not add to our comfort. Not a great deal of firing, except at one place on the right, where there is a continual firing night and day. In the heavy firing of yesterday morning on the right, report says the Rebs charged our works, but were driven back. The 12th Mass start for home today."

June 26 "As hot as ever; the ground all parched up; there has not been a drop of rain for twenty days; all is still on our front; both sides are willing to rest during this hot weather. There is no picket firing—the pickets are in friendly intercourse. Saw some of the 40th New York, whose time is out and are going home, also saw George Walker of the 16th Mass."

June 27 No change in the weather. The 3d Division of the 2d Corps go out in front of our lines and build a line of works, but left them and went back to the rear before night. The continual firing on the right are mortars. Report says that heavy guns are coming up, and the siege of Petersburg will commence in earnest. Rev Mr Sheldon from Westboro Mass., a member of the Christian Commission, visited the front today."

June 28 "Detailed for picket last night at 9 P.M. Went out and found the line with out any difficulty. A shower in the night and quite cool this morning. Was on the extreme left of the line, every thing was still, the pickets of both lines lying around loose. The 3rd Division of the 2nd Corps again came up and built a new line of works. Our Brigade move[d] to the right of the 2nd Corps, and buil[t] works, or were building when I came off picket." Capt Kimball was sick and went to the rear, and Rawson was supposed to be in Command; we were building breastworks and cutting down trees in our front, [which] with the picket duty, made it exceedingly hard for the boys. Walker and I were the two Sergeants of K who reported for duty. When I was relieved from the picket and came in, the orderly of the Commanding Officer of the Regiment was there when I came in and wanted the officer in command of K Company to report to him at once. Walker, who had just gone on the picket line, left K without a Commander; [as] for Rawson, no one knew where he kept himself in the day time. He would get up and be off before light and not come back till into the night, so his duties and our own were performed by either Walker or myself, and we did a good deal of grumbling. I, just coming in off the picket line hungry and tired, refused to go to Headquarters. The Orderly went away and soon returned with the orders that the Officer in command of K Company report at Headquarters forthwith. I then went down to headquarters, Major Pierce in Command. When I entered his tent he looked up and wanted to know if I was in Command of K Company. I told him I supposed I was, [and] he asked why I had refused to come at this first request. I told him that I had but just come in from picket. He wanted to know, if I was in Command of the Company, why was I on picket. I told him that there was an orderly and two Sergeants in K Company reported present for duty daily, and that one or the other of the two duty Sergeants were on duty all the time. That Rawson, the orderly who was reported as present, was away all the day. The Major said "I'll look into this," and told me to go back to the

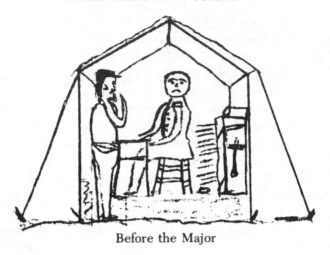

Before the Major

company, and when Rawson came in to send him up forth-with. I went to the Company and the boys gathered around and wanted to know what was up. I told them it was all right with me, and when Rawson came in, if I didn't see him, to tell me. Rawson soon came in as chipper as a bird in spring. I told him that the Major desired his presence at Headquarters forthwith. He went down and after a little came back, and the next morning took his traps and moved up to the works and never left again to visit his friends, as he said he was doing. It was a comfort to us to know where he was, even if he was of no help. Some one had told the Major how we were situated during the absence of Capt Kimball, and he had taken this way to right it.

June 29 "Finished the work by cutting down all the trees in our front. We have a splendid work and have a nice shade a few rods back to lay in. The firing on the right the same.

At eve visited the boys of the 1st Mass. Heavy Artilery; was glad to see them."

June 30 "Mustered for pay by Capt Carey in the forenoon. In the afternoon went over to the Sutlers with a $5.00 check, and brought back my arms full of salables. Report says that stirring times may be expected, about the 4th of July. Jim Elery of the 1st Mass Heavy came over to see us and we got him up a supper of potatoes, fried pork, eggs, cakes, coffee, tea and hardtack with plantation bitters thrown in. When he went back to his camp he told the boys there that we had a better commissary than they had, for we had issued to us, in addition to our regular rations, eggs, cakes and bitters." While over at the Sutlers I saw Sawyer, who was quite sick, barely able to keep around. Had not seen him since we crossed the James, thought he would hardly live to get home.

July 1 "The day is awful hot. Heard several reports of a cavalry fight, in which we got the worst of it. Dont believe all I hear. Two deserters came in last night. Policed up our quarters. Several more of the 1st Heavy came up to see us. The Sanitary Commission sent up several things for the Brigade. Sanborn promoted to a Sergeant, and Slatery to a Corporal."

July 2 "No change from yesterday. George Walker came up yesterday, and said he had no paper, and no means to get any with. I gave him a quarter for that purpose, as I had none myself, but there is plenty more that he can buy at any Sutlers. At night I again visited the 1st Heavy, and saw more boys from Hopkinton." George Walker was one of the bluest men I had seen for many a day; he had reenlisted and went home on his 30 days furlough, and while there had got married, and had now but recently returned, and the hard work, and fighting, without money had made him blue. He was almost tempted to desert. I tried to cheer him up, by saying the harder the fighting now, the sooner he would get home, although I would not exchange places with him for any three hundred dollars made. I gave him a quarter from my slender store, enough to relieve his present wants, and I have never seen him since.

July 3 "A warm day. Inspection ordered at 12 noon. Cleaned up my gun and got ready, when it was postponed. The firing on the right still continues. Strengthened our work by putting in traverses. The Cavalry not so badly used up as reported; they succeeded in cutting the Danville road."

July 4 "A stiller day than yesterday. The great fight that was expected did not come off. The 105th P.V. had a dance in the evening. Gen'l Crawford,[1] our Division Commander, had a great dinner, rather a jolly time I think they had. Our bands in the rear played the National Airs, while we could hear the Johnnie bands playing Dixie, the Bonny Blue Flag, and other of their Airs."

July 5 "The weather still continues warm. No change in affairs. Policed up our quarters and built us bunks, pitching our tents over them for a shade—all but Rawson, who sticks to the works, preferring to lay in the hot sun rather than to build a bunk in the shade, he was so afraid of the shells. Reported that Ewell[2] with his Corps is at or near Harpers Ferry. Commissary, half a canteen for two."

July 6 "The same daily routine to perform. The 1st Heavy go to the rear to sort over and pick out those whose time is out. Two redoubts commenced, one at Division and the other at Brigade Headquarters. The 3d Division, 6th Corps sent away this morning. Fighting reported to be going on at Harpers Ferry and Falling Water."

1. Brig. Gen. Samuel J. Crawford, USA.
2. Lieut. Gen. Richard S. Ewell, CSA.

July 7 "About the same as yesterday, comparative quiet all along the line. Strengthened our work by building an abatis in front. At night when the pickets were relieved, the rebs threw a shell which burst on the line, wounding two from the 104th New York and one from the 39th Mass. No return was given, although it was hard to keep the boys from doing so. Heard the Alabama was sunk off Cherbourg, France, by the Kearsarge. [3] Semmes, [4] the Commander, rescued by an English Yacht."

July 8 "The weather the same—hot and dry. Was in fatigue duty in the afternoon. Repitching Headquarters tents. The petition to be releived from the line on the 10th came back disapproved, our time out on the 16th. About 5 P.M. there was quite an artilery duel; the rebs threw shot and shells in all directions. Quite a lively time in getting into our works. None hurt in the Brigade. Went on picket as soon as the thing settled down. No firing by the picket." It is as well to state here that there was an understanding between the pickets of both sides that there should be no firing between them; if we were ordered to fire, the first volley over their heads, so they could get in their works, and they were to do the same by us; this related only to the picket line, they had nothing to do with the line of battle or the Artilery, and regretted very much when the Artilery shelled the picket.

We had the best of them, for our line was at the edge of the woods, while they were in the middle of a field. The picket line at places was so near that we could talk with each other, and at one place on our right the brush reached almost to their line, and Yank and Johnnie used to meet there and trade. I have got a Richmond paper that was

3. The famous Raider CSS *Alabama* was sunk by the USS *Kearsarge,* commanded by Capt. John A. Winslow, on June 19, 1864.
4. Captain (later Rear Admiral) Raphael Semmes, CSN, Commanding Officer of the CSS *Alabama.*

printed as a morning issue by noon. They used to grumble because our papers were so old. A Washington paper would be a day old before we could get it, New York two, and Boston three. A spring at the edge of the brush was visited by both sides. Just at our right and less than half a mile, was a strong fort bristling with cannon, while their line of works stretched on either side as far as we could see. The Rebs would open their Artilery from this fort every time they saw four or five Yanks together. We used to relieve pickets every night at sundown, and if when relieving some of the boys would be careless and wanted to see more than the Johnnies thought was best, a shot would surely come over from the fort, and then every one, Johnnies as well as Yanks, would hunt his hole. Almost all the annoyance we received came from that fort, and almost always came just at night. Our batteries would sometimes reply, and at other times remain silent. The next morning the Johnnie pickets would apologize for the shots being fired, laying the blame on the battery boys who, they said, never had to go on picket, and did not know the difficulty and the danger attendant upon that duty. Sometimes we would tell them, if the thing was repeated we would fire on them without any warning, but we never did so.

July 9 "Was up all night and day, till half past 2 P.M., when I lay down; was relieved at 6 P.M. Considerable firing all day by both sides. In the afternoon a battery on the left fired a few shots. In the shelling last night the Capt of the 20th Indiana was killed. No news from the invasion of Maryland.[5] Heard that Gov. Andrew[6] had called for five thousand, one hundred day men, their pay to be $20.00 a month."

5. Lieut. Gen. Jubal A. Early's (CSA) advance down the Shenandoah Valley and approach on Washington, D.C., in July 1864. In the Shenandoah Valley, going from Virginia toward Washington is called "going down the Valley" due to the terrain.

6. John A. Andrew, Governor of Massachusetts.

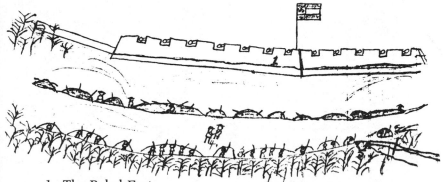

1. The Rebel Fort
2. Reb Picket Line
3. Union Picket Line
4. Where the Union and Johnnies used to meet and trade
5. Spring

30

Headed Home

July 10 "An early revillie in the shape of minnié bullets that sang merrily through the leaves; did not last but a few minutes, for the rebs found that we had not left. They as well as we heard the rumbling of wheels all night and thought that we were trying to get away, [but] it was a part of the 6th Corps going back to Maryland. Two more deserters came in today. A Brigade of colored troops came up to build a fort. John Hagar of the 16th Mass, Billy Foreman of the 32d, and Quartermaster Stone visited us today. Capt Kimball returned to duty. Col. Leonard came up."

July 11 "Quiet till near night, when the Rebs opened with shot and shell. We were out drawing rations at the time; none of us were hurt. In at the line of works a shell struck Col Davis of the 39th Mass. as he was sitting at the door of his tent, killing him almost instantly; a piece went through the Majors tent, of our Regiment, and another piece struck the Col. of 105th P.V., inflicting a slight wound." Drawing rations was under some circumstances rather dangerous work, especially if it were prolonged, so when we went out to draw them, each one that went was to get a certain thing, and when he got it he could go back to the line without waiting for the others. On this night almost all the boys were either on picket or fatigue; it was the orderly's business to see that the rations were drawn and distributed equally to each man, and so we Sergeants, Rawson, Stearns, Walker, and Sanborn, started for the ration wagons about a half a mile distant. The Rebs saw the white covering, and before we had time to commence weighing, they began to shell. At first their shots went wild, but soon they had the range and they came pretty near. I saw one pass under the belly of a horse that an officer was riding, that I thought would kill both horse and rider. The animal reared, and I expected to see both horse and rider go over backward. The Commissary Sergeant and the driver were very nervous and threw the rations out in a hurry, telling us to help ourselves. They disappeared. Walker, Sanborn, and myself got what we were expected to get, and also what Rawson was, for Rawson on the first shot being fired, had started on the run for the rear of a place where he thought he was safe, leaving the hardtack to its fate. We gathered up the rations and went back to the works as quickly as we could, not knowing what might be up. We met the stretcher bearers carrying the body of Col Davis to the rear. The shelling was all over before we reached the works. We portioned out the rations to the boys, saving Rawson some of all but the hardtack, and when he came in, sneaking in after dark, told him his tack was out where he left it. Al Sanborn wanted to know where he was going so fast; he said he got turned round and thought he was coming in towards the front when he was going to the rear. Al asked him how far he had got before he discovered his mistake and if he had been all this time coming back. Poor fellow, he had no answer to give.

July 12 "About 12 at night received orders to pack up, left the works about 2 A.M., and went back into the Fort that the Colored troops were building. 2nd Corps tear down their works and fall back. A change in the line. The Brigade set to work building the Fort. The Rebs shelled the pickets of the 2d Corps. Another Regiment of Colored troops arrived to work on the Fort. Heard the Rebs had taken Frederick Maryland, and were moving on Baltimore."

July 13 "My birthday, and the fourth one since I have been in the service. Spent the day in looking at the works and watching the colored men work. The Rebs were quite uneasy and kept up a shelling on Griffin all day. The news from Maryland is not very good. They are raising the Devil there, and want a few of the old Potomac army to keep them straight. Gen'l Warren working around the Fort all day." We are quartered inside the Fort, which is a large five sided one, containing about two acres, with a traversee running through the middle. We are behind the traversee, and as our time is about out we do not feel like work. I was up on the ramparts watching the Colored men work when Gen'l Warren and Crawford came along. I heard Warren tell Crawford that he must have some traversees put in on that side, for if the Rebs should shell it there would be nothing to protect the men. A little while after I saw Rawson up there taking his ease, for it was a great deal cooler there then down in the centre where there was not a breath of air, and the sun pouring down his hottest rays. Giving Sanborn the wink, and going up so Rawson could hear, I said to Al, "Did you hear what Gen'l Warren told Crawford." "No," said Al, "what is it?" "Well," said I, "Warren told Crawford that if the Rebs should open fire this would be a very

unsafe place to be in." Rawson said nothing, but got up and
went down into the Fort, and didn't go a rod away from the
traversee all day. I really pitied him. We boys stayed up, laying
around where there was a shade while Rawson lay down,
pretending to be asleep in the sun.

In the Fort

A brigade of Penn troops were sent to work chopping
down the trees in front of the fort. They went to work in a
very systematic manner, cutting the trees part way down
and then cutting one at the edge and having it fall on the
others, would take down an acre or more.

The Officers that commanded the colored troops here, to
my mind, were not of the sort to inspire much confidence
in the men. They were nothing but boys and were a swear-

ing, blustering, drinking set, not so capable to command as some of the Sergeants. I was disgusted with them. This fort was named in honor of our Corps Commander Warren, and was now to be the left of the line. In a later period of the war the rebs tried to blow it up, but their mine was some rods outside and it did but little damage. It was built of earth with walls at least ten feet thick and eight high, with a wide and deep ditch all around, [which] when filled would make it a hard place to take. There were embrasures for the guns.

July 14 "Received orders last night to pack up, and turn over our recruits and reenlisted men to the 39th Mass and go to the rear. The officers were busy all night accounting for the men, as some were on detail, others wounded, and the Commanding Officer refused them unless he knew where they were. At last, just before sunrise, all was arrainged and we were permitted to depart. It was growing light very fast, and as the woods had been partially cut away we should be in plain sight of the rebels and sure to get some shells if they saw us. Fortune favored us, for there was a little fog that hid us from their view. We could by straining our eyes see the dim outline of their works as we bid good by to the front.

We marched from the fort with eighty guns, but when we reached the rear and the teamsters, detailed men, and sick and wounded reported, we had a very respectful regiment.

We halted by the teams all day, when just at night we started for City Point. Capt Bucklin, the old Commissary, treated the whole regiment to a ration of whiskey. With three cheers for him and three more for the success of the Union army, we marched away. We were going home, and how light we stepped over the fields without much regard to order or rank. Al Sanborn, as usual, who could never smell of Whiskey but what he wanted to fight with some one, had a fighting fit on. Capt. Kimball, [who] wanted to get him home as a Sergeant if he could, for his friends sake if not for his own, wanted me to look after him.

We got along firstrate for a while, and I was in hopes of getting him through without any trouble, for I kept his jolly side out by talking and trying to have him sing. We were seperated from the reg't, for they marched faster then I could get Al along. Bummers from other regiments, teamsters and the like going both ways served to make an interesting time, and Al must have a word in with a good many of them. At last we struck one after the same stamp as Al; they both had to talk. I tried to have Al come along, but no, he must argue, and from argument they were coming to blows when we interfered and I got Al to go along, and the friends of the other man took care of him. I thought now it was all right and my troubles would soon be over, for we were near where the regiment stopped for the night, when Al all at once stopped and said he was going back to lick that fellow and if any one tried to stop him he would lick them. I tried to reason with him but he would not listen. Then I told him I should leave him to take care of himself, for I was going home and was not going to get into any row for him. I went on and left him; when he found himself alone he thought better of it, and concluded to come on and soon found the regiment. We bivouacked about two miles from the Point.

July 15 "Left at light and arrived there soon after. Went down to the Appomattox,[1] where we took a bath. Expected to leave on the Mail boat but the necessary papers failed to arrive, so we had to wait. In the afternoon the "City of Bath," a boat, was ready to leave, so we took passage on

1. Appomattox River.

her for Washington, left at four P.M., and went down and anchored for the night near Jamestown. I took a deck passage."

July 16th "Weighed anchor at four A.M. and steamed down the river. Arrived at Fortress Monroe at eight, stopped to let the pilot go ashore, when we steamed around and up into the Chesapeake. It was a little rough and many of the boys were seasick. The machinery got out of order and we had to lay by about two hours, when we steamed ahead at a slow rate of speed. Reached the mouth of the Potomac at dark and anchored for the night. As we came down by Newport News we saw the tops of the masts of the ill fated vessels that the Merrimac sent to the bottom. At the Fortress we saw the famous Rip Raps, where the unruly soldiers were sent. Saw the Ironclad Roanoke anchored there. We passed the Ram Atlanta in the bay."

Sunday July 17th "Weighed anchor at four A.M. and steamed up the river for Washington, arrived there at five P.M., and marched up through the city to the Soldiers Home. The old regiment made a splendid show of marching through the streets of Washington. Jim Shedd and Warren Williams, formerly members of K company, came to see us. The boys all feeling gay and happy and we passed a jolly night."

July 18th "Haskell, who was wounded the first day in the Wilderness, joined us today. A party of us went out to see the City, Haskell as guide. Went to the Mass soldiers Relief Association rooms. After went to the Capitol and looked it over, went into the Senate Chamber and sat down in the Vice President chair. The Hall of the House of Represen[ta]tives was locked, so we could not enter there. Spent about three hours in the Capitol and wished we had three hours more. At five marched to the depot to take the train for Baltimore, but did not leave till about ten. The cars were of

the box pattern, but it was a great deal better then walking."

July 19th "Arrived at Baltimore at half past one A.M.
Marched to the Soldiers Home and had breakfast at three,
after which we laid down on the sidewalk and slept till
morning. Laid around all day in the streets getting our
grub of salt horse, bread and coffee at the Home. Marched
at dark for the depot and took the cars for Philadelphia."

Just before leaving Washington a boy came to me and
said he wanted to go to Baltimore, and asked if we could
take him. I didn't know whether the boy was honest or
whether he was beating a ride out of every regiment that
went home, and what was more didn't care if there was a
dozen went, so I told him to wait until we found out what
our conveiance would be. When we found out, I told him
to get aboard. We were in box cars [and] there were some
enquires as to who the boy was, but I said "he is all right"
and we went on. He was a bright smart boy and, before we
reached the city, made friends with all. After reaching the
city and when we were going to breakfast, he asked me if I
would bring him out something to eat as he was afraid to go
in for fear of being arrested. I told him to wait at the door,
and I would come back and get him if everything was
lovely. If there was policemen around I would bring him
out some. When we were going in, Jordan cried out,
"Where the boy?" "Stearns, where the boy?" I told him if
he would keep still the boy would be all right, but he was
very impatient and wanted to know then. I told him again
to keep still, as the boy was none of his business. He was
getting mad fast, and the Captain, who had heard all, told
Jordan to keep quiet. The boy came in and had as good a
breakfast as any one of us. After we went out and were
preparing to lay down, Jordan, who was not satisfied, commenced again by dunning me for the dollar that he said I

owed him for tobacco I had bought of him when we first started in the spring. A dollar in money could not be found in the whole company and Jordan knew it as well as any one, but he felt ugly about the boy yet and wanted to let it out. I did not relish the idea of being dunned there before the whole regiment with out fighting back, so instead of trying to pacify him I rather goaded him on; I told him I did not owe him a dollar, that it was only fifty cts, and brought to his rememberence the time when he took my money and bought tobacco and sold it to the Col. Jordan was now raving and he swore he would lick me, let the consequences be what they might, and started towards where I was laying down. I jumped up, for I was not going to be licked if I could help it, or at least the fighting was not to be all on one side, but before he reached me, some of the other boys interfered and they soon quieted things down. Sanborn, as usual, had urged Jordan on as long as there was a prospect for sport, but when things took a more serious turn, was one of the first to help heal the breech. It was a long time before it was fully healed.

July 20 "Arrived at Philadelphia about six A.M. and marched directly for the Soldiers Home for breakfast, had a good one. Philadelphia was noted for the good meals it furnished the soldiers; started at eight A.M. for New York. Arriving there about three P.M., the Soldiers Home was visited and another meal obtained. At six marched to the depot and at eight left for Boston. Dorkham joined us in N.Y."

July 21 "Rode all night and reached Boston about eight A.M., where a large crowd was in waiting to welcome us home. Marched to Boylston Hall, where we left our traps, and went to the United States Hotel for breakfast at the Sutlers expense. Went back to the hall, where we formed again, and after marching through some of the principle streets, we were assembled in "Old Faneuil Hall," where we were welcomed home by the State, and partook of refreshments. Again at Boylston Hall when the Col. furloughed us until the 1st day of August. "K company" took the train for Westboro, arriving there about six, without a cent of money. A crowd of people was at the depot to welcome the boys, and we out of town were not forgotten. Through the kindness of Al Sanborn, we went over to his Fathers store, where we left our gun and other equipments until the next day, when we were to be welcomed by a parade and dinner in the Town Hall. Without a cent of money Warren Bruce, whose friends were in Vermont, John Stearns, and myself went to the stable after the boys had gone to their homes and the crowd dispersed, to see if we could get a team to carry us to Mothers six miles away. Bruce was going at our invitation. We told the stable keeper what we wanted and that we would pay him the next day. A team was quickly at our disposal and, seated in it, we were soon on the road to Bear Hill.

Brother Gilbert went with his team to Cordaville to meet us, but not finding us there, went to Hopkinton centre, and not finding us there either, started for Westboro. We met him soon after we had left the village, and we dismissed our team and rode with him, arriving at Mothers in the gathering gloom of a summers day. Gilberts little child lay dead in his house, so in the midst of joy there was sorrow. We went to the reception the next day, hardly getting there in time, we slept so late. From the 22d until the 1st of August we just rested and slept, trying to make up for lost time. On the 1st of August we were in Westboro to take the first train for Boston. The boys were all on time.

Going down in the cars that morning, the car that we were in was composed of soldiers, except three men in citizen dress. At South Framingham a soldier got aboard that some of us knew, but all soldiers were friends. He had a lighted cigar in his hand when he came in and, finding so many there that he knew, stayed. The conductor came around and ordered him to throw the cigar out of the window. He told the conductor the cigar had gone out, or the fire, and he refused to do so. The conductor says "I'll see you again," and went on through the train. Soon he came back and enquired about the cigar. The Soldier, whose name was Norcross, from Upton, told him again the fire was out. The conductor says "The cigar will go or you will"; he still refused, when the conductor laid hold of him and tried to pull him from the seat. We boys had had nothing to say until now, although our sympathies were all with the soldier. We told the conductor that he was going too fast and that he had better let the man stay where he was. He was quite indignant and, replying, said he was running that train. He then went to where the citizens were sitting and held a short talk with them. They arose and came up where the scene of the trouble was, when they made as though they would lay hold of the soldier. All of the boys were standing up, and all were ready to help, and we told the citizens that they too had better stop for there might be more trouble then they would wish for, that we were going to Boston and going in that car, all of us. One of the citizens straightened himself up and said, "I am Dwight Foster, the Attorney General of Massachusetts, and you had better be careful what you do." We laughed and told him we had seen as big a man as he was, and we wan't a mite afraid either. He thought discretion the better of valor, I think, for he went no farther, but said they would report us at Headquarters, and they took their seats. We heard no more of the affair.

We assembled at Boylston Hall, where we formed for the last time, and marched out to Boston Common and were mustered out of the United States service, marched back to the hall where we surrendered our guns and equipments, then to Old Faneuil where the Paymaster was ready to settle all claims. After receiving my pay I went to Jordan and handed him a dollar bill in payment of what I owed him; he was still grouty and would not take anything, saying in a very hateful manner that I owed him nothing. I told him I did, and wanted to pay all of my just bills. I laid the money besides him and turned to leave when he got up and hurried off, leaving the money there. I called again, but he paid no attention. I then said I had worked too hard for it to go and leave it there, picked it up, and put it in my pocket. When next we met we had both forgotten all our differences, and were the best of friends.

We then as a regiment seperated, each going his way to join in his chosen path in life.

The friendships that had been formed and welded through more than twenty battles, long marches, and privations incident to a life of a soldier through three years of service will last as long as life its self, and today after a lapse of twenty years, whenever I see or hear of a 13th man, I feel a thrill of pleasure and long to grasp him by the hand and say Comrade.

Of my life as a soldier, I can say that although serving in a humble capacity I was on every march, in every battle and skirmish—never was sick. Always did *my part* whether on drill, fatigue, guard or picket—wherever duty called I was there. Whoever reads this narrative may form their own opinion.

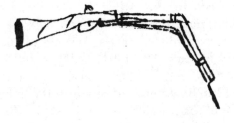

Appendix A

The records in the Adjutant General's Office, Boston, Mass., show that Austin C. Stearns, age 24, of Hopkinton, Massachusetts, enlisted in the service of the United States Volunteers on July 16, 1861, at Fort Independence, Boston, Mass. He began active service as a Private in Company K, 13th Regiment, Massachusetts Volunteer Infantry. His service terminated on August 1, 1864, at Boston, Mass., as a Sergeant in Company K, 13th Regiment, Massachusetts Volunteer Infantry, being honorably mustered out of Civil War service.

Remarks:

His occupation was bootmaking.

He was appointed Corporal on Sept. 12, 1862, and appointed Sergeant on Nov. 1, 1863.

He participated in the following engagements:

Second Bull Run	Antietam
Fredericksburg	Chancellorsville
Gettysburg	Mine Run
Wilderness	Spotsylvania
North Anna River	Totopotomoy
Cold Harbor	Petersburg

Austin C. Stearns's Service Record is on file in the National Archives. This record consists mostly of verifications that he appeared on Company K's Muster Roll from July 16, 1861, until the Company's "Muster-out Roll" on August 1, 1864. On the verification for March and April 1863 appears a notation that states "Promoted to Sgt., vice Warner promoted Mch 1, 63." All verifications thereafter carry him as a Sergeant. There is also a notation on the "Co. Muster-out Roll" that states "Promoted to Corpl. Sept. 12/62, to Sergt. Nov. 1/63."

The Historical Society of Westboro, Mass., has in its possession an old photograph of Stearns, with the following information written on the back:

AUSTIN C. STEARNS   Co. K—13th Age 24—Height 5-6 ¾—Hair, black Born in Upton, Enlisted July 16, 61. Was present in every battle Regiment was engaged in. Taken prisoner at Gettysburg.
Appointed Corporal Sept. 12/62
Appointed Sergeant March 1/63
Picture taken in 1864—Age 27

In summary, it would appear that Stearns was promoted to Sergeant on March 1, 1863, since in the narrative (chapter 15) he tells of Cordwell the Orderly's being promoted to Lieutenant, Warner to Orderly Sergeant, and Wheeler and himself to Sergeants. The notation on the March/April 1863 Verification of Muster Roll leads one to believe that he was promoted to take Warner's place as Sergeant (see preceding paragraphs). Further, he is listed as a Sergeant on the Company Muster Roll from March 1863 on.

Some brief notes on the life of Austin Calvin Stearns

He married in May 1865, had one daughter, and was widowed in October 1879.

He was born on July 13, 1835, in Upton, Mass., the son of Alanson Stearns and Maria Gibson Stearns, and lived in the area until he enlisted in June 1861.

He married in May 1865, had one daughter, and was widowed in October 1879. He remarried in September 1880 and had one son, Austin Eaton Stearns, who was my grandfather.

Most of his life was spent in Westboro and some surrounding towns with the exception of the war years and a short while in New Hampshire.

He maintained the occupation of bootmaking as long as he was able to work.

He died in Westboro, Mass., on July 8, 1924, five days before his 89th birthday.

Appendix B

SOME NOTES ON COMPANY K AND THE 13th MASS.

(From *Record of The Massachusetts Volunteers. 1861-1865,*
vol. 2, published by the Adjutant General of Massachusetts,
Boston, 1870.)

Company K was an average company in an average
three-year Volunteer Infantry Regiment. The Company
mustered in 94 men (excluding officers) on July 16, 1861,
and received approximately 50 recruits, substitutes, and the
like during its three-year existence. The original members
were from the following cities and towns:

44	Westborough, Mass.
1	Boston, Mass.
2	Framingham, Mass.
8	Hopkinton, Mass.
1	Kendall's Mills, Maine
2	Northborough, Mass.
1	North Bridgewater, Mass.
8	Shrewsbury, Mass.
18	Southborough, Mass.
8	Upton, Mass.
1	West Brookfield, Mass.

The recruits and substitutes were from two dozen various cities and towns in Massachusetts, with Westborough contributing five.

A recapitulation of Company K is as follows:[1]

Original Co.		*Recruits/Subs.*
4	Killed in battle*	1
0	Supposed killed**	1
6	Died of wounds***	1
4	Died of other causes	1
6	Deserted	11
0	Reenlisted and deserted	1
3	Promoted out of the company	0
3	Transferred out of the company	2
31	Disability discharge****	11
0	Sentenced to prison	1
0	Deserted, captured, sent to prison	1
1	Discharged per order President	0
1	Discharged per order Sec. of War	3
1	Reenlisted and transferred to the 39th Reg., Mass. Volunteers prior to Co. K's mustering out	2
0	Transferred to the 39th Reg. M.V.I. to finish out enlistment	7
1	Transferred to the Veteran Reserve Corps	1
30	Expiration of Service—Aug. 1, 1864	6

* 2 were killed at the Battle of 2nd Bull Run (2nd Manassas) 8/30/62.
  2 were killed at the Battle of Antietam (Sharpsburg) 9/17/62.
  1 was killed at the Battle of Gettysburg 7/1/63.
** 1 was supposed killed at the Battle of Spotsylvania Court House on 5/8/64.
*** 5 died of wounds received at Gettysburg 7/1/63.
  2 died of wounds received at Antietam (Sharpsburg) 9/17/62.
**** Disability discharges were granted for sickness and to men who had been wounded and were considered no longer fit for military service.

| 1 | Expiration of Service prior to 8/1/64 | 0 |
| 2 | Expiration of Service after 8/1/64 | 0 |

The 13th Regiment mustered a total of approximately 1,451 men and 72 officers during the three years, their disposition being as follows:

Officers

- 3 Killed in battle
- 1 Died of other causes
- 10 Promoted and left regiment
- 3 Disability discharge
- 1 Dismissed
- 1 Unknown
- 26 Resigned
- 27 Expiration of Service

Enlisted

- 68 Killed in battle
- 74 Died of wounds, sickness, and other causes
- 171 Deserted
- 100 Transferred out of Reg.
- 9 Missing
- 20 Unaccounted for
- 32 Promoted to officer or promoted and left the Reg.
- 225 Honorable discharge
- 5 Dishonorable discharge
- 414 Disability discharge
- 333 Mustered out at or for expiration of service.

Appendix C

The following roster was compiled utilizing all available data. In view of the differences noted in some dates, names, and reasons for termination of service, it appears that the roster contains errors. These are unavoidable, because the record-keeping procedures used 100 years ago leave something to be desired; the problem is further compounded by loss of documents and information in the interim. Every one of the facts listed in this Appendix has been published, however, and is a matter of public record.

It is entirely possible that one or more of those men listed as deserters may have met with a different fate. While foraging for food it would not have been difficult for a soldier to become the victim of an enemy patrol, or, in the heat of battle, advances, and retreats, a body may not have been found. In the many thousands of graves marked "Unknown" and in the many unmarked graves, there undoubtedly lie many, many, upright, patriotic Americans who have been unjustly labeled "deserter." However, that is fate and is unavoidable, even today.

The regiments listed here are Mass. Volunteers or Mass. Volunteer Militia, unless otherwise noted.

SECTION I

Officers

In addition to the officers promoted from the ranks (listed in Section II) the following officers served with Company K:

> KEY: *1st line:* Name, Age, Place of Birth, Occupation
> *2nd line:* Home, Rank, Muster Date, Termination, Reason
> *3rd and additional lines:* Notes and Remarks

BACON, William B.   19   — — —   — — —
   Worcester   1st Lt.   7-16-61   7-25-62   Resigned
   Resigned to accept appointment as Captain in the 34th Reg. He was killed 5-15-64.

FOX, Charles B.   28   Newburyport   Freight Agent
   Boston   2nd Lt.   7-16-61   12-62   Mustered Out
   Promoted to 1st Lt. 8-16-62. Later 1st Lt. in 2nd Mass. Cavalry, Major in the 55th Reg., promoted to Lt. Col. on 12-1-63, and Brevet Col. U.S. Volunteers on 3-13-65.

HOVEY, Charles H.   31   Boston   Clerk
   Boston   1st Lt.   7-16-61   8-1-64   Mustered Out
   Promoted to Capt. and assigned to Co. K on 11-6-61. Was wounded at Antietam 9-17-62. Detailed as Brigade Insp. on 1-15-63. Promoted to Division Insp. on 5-7-63. Was wounded and taken prisoner at Gettysburg on 7-1-63, and returned to Union control on 7-4-63. Promoted to Lt. Col. 4-16-64.

SECTION II

Original Members of Company

> KEY: *1st line:* Name, Age, Place of Birth, Occupation

BLACKMER, William P.   31   — — —   Clergyman
  Westboro   Captain   7-16-61   11-5-61   Resigned
  Was original Captain of Company.

WINSLOW, Charles P. — — — — — — — — — — —
  — — — — — — — — — Did not muster
  Was original 1st Lt. of Company but was replaced at
  time of muster. Later 1st Lt. in 51st Reg., Capt. in
  6th Unattached Co. Infantry, and Capt. in 4th Reg.
  Heavy Artillery. May have been in other regiments as
  well.

BULLARD, Ethan — — — — — — — — — — —
  — — — — — — — — Did not muster
  Was original 2nd Lt. of Company but was replaced at
  time of muster.

SANDERSON John W.   30   NEW YORK   Wireworker
  Westboro   Sgt.   7-16-61   7-22-62   See below
  Was original 3rd Lt. in the Co. but was replaced on
  7-16-61 and was mustered as Sgt. in Co. C. Later he
  was promoted to 1st Lt. He resigned on 7-22-62.

KIMBALL, William B.   28   Oakham   Farmer
  Westboro   Corp.   7-16-61   8-1-64   Exp. of Service
  Promoted to 1st Sgt. on 7-19-61, to Commissary Sgt.
  on 3-1-62, to 2nd Lt. on 5-25-62, to 1st Lt. on 2-27-63,
  and to Capt. on 10-4-63.

CORDWELL, William   31   Boston   Boot-Finisher
  Westboro   Sgt.   7-16-61   4-30-63   Killed in Action
  Promoted to 2nd Lt. on 2-14-63. Was killed at Fitz-
  hugh Crossing opposite Fredericksburg, Va.

FAY, William W.   25   Bernardston   Bootmaker
    Westboro   Sgt.   7-16-61   12-18-62   Disability
    Was wounded at Antietam 9-17-62. In 1864 was 2nd
    Lt. in 6th Co. Unattached Inf., and Co. E, 4th Reg.
    Heavy Artillery.

GREENWOOD, Abner R.   20   Ashland   Bootmaker
    Westboro   Sgt.   7-16-61   10-27-63   Disability
    Was original 4th Lt. in Co. but accepted Sgt. at muster.
    He was badly wounded at Antietam 9-17-62.

WARNER, William R.   19   Walpole   Student
    Upton   Sgt.   7-16-61   8-1-64   Exp. of Service
    Was assigned to Depot Commissary Dept. 7-8-62 to
    10-62. Prom. to 1st Sgt. 3-1-63, to 2nd Lt. 5-1-63, to
    1st Lt. on 3-10-64.

ALLEN, Augustus   25   Franklin   Machinist
    Westboro   Corp. 7-16-61   9-5-62   Disability

HODGKINS, Hiram G.   24   VERMONT   Boot Treer
    Westboro   Corp.   7-16-61   8-1-64   Exp. of Service
    Assigned to the Quartermaster Dept. after 8-2-62.

JONES, John   25   MAINE   Carpenter
    Westboro   Corp.   7-16-61   1-9-63   Disability
    Later 1st Lt. in the 6th Co. Unattached Inf., and 1st
    Lt. in the 4th Reg. Heavy Artillery.

PARKER, Charles F.   37   Southboro   Shoe-Click
    Southboro   Corp.   7-16-61   4-6-63   Disability
    A Veteran of the Mexican War.

SANBORN, Alfred L.   26   Boston   Carpenter
    Westboro   Corp.   7-16-61   8-1-64   Exp. of Service
    Promoted to Sgt.

SIBLEY, William H.   40   Westboro   Wheelwright
  Westboro   Corp.   7-16-61   8-1-64   Exp. of Service
  Wounded at Antietam 9-17-62. Spent some time as
  acting Commissary Sgt. at Cuyler Gen. Hospital,
  Germantown, Pa.

STONE, Frank L.   26   Westboro   Bootmaker
  Westboro   Corp.   7-16-61   9-5-62   Disability
  Later was 2nd Lt. in 35th U.S. Colored Reg., promoted to 1st Lt. and assigned as Quartermaster in
  37th U.S. Col. Reg.

TURNER, Melzar G.   19   Maine   Mechanic
  Westboro   Corp. 7-16-61   9-4-62   Order of Pres.
  Was discharged by order of President Lincoln.

SAWYER, Appleton L.   20   Shrewsbury   Clerk
  Shrewsbury Drummer 7-16-61 8-1-64 Exp. of Service
  Promoted to Principal Musician in the Regiment
  1-1-64.

DONOVAN, Ira L.   22   NEW HAMPSHIRE   Laborer
  Westboro   Wagoner   7-16-61   8-1-64   Exp. of Service

BALDWIN, Charles 44 NEW HAMPSHIRE Stonecutter
  Southboro   Pvt.   7-16-61   5-21-62   Disability
  Appointed Fifer 2-62. Muster out date may have been
  8-31-62 vice 5-21-62.

BARSTOW, Sidney   19   Hanover   Clerk
  Westboro   Pvt.   7-16-61   3-27-63   Disability

BATES, John F.   26   Weymouth   Shoecutter
  Southboro   Pvt.   7-16-61   8-1-64   Exp. of Service
  Was taken prisoner 12-13-62 and again at Gettysburg.

BEALS, Isaiah   29   ENGLAND   Shoemaker
  Westboro   Pvt.   7-16-61   11-7-62   Disability
    Also listed as BEALES, Josiah. Wounded at Rap-
    pahannock Station 8-62. Later was a Corporal in Co.
    A, 59th Reg. and was transferred to Co. A, 57th Reg-
    iment.

BLACKMER, Jabez A.   18   CONNECTICUT   Shoemaker
  W. Brookfield   Pvt.   7-16-61   11-18-63   Disability

BRADFORD, James E.   23   RHODE ISLAND   Bootmaker
  Hopkinton   Pvt.   7-16-61   3-2-63   Deserted
    Was Company Musician. Never returned from being
    on furlough.

BRIGHAM, Charles R.   19   Boston   Shoemaker
  Westboro   Pvt.   7-16-61   5-23-62   Disability

BRIGHAM, Francis A.   22   Westboro   Shoemaker
  Westboro   Pvt.   7-16-61   4-2-62   Disability
    Later was a Pvt. in Co. E, 51st Regiment.

BRIGHAM, Harrison M.   23   Grafton   Mechanic
  Westboro   Pvt.   7-16-61   — — —   — — —
    Was on detached duty from 7-4-62 to 2-15-64. Trans-
    ferred to the Veteran Reserve Corps on 2-15-64.

BROWN, David   29   Milford   Teamster
  Upton   Pvt.   7-16-61   8-1-64   Exp. of Service
    Was assigned to the Quartermaster Dept.

BRUCE, Warren E.   23   VERMONT   Teamster
  Upton   Pvt.   7-16-61   8-1-64   Exp. of Service
    Was assigned to the Quartermaster Dept. after
    3-13-63.

BRYANT, Stillman F.   21   Westboro   Shoemaker
  Hopkinton   Pvt.   7-16-61   8-31-62   Disability

BULLARD, Emery   37   Westboro   Joiner
  Westboro   Pvt.   7-16-61   5-10-62   Disability

BURKE, John   25   IRELAND   Shoemaker
  Northboro   Pvt.   7-16-61   7-26-61   Deserted

BURNAP, John S.   21   Westboro   Painter
  Westboro   Pvt.   7-16-61   12-10-61   Died
  Died at Williamsport, Md.

CHAMBERLAIN, Althama   24   Southboro   Shoemaker
  Southboro   Pvt.   7-16-61   3-7-63   Disability
  Was wounded at Antietam 9-17-62.

CHAMBERLAIN, Dexter A.   25   Southboro   Shoemaker
  Southboro   Pvt.   7-16-61   8-1-64   Exp. of Service
  Was promoted to Corporal.

CLEARY, Patrick H.   20   IRELAND   Sailor
  Southboro   Pvt.   7-16-61   4-2-62   Died
  Died at Manassas, Va.

COMSTOCK, Charles W.   18   Westboro   Laborer
  Upton   Pvt.   7-16-61   8-1-64   Exp. of Service
  Was promoted to Corporal.

COPELAND, John   20   IRELAND   Laborer
  Westboro   Pvt.   7-16-61   1-7-63   Disability
  Later a Pvt. in Co. A, 57th Reg., and was either killed
  at the Wilderness or died at Andersonville. References
  vary.

COPELAND, Thomas   18   IRELAND   Laborer
Westboro   Pvt.   7-16-61   8-30-62   Killed in action
Killed at 2nd Bull Run (2nd Manassas).

CROSBY, Robert   20   Boston   Shoe Finisher
Southboro   Pvt.   7-16-61   8-1-64   Exp. of Service

CROWLEY, John H.   21   East Boston   Lastmaker
Westboro   Pvt.   7-16-61   — — —   — — —
One reference lists as Dropped from Rolls 8-16-63 and
another as Exp. of Service 8-1-64.

CUSHMAN, William W.   20   MAINE   Shoemaker
Westboro   Pvt.   7-16-61   3-23-63   Disability
Promoted to Corporal. Was wounded at 2nd Bull Run.

CUTTING, James H.   18   Boylston   Laborer
Shrewsbury   Pvt.   7-16-61   — — —   — — —
Was wounded at Antietam. Transferred to the 18th
U.S. Infantry on 12-9-62 and killed at the Wilderness.

DAVENPORT, Melvin A.   21   UPTON   Bonnet-Presser
Framingham   Pvt.   7-16-61   2-17-63   Disability
Wounded at Antietam 9-17-62. Promoted to Corporal.

DAY, Warren W.   23   NEW HAMPSHIRE   — — —
Southboro   Pvt.   7-16-61   8-16-63   Deserted
One reference gives date of desertion as 8-13-61. 1863 is
probably more correct. Deserted from Hospital.

DOCKHAM, Edward C. 23 NEW HAMPSHIRE Blacksmith
Southboro   Pvt.   7-16-61   8-1-64   Exp. of Service
Also listed as Edwin C. Wounded 5-8-64 (probably at
or near Spotsylvania Court House).

DOUGLAS, George R.   20   NEW YORK CITY   Clerk
Westboro   Pvt.   7-16-61   1-29-63   Disability
Later a QM Sgt. in Co. E, 4th Reg. Heavy Artillery.

DRAYTON, Charles   18   N. Bridgewater   Painter
N. Bridgewater   Pvt.   7-16-61   3-30-63   Disability
Was promoted to Corporal. Later in the 37th U.S.
Colored Regiment, as a Lt.

EATON, Thomas B.   18   Worcester   Bootmaker
Shrewsbury   Pvt.   7-16-61   6-1-62   Died
Died at Washington, D.C.

EMORY, George F.   19   MAINE   Carpenter
Westboro   Pvt.   7-16-61   8-1-64   Exp. of Service
Also listed as EMERY. Was promoted to Corporal.

FAIRBANKS, Henry A.   18   Shrewsbury   Shoemaker
Westboro   Pvt.   7-16-61   4-23-63   Disability
Was wounded at Antietam 9-17-62. Later was Corporal
in the 6th Co. Unattached Infantry.

FAIRBANKS, Hollis H.   18   Shrewsbury   Bootmaker
Westboro   Pvt.   7-16-61   8-30-62   Killed in action
Killed at 2nd Bull Run (2nd Manassas).

FAIRBANKS, Joseph   55   Shrewsbury   Sleigh-Maker
Westboro   Pvt.   7-16-61   5-11-62   Disability

FAY, Charles M.   17   Montague   Laborer
Westboro   Pvt.   7-16-61   1-26-65   Exp. of Service
Wounded accidently at Harpers Ferry 9-61, wounded
at Gettysburg 7-1-63, taken prisoner at Spotsylvania
5-21-64 and held until 11-25-64. Went to Hancock's

Veteran Reserve Corps for one year.

FLY, John   29   MAINE   Blacksmith
  Westboro   Pvt.   7-16-61   7-26-63   Died of wounds
    Also listed as FLYE. Died at Gettysburg of wounds
    received there.

FURBUSH, William H.   18   Westboro   Sleigh-Maker
  Westboro   Pvt.   7-16-61   — — —   — — —
    Transferred to the U.S. Army on 1-15-63.

GASSETT, Thomas R.   21   Hopkinton   Bootmaker
  Hopkinton   Pvt.   7-16-61   9-17-62   Killed in action
    Killed at Antietam.

GASSETT, William H.   18   Hopkinton   Bootmaker
  Hopkinton   Pvt.   7-16-61   3-23-63   Disability
    Wounded at Antietam 9-17-62.

GATES, George H.   28   New York   Brewer
  Northboro   Pvt.   7-16-61   8-1-64   Exp. of Service

GLIDDON, John   20   NEW HAMPSHIRE   Laborer
  Westboro   Pvt.   7-16-61   8-1-64   Exp. of Service
    Also listed as GLIDDEN.

GOULD, Frank A.   20   Clinton   Mechanic
  Southboro   Pvt.   7-16-61   7-14-63   Died of Wounds
    Died at Gettysburg of wounds received there.

HANEDEN, George C.   18   Westboro   Shoemaker
  Westboro   Pvt.   7-16-61   12-22-61   Died
    Died at Williamsport. Also listed as HARADEN.

HARRINGTON, Frank A.   18   Boston   Mechanic
  Westboro   Pvt.   7-16-61   7-20-64   Exp. of Service

HASKELL, Lyman   23   Westboro   Bootmaker
  Westboro   Pvt.   7-16-61   8-1-64   Exp. of Service
    Wounded 5-5-64 (probably at or near the Wilderness).

HOYT, Dixi C.   27   NEW HAMPSHIRE   Physician
  Milford   Pvt.   7-16-61   — — —   — — —
    Never left the State with the Regiment. Later was an
    Assistant Surgeon in the 2nd Reg. Heavy Artillery.

JOHNSON, John H.   24   Upton   Shoemaker
  Upton   Pvt.   7-16-61   8-1-64   Exp. of Service

JONES, Lyman A.   30   Sudbury   Shoemaker
  Southboro   Pvt.   7-16-61   10-13-62   Disability

LACKEY, John   25   Hopkinton   Laborer
  Westboro   Pvt.   7-16-61   8-1-64   Exp. of Service
    Served as Teamster with the Quartermaster Dept.

LEE, Edward   30   IRELAND   Tailor
  Westboro   Pvt.   7-16-61   8-1-64   Exp. of Service
    Wounded 5-9-64 (probably at or near Spotsylvania).

LOVELL, Alden   29   WORCESTER   Shoemaker
  Westboro   Pvt.   7-16-61   2-14-63   Disability
    Wounded at 2nd Bull Run (2nd Manassas).

LYNCH, Michael   20   IRELAND   Bootfitter
  Westboro   Pvt.   7-16-61   8-1-64   Exp. of Service
    Wounded at Petersburg, 6-17-64

MARTIN, Joseph   26   CANADA   Shoemaker
  Southboro   Pvt.   — — —   7-23-62   Deserted
    Various references list muster dates of 7-16-61 and
    7-27-61. Questionable if he is one of the original
    members of the Company.

MORTON, Edward J.   22   NEW YORK   Currier
Shrewsbury   Pvt. 7-16-61 8-31-62 Order of War Dept.
Also listed as MORETON, Edmund J. or combination
of both. Transferred to the Reg. Band as Musician on
7-16-61 (day of muster).

NELSON, Dexter C.   18   Shrewsbury   Clerk
Shrewsbury   Pvt.   7-16-61   7-21-62   Disability
Later 1st Sgt. in Co. A, 57th Regiment.

O'LAUGHLIN, Michael 21 IRELAND Shoemaker
Shrewsbury Pvt. 7-16-61 10-8-63 Died of wounds
Died of wounds received at Gettysburg.

ONTHANK, Dexter D.   29   Southboro   Carpenter
Southboro   Pvt.   7-16-61   7-21-62   Disability
Later a Pvt. in the 6th Co. Unattached Infantry.

PARKER, Gardner R.   24   Lowell   Freightman
Southboro   Pvt.   7-16-61   4-20-63   Disability
Wounded 12-13-62 (probably Fredericksburg).

PLUMMER, John D.   29   Upton   Bootmaker
Upton   Pvt.   7-16-61   8-1-64   Exp. of Service

RAWSON, William   18   Worcester   Mechanic
Upton   Pvt.   7-16-61   8-1-64   Exp. of Service
Promoted to Corp. 8-1-62, to Sgt. 1-1-63, and to 1st
Sgt.

RICE, Arthur T.   21   Framingham   Clerk
Framingham Pvt. 7-16-61 3-31-64 Order of Sec. War
Wounded at 2nd Bull Run (2nd Manassas). Declined
promotion to Orderly Sgt. 5-8-62 to accept Clerkship
at the Adj-Gen. Office in Washington, D.C.

ROBBINS, Chandler   41   Plymouth   Wheelwright
Westboro   Pvt.   7-16-61   8-1-64   Exp. of Service
Worked as Hospital Steward and was taken prisoner
while at Fitzhugh Hospital opposite Fredericksburg.

ROSS, Harvey C.   31   VERMONT   Bootmaker
Westboro   Pvt.   7-16-61   8-1-64   Exp. of Service
Badly wounded at Gettysburg.

SARGENT, Amos P.   18   NEW HAMPSHIRE   Painter
Southboro   Pvt.   7-16-61   8-1-64   Exp. of Service
On detached duty as Hospital Steward much of the
time.

SHEA, Thomas   26   NEW YORK CITY   Carpenter
Boston   Pvt.   7-16-61   7-29-61   Deserted
Deserted while Company was passing through Boston.

SLATTERY, James   20   IRELAND   Shoemaker
Westboro   Pvt.   7-16-61   8-1-64   Exp. of Service
Promoted to Corporal 3-1-64.

SMITH, Edwin   21   NEW YORK   Nurseryman
MAINE   Pvt.   7-16-61   4-1-63   Disability
Badly wounded on Maryland Heights (Harpers Ferry)
8-24-61.

SPRAGUE, George E.   27   Grafton   Shoemaker
Shrewsbury   Pvt.   7-16-61   7-16-63   Died of wounds
Died of wounds at Gettysburg.

STEARNS, Austin C.   24   Upton   Bootmaker
Hopkinton   Pvt.   7-16-61   8-1-64   Exp. of Service
Promoted to Corporal 9-12-62, and to Sgt. 3-1-63.
Wounded and taken prisoner 7-1-63 (Gettysburg),
paroled and to duty.

STEARNS, Jonathan   19   Hopkinton   Farmer's Son
Hopkinton   Pvt.   7-16-61   8-1-64   Exp. of Service

STEVENS, Warren H.   20   Holden   Bootmaker
Southboro   Pvt.   7-16-61   2-28-62   Deserted

THURSTON, John C.   29   Grafton   Farmer
Boston   Pvt.   — — —   11-23-62   Disability
Assigned as Musician. Various references list muster
date as both 7-16-61 and 7-29-61. Questionable if he is
one of original members of the Company.

TRASK, Charles A.   20   MAINE   Shoemaker
Southboro   Pvt.   7-16-61   10-2-62   Died of wounds
Died at Chambersburg, Pa. of wounds received at An-
tietam.

WALKER, Melville H.   19   Barre   Farmer's Son
Westboro   Pvt.   7-16-61   8-1-64   Exp. of Service
Also listed as Melvin. Promoted to Corporal on
1-10-63, and to Sgt. on 11-1-63.

WARREN Daniel S   36   Hopkinton   Bootmaker
Hopkinton   Pvt.   7-16-61   6-29-65   Exp. of Service
Reenlisted 7-13-64. Transferred to Co. G, 39th Reg.
on 7-13-64 and to Co. H, 32nd Reg. on 6-2-65.

WARREN, Stephen   27   Westboro   Laborer
Westboro   Pvt.   7-16-61   8-1-64   Exp. of Service
Detailed as Attendant at the U.S. General Hospital,
Frederick, Md. for 20 months.

WELLINGTON, Charles H.   23. Holden   Bootmaker

Upton   Pvt.   7-16-61   10-2-62   Died of wounds
Died at Chambersburg, Pa., of wounds received at
Antietam.

WHEELER, Willard   25   Hopkinton   Bootmaker
Hopkinton   Pvt.   7-16-61   7-1-63   Killed in action
Promoted to Sgt. 3-1-63. Killed at Gettysburg.

WILLIAMS, Charles H. 32 NEW YORK CITY Carpenter
Westboro   Pvt.   7-16-61   8-31-62   Order of War Dept.
Transferred to Reg. Band as Musician 8-7-61.

WILLIAMS, Warren W.   21   Ashland   Machinist
Southboro   Pvt.   7-16-61   1-9-63   Disability

WILLSON, Frank P.   20   ENGLAND   Bootmaker
Shrewsbury   Pvt.   7-16-61   8-1-64   Exp of Service
Also listed as WILSON. Promoted to Corporal 11-1-63
and to Sgt. 7-1-64.

WILLSON, William H.   18   ENGLAND   Shoemaker
Shrewsbury   Pvt.   7-16-61   12-29-62   Disability
Later was 1st Sgt. in Co. A, 57th Regiment, killed
5-6-64.

Company K departed for Boston on 6-29-61 with 101 officers and men; the preceding roster lists 102. Either MAR-
TIN or THURSTON was not an original member but both
are included because of the double listing of muster dates.
When the Company mustered into Federal service on
7-16-61, 2 officers were replaced and 1 officer mustered in
Co. C as a Sergeant. One man never left the state with the

Company, one was transferred to the Regimental Band, and two deserted shortly after muster, therefore there were effectively 94 men (less officers) who mustered and did service with the Company (See Appendix A).

SECTION III

Recruits and Substitutes sent to Company

KEY: *1st line:* Name, Age, Place of Birth, Occupation
2nd line: Home, Rank, Muster Date, Termination, Reason
3rd and additional lines: Notes and Remarks

BLUCHER, Charles   20   PRUSSIA   Machinist
    Swanzey   Pvt.   7-28-63   9-19-63   Deserted
    Age may be 26. Was a Substitute.

CHAPMAN, Lorenzo A.   34   Princeton   Bootmaker
    Westboro   Pvt.   8-14-62   8-1-64   Exp. of Service

CLIFFORD, George W.   18   VERMONT   Farmer's Boy
    Cambridge   Pvt.   8-16-62   8-1-64   Exp. of Service
    Promoted to Corporal. Wounded 5-8-64 (Spotsylvania).

COLLINS, John   18   Southboro   Shoemaker
    Southboro   Pvt.   3-19-62   — — —   — — —
    Transferred to the 18th Co., 2nd Batt., Veteran Re-
    serve Corps on 9-1-63.

COLLINS, Lowell T.   29   Southboro   Shoemaker
    Southboro   Pvt.   2-6-62   2-17-64   Disability
    Muster date may have been 2-16-62.

CUTTING, Horatio A.   44   Attleboro   Bootmaker
    Shrewsbury   Pvt.   8-1-62   7-22-63   Died of wounds
    Died at Ft. Schuyler, N.Y., of wounds received at
    Gettysburg.

DAVIS, Francis   30   Southboro   Shoemaker
    Southboro   Pvt.   3-6-62   9-30-62   Disability

DRAYTON, Otis   18   N. Bridgewater   Clerk
N. Bridgewater   Pvt.   8-17-62   11-19-63   Deserted
Never rejoined Regiment after being in hospital.

EDMOND, William H.   25   Taunton   Blacksmith
Westboro   Pvt.   8-14-62   6-11-63   Disability
Also listed as EDMANDS.

FLAGG, Henry L.   31   Ashland   Carpenter
Southboro   Pvt.   3-5-62   2-20-63   Disability
Was later in Co. E, 4th Reg. Heavy Artillery

HALL, George W.   18   Boston   Mariner
Boston   Pvt.   8-18-62   6-29-65   Exp. of Service
Was taken prisoner at Gettysburg. Reenlisted on
1-4-64 and was transferred to Co. F, 39th Reg. on
7-13-64, and to Co. E, 32nd Reg. on 6-2-65.

HARTWELL, George E.   38   W. Boylston   Carpenter
Westboro   Pvt.   8-14-62   1-9-63   Disability
Badly wounded at Antietam 9-17-62.

HEATH, Walter S. C.   29   CANADA   Watchmaker
Boston   Pvt.   8-2-62   4-10-64   Deserted

HILL, John M.   32   Worcester   Bootmaker
Westboro   Pvt.   2-17-62   2-17-65   Exp. of Service
Declined promotion to Corporal in order to be de-
tailed as a Mounted Pioneer at Headquarters 11-1-63.
Transferred to Co. G, 39th Reg. on 7-13-64.

HOLDEN, Hollis   44   VERMONT   Farmer
Shrewsbury   Pvt.   8-11-62   9-17-62   Killed in action
Killed at Antietam.

JONES, William   28   OHIO   Sailor
Boston   Pvt.   7-31-61   — — —   — — —
Transferred to the U.S. Navy on 11-16-63.

JORDAN, Samuel   (37)27   MAINE   Wheelwright
Shrewsbury   Pvt.   8-9-62   8-1-64   Exp. of Service
Promoted to Corporal. Was a prisoner at Gettysburg.

KELLAR, Balthasa   24   GERMANY   Clothier
Littleton   Pvt.   11-5-63   6-29-65   Exp. of Service
Also listed as Balthasen. Transferred to Co. F, 39th
Reg. on 7-13-64 and to Co. G, 32nd Reg. on 6-2-65.

KING, William   27   Plymouth   Mariner
Plymouth   Pvt.   8-21-62   12-20-62   Disability
May never have been with Company.

MARVIS, Frank   21   GREECE   — — —
Chelmsford   Pvt. 7-28-63   — — —   Dropped from rolls
Also listed as MAUVRIS. Deserted 8-22-63, was ar-
rested and sent to prison on Tortugas.

MILLER, James   24   PRUSSIA   Clerk
Dedham   Pvt.   7-28-63   9-19-63   See below
One listing shows that he died at Rappahannock Station on 9-19-63, while another lists him as having deserted on the same date (9-19-63).

MINARD, Nelson C.   21   VERMONT   Clerk
Chelsea Pvt.   8-1-62   7-12-65   Order of War Dept.
Reenlisted 3-31-64. Transferred to Co. G, 39th Reg.
on 7-13-64 and to Co. H, 32nd Reg. on 6-2-65.

MURRAY, John   22   IRELAND   Blacksmith

Paxton   Pvt.   7-28-63   11-25-63   Deserted
May have been Thomas vice John.

PALMER, Joseph   25   IRELAND   Sailor
Bedford   Pvt.   7-27-63   10-28-63   Deserted

PARRE, John   32   CENTRAL AMERICA   Cigar Maker
Worcester   Pvt.   7-24-63   — — —   — — —
Also listed as PARRA. Was a deserter from the Con-
federate Army. Transferred to the Dept. of Northwest
Territory on 4-20-64.

PERRY, Abel O.   23   Shrewsbury   Farmer
Shrewsbury   Pvt.   8-2-62   12-27-62   Disability
Wounded at Antietam 9-17-62.

RAPP, Robert   28   FRANCE   Painter
Northbridge   Pvt.   7-24-63   10-24-63   Deserted

RICE, Charles F.   19   Danbury   Farmer
Shrewsbury Pvt. 8-1-62 5-8-64 Supposed killed
Missing and supposed killed at the battle of Spotsyl-
vania.

RILEY, John   22   IRELAND   Carpenter
Brighton   Pvt.   7-24-63   2-3-64   Deserted

ROGERS, John   20   NEW YORK   Laborer
Provincetown   Pvt.   7-28-63   12-17-63   Deserted

ROGERS, Thomas   29   WALES   Sailor
Ashby   Pvt.   7-24-63   8-22-63   Deserted

SEAVER, George H.   25   Holden   Farmer
Holden   Pvt.   8-1-62   8-1-64   Exp. of Service

SHEDD, James A.   23   Cambridge   Clerk
   Cambridge   Pvt.   8-22-62   3-1-64   Order of Sec. War
     Was a clerk at Headquarters, 2nd Div., 1st Army
     Corps and Chief Clerk in the draft bureau at the Adj.
     Gen. Office, Washington, D.C. Discharge date may
     be 3-31-64 vice 3-1-64.

SHEDD, William E.   21   Cambridge   Clerk
   Cambridge   Pvt.   8-14-62   12-1-63   Order of Sec. War
     To duty in Adj. Gen. office, Washington, D.C.

SKINNER, John B.   40   MAINE   Furrier
   Boston   Pvt.   11-5-63   6-29-65   Exp. of Service
     Transferred to Co. G, 39th Reg. on 7-13-64 and to Co.
     C, 32nd Reg. on 6-2-65.

SMITH, Charles H.   26   ENGLAND   Tailor
   Lowell   Pvt.   7-29-63   6-29-65   Exp. of Service
     Deserted 11-25-63, was arrested at Boston on 1-6-64.
     Transferred to Co. B, 39th Reg. on 7-13-64 and to Co.
     D, 32nd Reg. on 6-2-65.

SMITH, Frank   22   IRELAND   Sailor
   Princeton   Pvt.   7-29-63   11-25-63   Deserted

STOREY, Edward A., Jr.   20   — — —   — — —
   Brighton   Pvt.   8-18-62   2-19-63   Disability

SYLVESTER, Horace C.   19   VERMONT   Clerk
   Boston   Pvt.   8-14-62   4-1-63   Order of Sec. War
     Wounded at Antietam 9-17-62. Discharge date may be
     12-3-63 vice 4-1-63.

TREATEST, Edmund   30   FRANCE   Sailmaker
   Worcester   Pvt.   7-24-63   10-19-63   Deserted

TROWBRIDGE, Alfred L.   18   Westboro   Wheelwright
Westboro   Pvt.   3-21-62   5-24-62   Disability
Later was in the 6th Co. Unattached Infantry.

TUCKER, Smith   34   Shrewsbury   Farmer
Shrewsbury   Pvt.   7-26-62   3-27-63   Disability

VAN DOREN, Lewis   26   HOLLAND   Cook
Dedham   Pvt.   7-27-63   10-24-63   Deserted
Also listed as VANDOINE.

VINING, Albion L.   18   MAINE   Farmer
Shrewsbury Pvt.   7-29-62   8-1-64   Exp. of Service
Wounded 7-1-63 (Gettysburg).

VINING, Henry C.   24   MAINE   Shoemaker
Shrewsbury Pvt.   8-1-62   8-1-64   Exp. of Service
Was taken prisoner at Gettysburg.

WALCH, William   22   IRELAND   Laborer
Charlestown Pvt.   7-25-63   6-29-65   Exp. of Service
Also listed as WELCH. Transferred to Co. F, 39th
Reg. on 7-13-64, and to Co. B, 32nd Reg. on 6-2-65.

WILSON, John   21   ENGLAND   Caulker
Billerica Pvt.   7-28-63   6-29-65   Exp. of Service
Deserted 8-19-63, was arrested and sentenced to hard
labor on Government Fortifications for one year.
Transferred to Co. C, 39th Reg. on 7-13-64, and to
Co. H, 32 Reg. on 6-2-65.

WILSON, John   23   ENGLAND   Sailor
Charlestown Pvt.   7-27-63   6-29-65   Exp. of Service
Deserted 8-19-63, was arrested, and returned to duty.

Was wounded 5-8-64 (probably at or near Spotsylvania). Transferred to Co. G, 39th Reg. on 7-13-64,
and to Co. E, 32nd Reg. on 6-2-65.

WILLIAMS, John   32   ENGLAND   Sailor
Boston   Pvt.   7-29-63   — — —   Dropped from rolls
Deserted 8-22-63, was captured, and sent to prison on
Tortugas.

There were 50 Recruits and Substitutes sent to Company K
during the three years. Forty-nine are listed in this section.
Either MARTIN or THURSTON, who are listed in Section
II, was a Recruit; however, because each has a listed Muster Date of 7-16-61 (one apparently in error), they are included with the original members.

Bibliography

Davis, Charles E., Jr. *Three Years in the Army. The Story of the Thirteenth Massachusetts Volunteers from July 16, 1861 to August 1, 1864.* Boston, Mass.: Estes and Lauriat, 1894.

Record of The Massachusetts Volunteers. 1861-1865. Vol. 1. Published by The Adjutant General, Boston, Mass., 1868. Vol. 2. Published by The Adjutant General, Boston, Mass., 1870.

Index

346]   THREE YEARS WITH COMPANY K

Admiral), CSN, 297
Sharpsburg. *See* Antietam
Sheridan, Philip H., Maj. Gen., USA, 262
Shields, James, Maj. Gen., USA, 59, 60-61, 77
Shiloh. *See* Pittsburg Landing
Sibley tents, 69
Sigel, Franz, Maj. Gen., USA, 85, 105
Sixth Army Corps, 149, 167, 264, 266, 296, 300
Skirmishers, 125
Slaughter Mountain. *See* Cedar Mountain
Slidell, John, 58
Smith, William F. (Baldy), Maj. Gen., USA, 261
South Carolina: Infantry: 4th Regiment, 283; 16th Regiment, 273
South Mountain: battle, 121
Spotsylvania: battle, 262-70
Sprague, William, Governor of R.I., 36-37
Stuart, James E. B. (JEB), Lieut. Gen., CSA, 102, 135

Styles, John W., Col., USA, 100, 126, 134-35
Substitutes, 214-18
Sumner, Edwin V., Maj. Gen., USA, 138
Sutlers, 158, 257

Taylor, Nelson, Brig. Gen., USA, 137, 146-47
Third Army Corps, 261, 265, 278; combined with Second Corps, 256
Totopotomoy Creek: engagement, 275
Twelfth Army Corps, 221

Wadsworth, James S., Maj. Gen., USA, 211; killed, 261
Warren, Gouverneur K., Maj. Gen., USA, 238, 264, 267, 270, 288, 302, 304
Washington, D.C.: threatened, 73
Webster, Fletcher, 85
Wilderness: battle, 258-61
Winchester, Va.: battle, 61
Wisconsin: Infantry: 3rd Regiment, 36, 37